Zonpower

PART I
Neo-Tech Physics
The Foundation

PART II
The Anticivilization
The Problem

PART III
The Civilization of the Universe
The Solution

for limitless

Money, Romantic Magnetism
and a
Nonaging Body

Honesty
1. Fairness and straightforwardness in conduct.
2. Adherence to the facts: sincerity.

(Webster's Ninth New Collegiate Dictionary)

Your Route to Riches

Three thousand years ago, our nature-given bicameral minds broke down into chaos. To survive, we invented consciousness, which soon became corrupted with Plato's dishonesties and "noble" lies. Now, today, our corroded conscious minds are also breaking down. To survive, we are finally discovering the all-powerful Neothink mind that functions through wide-scope integrations and fully integrated honesty. Neothink brings eternal Zonpower — the power from the Civilization of the Universe. ...Zonpower provides everyone with riches, romantic love, and a god-like mind and body.

Zonpower
A Manuscript of Contextual Facts and Metaphors
dedicated to
Henrik Ibsen

ISBN# 911752-72-2
Library of Congress # 95-60719
Copyright © 1995
by the
Zon Association, Inc.

First Printing
June 1995
3 5 7 9 8 6 4 2
99 98 97 96 95

Cyberspace
email: zon@zon.neo-tech.com
WWW Home Page: http://www.neo-tech.com/zonpower/
Newsgroup: alt.neo-tech
Mailing List: talk@zon.neo-tech.com

Zonpower

A Communiqué from the Universe

Orientation

Zon is absent from the entire history of Earth's anticivilization. Yet, Zon embraces all the future. ...Zon answers the *how* and *why* questions of life and existence.

Zonpower has no authors. It has only editors backed by the power of *fully integrated* honesty, reason, and rationality. Zonpower arises from God — not the unreal God of mystical religions, but the *nonmystical* God of Zon.

Zon's editor is a professional scientist: Dr. Higgs Field, a former Senior Research Chemist at E. I. du Pont de Nemours, cuts across the boundaries of physics, chemistry, astronomy, mathematics, biology, medicine, chaos, economics, politics, business, philosophy, and nonmystical religion to integrate the widest knowledge into a single whole — *Zonpower*.

The reader needs only a brief orientation to *Zonpower* rather than an Introduction or Preface as found in most books. This orientation will help the reader capture the Zonpower dynamics that lead to limitless riches, romantic charisma, and nonaging beauty guaranteed by Zon.

Part I is a nonmathematical presentation of Neo-Tech Physics edited for all readers — from general readers to professional physicists. On initial reading, some general readers may think the scientific footnotes in Part I are perhaps too technical. But, do not worry. One does not even need to read the scientific proofs or technical footnotes to understand and fully use Zonpower.

After reading Part II, *The Problem*, and Part III, *The Solution*, one captures the Zonpower needed to collect limitless riches, romance, and a god-like mind and body.

Table of Contents

Table of Contents

Illustrations

Charts and Tables

New Words and Concepts

Zon is a collective word related to the fully integrated honesty of Neo-Tech and comprises (1) the Civilization of the Universe, (2) those operating from its wide-scope perspective, and (3) the power required to control existence — the integrated power to gain limitless wealth and eternal happiness. ...Zon is the mind of God. Zon *is* you!

Zonpower is the power to control existence. Zonpower is derived from applying the fully integrated honesty and wide-scope accountability of Neo-Tech to all conscious actions.

Neo-Tech is a noun or an adjective meaning *fully integrated honesty* based on facts of reality. Neo-Tech creates a collection of *new techniques* and *new technology* that lets one know exactly what is happening and what to do for gaining honest advantages in all situations. Neo-Tech provides the integrations to collapse the illusions, hoaxes, and irrationalities of any harmful individual or institution.

Anticivilization is the irrational civilization gripping planet Earth — an unreal civilization riddled with professional value destroyers causing endless cycles of wars, economic and property destructions, unemployment and poverty, suffering and death. The essence of the anticivilization is dishonesty. ...Through Neo-Tech, the Civilization of the Universe will replace Earth's anticivilization.

Civilization of the Universe is the rational civilization throughout the universe — a civilization filled with value producers providing endless cycles of wealth, happiness, and rejuvenation for everyone. ...Professional value destroyers and parasitical elites are nonexistent in the Civilization of the Universe.

Parasitical Elites are unnatural people who drain everyone. The parasitical-elite class lives by usurping, swindling, and destroying values produced by others. Their survival requires political-agenda laws, armed bureaucracies, ego-"justice" systems, and deceptive neocheating.

Neocheating is the undetected usurpation of values from others: the unsuspicious swindling of money, power, or values through deceptive manipulations of rationalizations, non sequiturs, illusions, and mysticisms. ...All such net harms inflicted on society can now be objectively measured by the wide-scope accounting of Neo-Tech.

Subjective Laws include political-agenda laws conjured up by politicians and bureaucrats to gain self-serving benefits, ego props, and unearned power. Enforcement of political-agenda laws requires the use of force and armed agents against innocent people. ...The only purpose of such laws is to violate individual rights.

Objective Laws are not conjured up by politicians or bureaucrats. Instead, like the laws of physics, they arise from the *immutable laws of nature*. Such laws are valid, benefit everyone, and advance society. Objective laws are based on the moral prohibition of initiatory force, threats of force, and fraud as constituted on page 188. ...The only rational purpose of laws is to protect individual rights.

Ego "Justice" is the use of political-agenda laws to gain harmful livelihoods and feel false importance. Ego "justice" is the survival tool of many politicians, lawyers, and judges. Ego "justice" is the most pernicious form of neocheating. ...Parasitical elites thrive on subjective laws and ego "justice" to the harm of everyone else and society.

Golden Helmets are all-revealing, wide-scope accounting tools that evolve naturally from the fully integrated honesty of Neo-Tech. Golden Helmets are the tools needed by businesspeople to generate limitless wealth for others and society. Golden Helmets are what economically control existence and will bring the Civilization of the Universe to planet Earth.

Cassandra's Secret revealed through Zon is the power of the conscious mind to accurately foretell the future through its power to control existence...and its future.

Intelligence is redefined by Neo-Tech as the *range of integrated thinking*. The range, width, or scope of valid integrations is more a function of honesty than of IQ. No matter how high is one's raw IQ, that person can be outflanked and outperformed by a lower IQ mind that is more honest, allowing wider-scope integrations. In the Civilization of the Universe, wide-scope integrations are what give conscious minds power. Neo-Tech intelligence supersedes the role of IQ detailed by Richard J. Herrnstein and Charles Murray in their controversial, best-selling book *The Bell Curve* (Simon & Schuster, 1994). Since fully integrated honesty, not IQ, is the key to long-range success and abiding happiness, all races have equal access to the limitless prosperity available from the Civilization of the Universe.

Purpose of Existence and Motive for Controlling Existence: Achieving and expanding happiness is the moral purpose of conscious life.[1] Happiness, therefore, is the ultimate motivator behind conscious-controlled existence. But, to control existence, one must realize that existence itself is *never* derived from thoughts or emotions. Instead, thoughts and emotions, including happiness, are *always* derived from the conscious control of existence. Thus, conscious control of existence is ultimately directed toward creating limitless prosperity, rejuvenated life, and eternal happiness for everyone and society.

---

[1]As identified in Aristotle's *Nicomachean Ethics*, happiness is the highest moral *purpose* of conscious life. ...Life is the moral *standard*. Reason is necessary for human survival. Reason *and* honesty are required to achieve happiness.

[See pages 323-327 for additional word usages]

PART I

Neo-Tech Physics

The Foundation

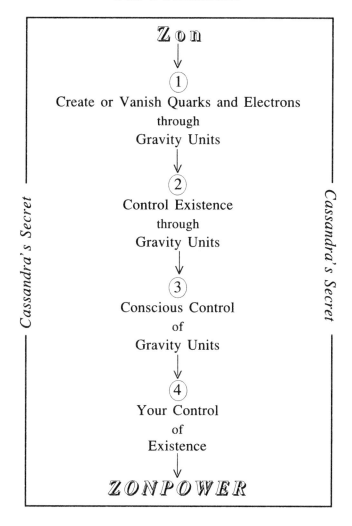

Cassandra's Secret

Zon

①

Create or Vanish Quarks and Electrons
through
Gravity Units

②

Control Existence
through
Gravity Units

③

Conscious Control
of
Gravity Units

④

Your Control
of
Existence

ZONPOWER

Cassandra's Secret

Existence Exists as Gravity Units

Gravity Units are the fundamental units of existence. They are indivisible, windowless units of submicroscopic geometries from which nothing can enter or exit. Yet, those geometries exist continuously — as a blended whole through wave-like dynamics and resonances. Each Gravity Unit can flux into a universe of gravity, mass, energy, and consciousness. ...All wealth arises from Gravity Units.

Chapter 1

Boundless Prosperity

through

SIGUs and Googolplexes

What are SIGUs and googolplexes? What connection do they have to boundless prosperity? First ask: How do conscious beings meet the energy and communication requirements of an eternally advancing civilization? How does one unleash nature's power to achieve near instant communication throughout the universe? How can one capture the power of universes spanning billions of light years across? How can one unleash the universal power locked in gravity units lurking beneath every subatomic particle? How can one direct the power of Super-Inflation Gravity Units[1] (SIGUs) to eternally expand life and prosperity?

Take a Numbers Ride

Take a ride to the big: The mathematical term googol is the number 1 followed by a hundred zeroes, or 10^{100}, meaning 10 raised to the power of a hundred.[2] How big a number is a googol? Astronomers estimate our universe is 15 billion years old...or 10^{18} seconds old. Over 22 centuries ago, Archimedes calculated that 10^{63} grains of sand would fill the then known universe.

Consider today's known universe contains at least a hundred-billion galaxies each containing an average of a

---

[1] A Super-Inflation Gravity Unit is equivalent to a symmetrical Geometry Unit of the entire universe.

[2] The power of the number 10 means the number of zeros after the number 1. For example, 10 raised to the power of 2 or 10^2 means 100, 10^3 means 1000, 10^{100} means 1 followed by a hundred zeros, $10^{10^{12}}$ means 1 followed by a trillion zeros. Likewise, 10^{-3} is $1/10^3 = .001$. Also, 10^{-43}, for example, is a decimal point followed by 42 zeros then the number 1. ...Human life expectancy is about 2×10^9 seconds. The passing of a light wave takes about 10^{-15} seconds.

hundred-billion stars. Now consider the mind-boggling number of electrons, protons, neutrons, and all other matter-and-energy particles in those stars, planets, dark matter...as well as all additional particles scattered throughout space. That number would equal 10^{86} particles, a number still considerably less than a googol! Now, if our entire universe of about fifteen billion light years across were packed *solid* with subatomic particles with zero space between them, the number of particles would rise to 10^{130}.

But, how large is a googolplex, $10^{10^{100}}$? Just to print the number of zeroes after the number 1 would require enough paper to pack solid our entire universe, fifteen billion light years across.[1] ...And a super googolplex is a googolplex that is raised to an additional 100th power. No scale is available for any conscious mind on Earth to grasp such a number.

Now take a ride to the small: Slice an average-sized pie in half ninety-one times. On the ninety-second slice, you would need to slice the nucleus of an atom in half. How small is the nucleus of an atom? Enlarge a baseball to the size of Earth. One would then see the atoms of that baseball as the size of cherries filling the entire planet. Now, enlarge one of those atoms to the size of the Astrodome. The nucleus would then become visible as the size of a grain of sand.

What about the smallest or shortest unit of time that the human mind can grasp: Planck's time of 10^{-42} of a second — about the time required for light travelling at 186,281 miles per second to traverse the diameter of the smallest subatomic particle of, say, a 2×10^{-33} centimeter

---

[1] Roger Penrose calculated that to emulate all possible quantum states of the known universe would require $10^{10^{123}}$ bits of information.

diameter, which is Planck's length. A time less than 10^{-42} of a second measured from the *theoretical* beginning of time in our universe[1] cannot be experimentally simulated or conceptually grasped.

Finally, grasping the smallest and the biggest in terms of eternity requires the axiomatic fact that *existence exists*. Thus, existence has no prior causes and is eternal. Relative to eternity, the smallest unit and the largest unit are equal in occurrence, time, or distance. For example, compare an incredibly fast event that occurs once every 10^{-42} of a second to an incredibly slow event that occurs once every googolplex years. The occurrence of those events are equal in eternity. For, each of those events will occur an infinite number of times in eternity.

The smallest units of existence, such as quarks or the even smaller Gravity Units as explained in Chapters 5 and 7, to the largest expansion of the universe with everything in between and beyond are all a part of eternal existence. Gravity Units, quarks, subatomic particles and energies; protons, neutrons, and electrons; electromagnetism, nuclear forces, and gravity; universes, galaxies, stars, and planets; atoms, molecules, and compounds; gasses, liquids, and solids; air, water, and land; mountains, oceans, and clouds; protoplasm, amoeba, plants, fish, animals, primates, *and conscious beings*...all are part of existence and its natural evolution that has occurred eternally. Indeed, each and every entity of existence has existed forever. Thus, conscious beings as entities of existence have also existed forever throughout the universes as shown in Chapter 6 and in Part III.

---

[1]Contrary to big-bang theories, universes have no natural beginnings or endings. In concert with the laws of physics, universes have conscious-controlled beginnings in quantum-fluxed Gravity Units as described in later chapters.

Rapid Communication Across Universes
by using
Super-Inflation Gravity Units Called SIGUs

Reality can never be contradicted. Thus, the laws of nature and physics can never be violated. That means nothing can exceed the speed of light. So, how can near instant communication occur across distances that require light (travelling at 186,281 miles per second) millions or even billions of years to traverse? Even more, how can communication occur between universes from which not even light can escape? Conscious beings and only conscious beings can accomplish such near instant communication. How do they accomplish that communication without violating the laws of nature or physics?

Conscious beings harnessing the Super-Inflation nature of Gravity Units (SIGUs) can produce near instant, gravity-pulse communication not only across an entire universe but possibly between universes — all without violating physical laws, including the speed of light. How? By gravity pulses transmitted through big-bang-type inflations radiating from exploded Gravity Units.

How do gravity pulses communicate faster than the speed of light with nothing exceeding the speed of light? First, realize that the smallest units of existence, Gravity Units, and the largest unit of existence, the full expanding universe, are one and the same: They each contain the same mass and energy potentials. The units are just in different modes throughout time and space. Next, examine the so-called big-bang or hypothetical spacetime birth of our universe from a gravity unit: At 10^{-42} of a second or Planck's time after its birth, the entire universe is 10^{35} times *smaller* than a subatomic proton. Doubling every 10^{-34} seconds or doubling 10^{36} times at 10^{-32} seconds from birth, the universe has grown to 12 centimeters across — about the size of a grapefruit. And then, doubling 10^{50} times by somewhat over 10^{-30} seconds from its hypothetical birth, the universe has exploded to the size of our solar system — all in that tiniest fraction of a second. ...In other words, during that instant in time, the universe has expanded trillions of times faster than the speed of light. Yet, nothing exceeds the speed of light. How can that occur?

The super-fast growth of the universe during its first moment in time can be explained by the Inflation Theory originated by Alan Guth of MIT in 1979. Such inflation involves the brief existence of "repulsive gravity" and the relative positions of spacetime coordinates in accord with Einstein's general relativity. ...That super-fast inflation can also be understood, without complete accuracy, in more simple Newtonian terms: Consider two entities starting at the same point and moving apart near or at the speed of light. At the end of one year, those entities will be about two light years apart. Thus, they will have "communicated" from their respective points A and B at about twice the distance covered by the speed of light without exceeding the speed of light.

Now, consider breaking the geometry or symmetry of a universe-containing Gravity Unit or Geometry Unit, causing a spacetime birth. That occurrence begins the near instant conversion of the smallest unit of existence, the universe-containing Gravity Unit, into the largest unit of existence, the entire expanding universe. Incredibly, that new-born exploding Gravity Unit has the same mass/energy total of an entire universe fifteen billion years old. Consider what occurs in the tiniest fraction of the initial second during a big-bang birth: a near instantaneous unit-after-unit multiplication, perhaps initially with repulsive gravity, into nearly the total number of entities (10^{86}) that will exist in the mature universe billions of years old.

Like the previous, simple example of two entities separating at nearly twice the speed of light, each of the rapidly multiplying, countless entities are also separating at or near the speed of light from all the previous and subsequent formed entities. That process multiplies distances of entity separation by trillions of times the speed of light without any individual entity exceeding the speed of light. In that way, the total range of expansion or "communication" announcing the big-bang birth occurs at trillions of times the speed of light without violating the laws of physics. (See pages 91-92 for another perspective.)

Conscious beings can control how and when to break the symmetry of Gravity Units. With conscious beings controlling the symmetry breaking of Gravity Units, the efficiencies and power of universe-creating energy and communication multiply. How can that multiplication occur? The most obvious way is by aiming or lasing each spacetime birth in specific directions as energy waves or gravity pulses, rolling out in multidimensional geometries ...rather than allowing the gravity explosion to convert into the "usual" universe-making energy and matter radiating in three geometric directions. ...Also, such communication could possibly flash through hyperspace to other universes.[1]

Note to General Readers

Understanding or reading scientific footnotes such as below are not necessary for understanding and acquiring Zonpower.

---

[1] In water, the speed of light slows by about 23% to 142,600 miles/ second. Thus, in water very high-energy, charged particles can exceed
(footnote continued on next page)

Boundless Prosperity

Business: The Power of the Universe

Competitive business is the eternal power of existence. It advances every level of society throughout the universe as described in Mark Hamilton's *Neo-Tech Cosmic Business Control*, 510 pages, Neo-Tech Publishing (1989) and in Eric Savage's *Neo-Tech Global Business Control*, 256 pages, Neo-Tech Worldwide (1992). Business is the natural mode of existence for conscious beings. What is business? Business is the *competitive production* and *voluntary exchange* of values among conscious beings. ...Conscious beings throughout the universe control nature through business.

Knowledge begets knowledge. Thus, knowledge is limitless — limitless power. Harnessing universal energy and communication through business represents one increment of productive achievement along the endless scale of knowledge throughout the Civilization of the Universe. Indeed, conscious beings exert business control over nature. Through the universal virtue of competitive business, advances in value production continue endlessly — beyond the imagination of conscious beings on Earth.

(footnote continued from previous page)
that slower speed of light to create a light-barrier shock wave producing Cerenkov radiation. Now, throughout existence, no total vacuum can exist in which to measure the ultimate speed of light. In our universe, the quantum vacuum state or the gravity-unit ether exists at a certain energy level. In a vacuum state at lower-energy levels, light could travel faster than 186,281 miles/second. Does that mean certain particles such as Gravity Units could travel faster than 186,281 miles per second through our universe and not exceed the speed of light travelling through lower energy-level vacuums? Could such particles set up a shock wave that would break or tunnel through the metastable vacuum of this universe into a lower energy state, thus, annihilating at light speed our entire universe as we know it? Or, could lower vacuum states be a conscious-controlled, advanced source of energy and communication? ...What about tachyons? They are hypothetical particles that can never travel *slower* than the speed of light and *increase* in speed as they *lose* energy.

9

Yet, someday, in the eternal Civilization of the Universe, immortal descendents from Earth will routinely function along all levels of unimaginable knowledge and accomplishments.

How can conscious life be immortal — eternal? First, examine the nature of existence: Existence is axiomatic. Existence simply exists — eternally, without prior cause. No alternative is possible. For, existence cannot *not* exist. Thus, as part of existence, the evolution of consciousness is also eternal. Countless conscious societies, therefore, exist throughout the universes with endlessly higher levels of knowledge — with millions or billions of years more advanced societies than ours. Because of such vast and endless differences in knowledge, conscious beings at any specific level of civilization cannot imagine the knowledge or activities of say a thousand years, much less a million or a billion years, more advanced societies.

If communication among conscious beings throughout the universe delivers rational benefits, such communication would develop through competitive-business dynamics. But, probably no net benefits would accrue from communicating with less advanced civilizations. Likewise, communicating with much more highly advanced civilizations would probably yield no net benefits. For, conscious beings in the Civilization of the Universe would not benefit by jumping significantly beyond their own ongoing, step-by-step integrations in developing knowledge and values. Indeed, no matter from what level of knowledge, the *continuity* of experiences and integrations needed to create ever expanding prosperity is the root cause of happiness in any civilization.

Why are net benefits impossible from big-gap jumps into realms beyond current knowledge? For example, conscious beings cannot benefit from "million-year" advanced-knowledge jumps without going through the integrated steps to acquire that knowledge. Indeed, to benefit from advances in knowledge requires meeting the criterion for advancing prosperity. That criterion throughout all universes and all time is fully integrated honesty combined with productive effort. In other words, that criterion *is* Neo-Tech.

On Becoming Zon

Most conscious beings among Earth's anticivilization will encounter the fully integrated honesty of Neo-Tech at least once by the year 2000. That encounter will knock each person down. But, most people will jump right back up. Still enclosed in their mystical bubbles, most will bounce away...never examining what happened, never discovering eternal life and prosperity. Yet, a few will stay to examine Earth-evolved Neo-Tech. They will benefit enormously from applying its fully integrated honesty *within* Earth's anticivilization. ...And, a small number of those people will go beyond Neo-Tech by entering the Civilization of the Universe. As explained in Part III, they will become Zons. For them, the anticivilization will vanish into its nothingness as they experience the power of the universe — the power of Zon.

With the power of Zon, all things throughout the universe can become nonmystical conscious thoughts — *and nonmystical conscious thoughts (T1) can become all things (T2) throughout the universe.* ...As explained in Part III, from the equation T1 equals T2k arises k as the universal constant of Zon. From the constant k flows the power of Zon.[1]

---

[1]The Zon constant k has not yet been determined. But, k would be the fifth and unifying universal constant: unifying the relativistic,

(footnote continued on next page)

Part I: Neo-Tech Physics

(footnote continued from previous page)
macroscopic universal constants of G (gravity) and c (velocity of light) with the quantum, submicroscopic universal constants of k (Boltzmann) and h (Planck). Perhaps k manifests itself in some sort of unifying ratio with the other four universal constants, such as k: *Gc/kh*. The Zon constant would relate energy, mass, gravity, and their velocities to the flow of *time* toward decreasing entropy, *not* toward increasing entropy. ...Universal constants, including the quantum cosmological constant, ultimately arise from a deep, compelling symmetry or geometry controlled by conscious beings. *The Zon constant fixes the values of all other constants.*

Except for consciousness, gravity is the weakest yet most pervasive force in nature. Indeed, gravity controls universal motion. But, the fifth force of nature — human consciousness — is the *grand-unifying* force controlling all existence. Conscious force is more subtle to specific measurement and mathematical quantification than gravity. Still, consciousness is the most noticeable force on planet Earth. Moreover, consciousness is the only force that can alter the otherwise predestined courses of the other four forces of nature: gravitational, electromagnetic, weak nuclear, strong nuclear. ...Consciousness is the force that unifies all forces and heals the seeming breaches of nature caused by quantum "uncertainties".

As a law of nature expressed by the Heisenberg Uncertainty Principle, facts asserted as truth are never certain. But, *principles* contextually determined through integrated honesty are always certain. Thus, for example, one can have certainty about the Heisenberg Uncertainty *Principle* without paradox or contradiction: (1) Metaphysically one can be certain that any particle always has an exact position and momentum at any exact time.   But, epistemologically one can be certain that exact position and momentum *cannot* be simultaneously measured...at least not directly. (2) Measurements can be validly done in Euclidean/Galilean/ Newtonian coordinate systems or in noneuclidean/relativistic/quantum-mechanical systems, depending on the object measured and the accuracy desired. And finally, (3) the indeterminate and probabilistic nature of quantum mechanics does not negate the laws of identity, noncontradiction, or cause and effect. The decay of radioactive atoms, for example, are both indeterminate and probabilistic. But, each decay has an identifiable, noncontradictory cause. ...That means Heracleitus, Plato, and Kant are out; Parmenides, Aristotle, and Rand are in.

As a side note important later: Plato is the father of organized deception through "noble" lies — the father of purposely dishonest government and science. Aristotle not only is the father of logic, science, and biology, but is the father of *rational* metaphysics and epistemology. Plato subjugated conscious life to higher mystical powers. Aristotle exalted conscious life on Earth as the highest value. Portions of Aristotle's ethics and politics, however, remained under Plato's influence, thus, are fallacious. ...Philosophically, Plato and Kant are mankind's villains, Aristotle and Rand are mankind's heroes.

Chapter 2
Your Journey to *Zonpower*

What is Zonpower? To answer that question, you must first take a journey that leads to the center of weirdness. Then, you must go beyond, into the realm of weirder-than-weird. That journey will lead you into the weirdest realm of the entire universe. And that realm is right here on planet Earth in its bizarre, upside-down, anti-power civilization. You must go to that black-hole apex in order to go through it and then out into the advanced Civilization of the Universe — the civilization of honesty, prosperity, and happiness.

Journey to the Weirdest Realm

Only from this anticivilization can you discover the realm of weirder-than-weird. Once there, you will find the key to Zonpower. Unlocking the door to all power and prosperity, you will escape the false journey that essentially everyone on Earth is traveling: As one example, consider the false search in today's sciences and religions, especially in astro/quantum/particle physics and the Vatican. That search is for a **Quantum/God Singularity** and the **Big Bang** — the fictional, wished-for birthplace of our forever evolving, plasmatic Universe.

World-class scientists have searched for that single point of creation. Yet, the notion of Singularity contradicts the laws of nature and physics, as do the mystical notions of perpetual motion, cold fusion, low-energy nano-technology, along with various mystical interpretations of chaos and quantum mechanics. Many brilliant scientists are pursuing never ending illusions that demand ever more tax money, such as the twelve-billion-dollar, super collider (SSC)[1] in Texas. Such pursuits can generate ever more intriguing but eventually meaningless science and mathematics.

Singularity is rationalized to occur in an infinite[2] black hole collapsed to an undefinable, single-point entity filled with mathematical stratagems involving infinities. From such a single-point entity or Singularity, certain physicists assert that our universe and all existence was born. In turn, certain religionists enthusiastically point to Singularity as scientific proof of "God". For, the creation of our universe from Singularity would require a "God"

---

[1] The SSC's mission to find the Higgs boson is a valid quest, especially under brilliant Nobelists such as experimentalist Leon Lederman and theorist Murray Gell-Mann...but not under the dishonesties and inefficiencies of tax-funded science.

[2] "Infinite" is a useful mind-created concept that cannot exist in reality. Except for existence itself, which is eternal and has no finites or boundaries, "infinity" violates the law of identity. In accordance with reality, at any point one stops in traveling toward infinity, the entity is defined and finite, never infinite. For example, one's mind knows that a curve can asymptotically approach a straight line forever. Yet, at any point on that curve, all becomes finite and definable about that curve and the straight line.

Now, consider how the notion of a single point can always be approached closer and closer, but can never be reached. For, like the notion of infinity, singularity does not and cannot exist beyond a mind-created notion. As an analogy, think again how a curve can asymptotically approach but never reach that straight line and become a straight line. Nothing in reality can justify a notion that such an ever approaching curve would suddenly contradict its nature — its never-ending course — by arbitrarily and inexplicably jumping over a quantum space to join, straighten out, and become a part of that never reachable straight line.

The laws of identity and noncontradiction always hold in reality. Those laws are eternally fundamental and axiomatic throughout existence. Moreover, existence is not in space or time. Rather, time and space are in existence. The universe is eternal, not infinite.

mystically preexisting in nothingness and creating a universe out of nonreality. ...What an unnecessary, impotent notion.

Why resort to mysticisms, nonrealities, and nothingness to explain the creation of our universe? Why be stuck within such unreal and harmful limitations? Consider the seemingly infinite number of ordinary conscious beings wielding Zonpower throughout the rational civilizations existing among the universes. Most of those conscious beings have the power to create far beyond any imagined creations of a mystical "God". And, unlike the miracles of a made-up "God", conscious-being creations are real — accomplished naturally, within the laws of physics.

Each such conscious being, for example, has the power to create an endless number of universes from an endless number of universe-containing black holes existing at every spacetime point throughout eternity. Even so, most of those conscious beings have technologically and economically advanced so far that they have long ago in their forgotten histories abandoned the creation of universes as an inefficient, primitive activity.

Vanish All "Gods"

With Zonpower, one captures powers far beyond any imagined powers of a "God" conjured up in Earth's anticivilization. Every such "God" is created to demand sacrifice — sacrifice of the productive class to the parasite class. But, with Zonpower, one escapes the "God" trap by entering the Civilization of the Universe.

Blasphemy? No. For, rational Zonpower, not imagined Godpower, is real and good. Zonpower, not wishful thinking, delivers open-ended prosperity and happiness to conscious beings throughout the universe.

Individual consciousness throughout the universes *is* the eternal, grand-unifying force of existence.

On planet Earth today, Albert Einstein represents the furthest advance in theoretical science and physics based entirely on a foundation of rationality and reality. Einstein avoided any arbitrary, quantum-mechanical retreats into fashionable nonrealities or Eastern mysticisms. With the recent discovery of Zonpower, Einstein arises anew. For science, physics, quantum mechanics, mathematics, and business can now advance in unison on Einstein's foundation of rationality and reality toward the promised land.

A Journey into the Black Hole

To discover Zonpower, you must first take a journey to the realm of weirder-than-weird.[1] This journey proceeds from Einstein's dual relativity viewpoints — first from the observer's viewpoint and then from the traveler's viewpoint:

THE OBSERVER

Through a special relativity telescope/microscope, you are observing a spaceship hurling toward a universe-containing black hole of such great mass that all matter will collapse seemingly forever.[2] You see the spaceship

---

[1]This metaphorical journey is contextually and descriptively quite accurate. But out of communication necessity, some descriptions may not be *precisely* accurate and await further advances in physics.

[2]Every black hole originates from less than infinite mass and energy. All black holes, therefore, will stop collapsing at some equilibrium point determined by its finite mass/energy: For example, stopping at the Chandrasekhar limit then at the Schwarzschild radius. That equilibrium point of finite size consists of various entities and energies that cannot by definition be a pure point of singularity. Instead, by nature, those entities and energies are simply new, valid, and real sets of physics definable by that particular condition for those entities, masses, energies, and finally gravity at a particular density.

cross the event horizon to be inescapably captured by the enormous, always increasing gravitational pull of that black hole. That overwhelming gravity continually accelerates the spaceship's plunge toward the center point with ever increasing speeds — speeds always approaching but never reaching the speed of light: 186,281 miles per second.

Observable only through your relativity telescope/microscope, the collapsing, mega-mass black hole itself is now submicroscopic. And that black hole continues to collapse at ever increasing speeds. With fuzzy thinking, you rationalize that the infinitesimally tiny black hole still collapsing ever faster, approaching the speed of light, should in the next instant crunch into one entity at a single-point center. Your fuzzy thinking continues: All entities and forces would then become Singularity — a unified, single-point entity or force describable only in terms of unreal infinities.

Yet, no such thing happens as you continue observing through your relativity telescope/microscope: The spaceship and all surrounding existence keeps hurling toward the center at ever increasing speeds with ever decreasing distances, but without ever reaching the center. How can that be?

By continuing to observe the spaceship, you discover the answer through the laws of physics and Einstein's Special/General Relativity: As any object approaches the speed of light, its mass density increases *toward* infinity and its size shrinks *toward* zero length from the observer's viewpoint. Accelerating toward the speed of light, that spaceship appears to you, the outside observer, to move forward essentially as fast as that same spaceship is shrinking backward. Also, time aboard the spaceship appears to slow toward zero. Thus, as with all the other entities of that black hole, the shrinking spaceship keeps approaching the black-hole center at ever higher velocities, but with ever slowing time, never reaching that center.

At some approaching equilibrium, the collapse will stop accelerating as determined by the laws of physics and the finite mass/energy/gravity geometry of the black-hole center. At that moment, the spaceship and all other surrounding entities of existence captured by the black hole will stop shrinking. All existence will then lock together in a black hole of finite size and specific nature — a nature or physics characteristic to its particular gravity or geometry. Moreover, that or any physics will always be in accord with reality. Thus, such a finite geometry of locked entities can, by definition and nature, never be a single point of mass or energy...or of Singularity. Instead, all that existence will be an energy/entity unit of gravity or geometry...not a single-point.

Without the mind-blocking, dead-end concept called Singularity, a new question and viewpoint arise: What or who could break a black-hole equilibrium of locked-together symmetries, entities, and energies? The answer, as described in later chapters, is that conscious people can break universe-containing black-hole symmetries to create universes and encoded cosmos systems observable today.

THE TRAVELER

Now, let us experience the same journey as a traveler on that spaceship in quest of Singularity. First, you would have to somehow acquire such a spaceship from some advanced civilization. For, if you were capable of building that spaceship, you would also have the knowledge to realize Singularity is a contradiction of reality and cannot exist. Thus, any such quest would be a fool's journey, forever wasting your life. Indeed, when that universe-containing black-hole equilibrium were finally reached, you would be locked together with all entities and energies, entombed apparently forever in that black hole.

Nevertheless, in that spaceship, you are now accelerating toward a seemingly infinite-mass black hole that will collapse almost forever toward its center. Crossing the event horizon, you see the center of the black hole. You fear an imminent crash into that center. But, soon, you realize something entirely different is happening. On looking outside the spaceship, time seems to pass so slowly and then ever slower. To travel the most minute distance seems to take forever. Every tiny incremental approach toward that black-hole center seems to take ever longer as time passes ever slower.

Soon you seem to be standing still with the black-hole center never again appearing to get closer. Yet, the spaceship's instruments show you are traveling at almost the speed of light and continually accelerating toward that center. You realize that you are experiencing not only Einstein's relativity in time and space, you are also experiencing relativity in gravity: Now, even the increases in gravity seem to have stopped. In fact, not even the quantized effects of gravity can escape that universe-mass black hole. ...You seem to be forever frozen in time, space, and gravity.

Finally, you the space traveler realize the ultimate fool's journey of boredom in which you have embarked and are forever trapped. You lose all that conscious life and valid knowledge have to offer. Your fool's journey offers only an endlessly changing physics, energy, and particles that at first seem rapid, interesting, important, and leading to new knowledge for answering questions. But now, your almost infinitely slow journey is leading to nothing new — nothing that can build new knowledge or answer questions in reality. You can only observe endlessly slower changing forms[1] of mass/energy that are forever predictable as a function of existence and its gravitational fields, geometries, and dimensions.

Yet, the moment you recognize what an endless, inescapable fool's journey you have traveled and are now stuck, the door to escape opens. Realizing existence is never born or created, it simply exists eternally, your mind is finally free. Your entire thinking and viewpoint change. You realize existence, *not* consciousness, is primary.[2] You can now gain valid, new knowledge — Zonpower knowledge — that will show you how to escape that meaningless pursuit of a nonexistent grail: the birthplace of existence. You realize existence has no birthplace. You realize conscious beings have always controlled eternal existence through Zonpower.

Indeed, Zonpower brings you into the all-powerful Civilization of the Universe. With Zonpower, you control existence and, thus, can break out of any black hole. ...With conscious beings, rotating black holes can actually become shortcuts through space and time.

---

[1]Changing from a black hole to a naked black hole from which nothing, not even gravity, can escape...and finally changing into the geometry of a Gravity Unit.

[2]Aristotle is the father of the philosophically correct *primacy-of-existence* concept — a concept fully validated by Rand and Peikoff in the late 20th century. Plato is the father of the philosophically false *primacy-of-consciousness* concept — a concept disastrously advanced by Augustine, Hobbes, Descartes, Hume, Kant, and Hegel. ...Totalitarian-trending governments and their destructive politicians, armed bureaucrats, and parasitical elites require a dishonest, primacy-of-consciousness philosophy to advance. *Zonpower in cyberspace vanishes Plato's philosophy, irrational acts, and government evils.*

Chapter 3

Seven Waves
to the
Civilization of the Universe

WAVE ONE

The Journey into a Black-Hole Civilization

* A spaceship travels into a universe-containing black hole: That spaceship can never reach Singularity, all in accord with the laws of nature as expressed by Einstein's general relativity, by *full-context* quantum/particle physics, and by multidimensional superstring theories.

* Singularity and the big-bang creation of existence is a mystical notion requiring an imagined "God". Thus, the astute Vatican and its Pope, as early as the 1950s, seized out-of-context quantum physics as the long sought-after-link of science to religion "proving" the existence of their mystical "God".

* The fundamental fact of existence is *existence exists.* That means existence is eternal without prior causes. Existence includes the full evolvement of each new universe: from subatomic gravity units, quarks, electrons to the elements and compounds...from land, water, life, conscious beings, buildings, computers to conscious-created civilizations...and finally to conscious-controlled universes — controlled from both above and below. Thus, life and consciousness — like geometry, matter, and energy — have existed throughout eternity. Indeed, conscious beings like us, not an imagined "God", have eternally controlled nature and existence. ...Consciousness within each human being *is* the controlling force of existence.

21

WAVE TWO
Discovering the Civilization of the Universe

* Consider the very few honest philosophers who have lived on Earth: Parmenides, Aristotle, Thomas Aquinas (variance with reason is evil), Baruch Spinoza, Adam Smith (economist), John Locke, Ayn Rand, Leonard Peikoff. Consider their struggle against the irrationality of an anticivilization. They all sensed increasing frustration at their inevitable failures because they too were an integrated part of irrationality — of anticivilization. They never knew how to leave or even knew that leaving an anticivilization was possible. They never considered themselves being able to create and then enter the Civilization of the Universe. ...They too were locked in a fool's journey within Earth's black-hole anticivilization.

* Not until mystical, wishful-thinking notions, such as a Quantum/God Singularity, are cut away and discarded can physicists, mathematicians, and astronomers once again move forward in generating major new knowledge. As new-age mysticisms multiply, all fields of knowledge shrink toward darkness. But, as Neo-Tech starts vanishing such mysticisms, those declines in physics, mathematics, astronomy, medicine, law, education, and philosophy will reverse. The resulting forward movement will bring a golden age of knowledge. From that new knowledge and prosperity, we shall learn to live forever with ever increasing wealth and happiness. We shall be in the Civilization of the Universe.

WAVE THREE
Zon Easily Outdoing "God's" Supreme Feat

* A century ago, no religious huckster could even imagine their mystical "God" could create a nuclear-power reactor or a computer. Yet, conscious beings easily do that today.

* Who would be the winner in any Zon-versus-"God" contest? All conscious beings have the capacity within the laws of nature and physics to outdo the greatest imaginable feat of that mystical "God" — the creation of our universe. Indeed, the creation of universes by conscious-controlled, Guth-type inflations of Gravity Units is elementary child's play long-ago left behind by the more advanced Zons.

* Unchain Jesus[1]: He was a hero of Zon, not "God".

* Cut away and vanish the nothingness trap of mysticism, such as Quantum/God Singularity. Then what happens? An entirely different view, thinking, experiments, and physics unfold:

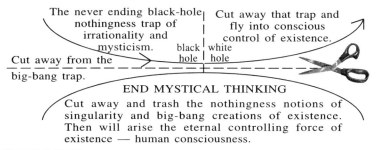

The never ending black-hole nothingness trap of irrationality and mysticism.

Cut away that trap and fly into conscious control of existence.

black hole | white hole

Cut away from the big-bang trap.

END MYSTICAL THINKING

Cut away and trash the nothingness notions of singularity and big-bang creations of existence. Then will arise the eternal controlling force of existence — human consciousness.

---

[1]Not the unreal, dead Jesus of establishment Christianity. Not the chained, captive Jesus manipulated by parasitical "authorities" and vested interests since 400 AD. But, the real, ever-living Israelite Jesus of Zon — the newly freed spirit of eternal prosperity and happiness.

The parasitical-elite class with its subjective laws and ego "justice" attacked, jailed, and finally killed Jesus. Why? For his trying to bring the prosperous Civilization of the Universe described in Part III to the harmful anticivilization described in Part II. ...The professional value destroyers of the Roman Empire convicted and crucified Jesus solely to protect their ego agendas and harmful livelihoods.

Brief, erratic contacts with the Civilization of the Universe described in Part III were perhaps experienced by Moses, Confucius, Socrates, Jesus, Bruno, Galileo, Spinoza, Newton, Brigham Young,

(footnote continued on next page)

* A century ago, any thought of human beings cracking the atom to convert mass into energy was inconceivable. Today, nuclear energy is routine. Likewise, today, any thought of human beings cracking super-dense black holes or Gravity Units (GUs) into new galaxies and universes is inconceivable. Yet, once free of mystical notions such as Singularity and the big-bang creation of spacetime, the cracking of black-hole symmetries will become understood. Then, universe-making energy can be harnessed by conscious beings breaking the symmetry of universe-containing Gravity Units — all consistent with the laws of physics. ...That process, in turn, will spin out the unlimited riches available from the conscious-controlled unleashing of matter and energy from those Gravity Units.

WAVE FOUR
Surpassing Einstein

* A universe-containing Gravity Unit (UGU[1]) is equivalent to all the mass and energy of a universe spun into a submicroscopic geometry of wound-up gravity or antimotion order at zero entropy — the pure, quantized geometry of gravity in which time and space do not exist. Advanced conscious beings create countless universes from such hidden quantized Gravity Units. How? By

---

(footnote continued from previous page)

Einstein. But, today, a consistent, nonstop journey from Earth to the Civilization of the Universe has begun. It began in 1976 with the publication of the *Neo-Tech Reference Encyclopedia*.

The future belongs to fully integrated honesty — to reason, rationality, Neo-Tech, and the Civilization of the Universe.

[1]Universe containing Gravity Units (UGUs) *are* existence, thus, have existed eternally. By contrast, universe-containing black holes (Chapter 2) form whenever an entire universe collapses into a black hole.

breaking symmetries to unwind the endless UGUs into universes of matter and energy...or perhaps into just gravity pulses for communication. Why do conscious beings create universes? To utilize nature's ultimate energy and communication source in advancing their well beings. ...That conversion of UGUs into endless riches and universes by conscious beings is expressed by the equation:

UGU energy/c2$\overset{Eq}{\longleftrightarrow}$UGU mass$\rightarrow\begin{bmatrix}\text{broken}\\\text{symmetry}\end{bmatrix}\rightarrow$Energy+Mass+Time

* The UGU state is near pure gravity in an existence field. UGUs are at once *all* energy and *all* mass. The quantized Gravity Unit is the basic unit of existence — the immutable source of all life and riches. Thus, all expanding values and riches rise from that single unit (*not* a single point) — the quantized GU. Additionally, GUs are the energy and communication means among the controlling force of existence — goal-directed conscious life.

* How does one prove conscious life is the only nongeometrically structured force of nature — the fifth and controlling force of the universe? By discovering anomalies in the universe that are unmistakably obvious as conscious creations — creations that could never be produced or configured by the other four universal forces — the geometrically structured forces of gravity, electromagnetism, weak nuclear forces, and strong nuclear forces. ...Consider one observing a planet in a distant solar system. Did conscious life ever exist there? What if that observer spotted a land-rover vehicle on that planet? That land-rover vehicle would be unmistakable proof of conscious existence. For, no geometric force of nature could produce or configure a land-rover vehicle. Now, extrapolate that example to anomaly configurations in the universe. Are those anomalies a part of a nongeometric,

consciously encoded cosmos system? Such anomalies will be resolved only by plugging in the purposeful, unifying force of conscious life into theoretical and mathematical models of our entire universe down to subatomic phenomena. ...Is existence itself encoded by conscious control?

* At every level, from distant quasars to subatomic quarks, from astronomy to quantum physics, certain anomalies will be resolved as purposeful, life-enhancing conscious actions. Within that resolution exists the proof that nongeometrically structured conscious life *is* the fifth and controlling force/dimension of existence.

* The conscious harnessing of Super-Inflation Gravity Units (SIGUs) allows near instant, gravity-pulse communication not only across our entire universe but possibly between universes — all without violating physical laws, including the speed of light. How? By rolling multidimensional geometries into lased gravity pulses transmitted via Guth-type inflations of Gravity Units.

WAVE FIVE
From Impossible to Succeed to Impossible to Fail

* Civilizations and anticivilizations are conscious-created, just as are land-rover vehicles, airplanes, and television sets. None exist in nature alone. None are created by the other forces of nature without conscious beings.

* The Civilization of the Universe is created by conscious beings objectively integrating reality. But an anticivilization is conjured up by humanoids subjectively disintegrating reality.

* In an anticivilization, endless volumes of philosophy arise in order to rationalize or counter the endless

contradictions of reality and rationality. The Civilization of the Universe **is civilization**. *For, civilization is the integration of reason and objective reality.* In such a civilization, philosophy simplifies to a few words and then disappears as self-evident.

* Civilization vanishes any anticivilization on contact — somewhat analogous to matter vanishing antimatter on contact. Both anticivilization and antimatter are anti *by nature*. Therefore, their natures can never be changed. But, they can be annihilated, vanished, or puffed away by actual matter and the actual Civilization of the Universe.

* Throughout the universe, the position of anyone or any civilization on the scale of knowledge makes no difference. Only the process of advancing unimpeded on that never ending scale of knowledge delivers prosperity and happiness to conscious beings.

* The Civilization of the Universe delivers far beyond any mystic's dream of a no-effort paradise. With Zonpower, one can solve life's problems to live eternally in ever expanding knowledge, prosperity, and happiness. For, the Civilization of the Universe is based on rational efforts integrated with reality — on disciplined thoughts, goal-directed actions, and iron-grip controls — not on lazy rationalizations, wishful thinkings, or sloppy mysticisms.

* In any civilization, the *only* legitimate or beneficial function of government is to **protect** individual property rights. The *only* legitimate use of force is self-defense in protecting those rights. By contrast, criminal-controlled governments of anticivilizations depend on political-agenda laws, ego "justice", initiatory force, threats, coercion, fake compassion, and fraud to survive. They survive by draining value producers and **violating** property rights.

* How can one escape parasitical elites while trapped

in their anticivilization? The trap is the attempt to reform their anticivilization, which cannot be done. The key is Zonpower. With Zonpower, one can cut away and vanish the anticivilization. Consider the following: (1) Zonpower is the tool for building unlimited prosperity available to every conscious being, (2) Zonpower is Neo-Tech applied from the Civilization of the Universe, (3) Zon is anyone who is applying Neo-Tech from the Civilization of the Universe.

* In an anticivilization, long-range successes are impossible. In the Civilization of the Universe, long-range failures are impossible.

WAVE SIX
The Source of Eternal Wealth

* Technically, gravitational "forces" do not exist. As Einstein discovered in surpassing Newton, gravity is the relative interaction among the geometries of mass, energy, space, and time.[1] Similarly, universal consciousness as promoted by certain physicists, Eastern religions, and pantheism does not exist. Rather, universal consciousness as the eternal interaction between individual conscious beings and existence is what dominates nature.

* As Einsteinian relativity overtook Newtonian gravity, astronomers and physicists went about empirically proving relativity. Likewise, as the Civilization of the Universe overtakes today's anticivilization, astronomers and physicists will go about empirically proving Zonpower: the control of the universe by conscious beings. ...Einstein's discredited cosmological constant will rise anew from

---

[1]Somewhat analogous to two-dimensional flatlanders feeling the tugs of geometric variances as "gravitational forces" when they traverse, for example, a crumpled sheet of paper.

Gravity Units containing the hidden Zon constant that brings eternal wealth and happiness to the universe.

WAVE SEVEN
The Product from Zon — Let There be Light!

* Civilizations are created by conscious beings applying the eternal principles of nature to life. Thus, civilizations can be created by billions of conscious beings or by a single conscious being. Moreover, as a conscious creation, civilizations can be created and expressed in writing — in a document. Once a Civilization of the Universe is created here on Earth, anyone can experience that civilization. And, once one experiences that civilization, he or she captures the power of Zon.

The ancients saw power in the gods among the stars. The golden-age Greeks brought power to man on Earth. Today, Zonpower brings the Civilization of the Universe to Earth. ...Zonpower gives conscious people power over existence.

* On capturing that wealth and power among the Civilization of the Universe, one can never again look back or waste a thought on the boring irrationality of today's anticivilization — today's insane civilization ruled by dishonest parasites who can only drain others and harm society.

* Thus, the first-and-final product from Zon *is* the **Civilization of the Universe**. As explained in Part III, once one receives that ultimate product, he or she becomes a citizen of the universe. With the resulting Zonpower, that person puffs away the anticivilization to gain eternal wealth, romantic love, and happiness.

Science, Physics, and Mathematics
merge into
Conscious-Controlled Cyberspace

Francis Bacon (1562-1626) the father of the Scientific Method developed inductive reasoning and formulated perhaps the most important maxim of Western thought: "Nature, to be commanded, must be obeyed." To be commanded, nature must first be understood. Thus, "knowledge is power". ...That power resides in conscious-controlled cyberspace.

Galileo Galilei (1564-1642) the father of modern science identified and demonstrated that mathematics was required for the development of physics — its theories and laws. Mathematics as the key to understanding nature was also demonstrated by Johannas Kepler (1571-1630) in his discoveries of algebraic geometries that codified the elliptical orbits and area sweeps of planetary motions.

The Zon Institute is seeking to develop the mathematical descriptions and field formulations of conscious-controlled physics. All universal constants and the laws of physics are formulated through the conscious unfurling of Gravity Units. Publishable contributions providing such mathematical descriptions may be submitted to John Flint, The Zon Association, P. O. Box 60752, Boulder City, NV 89006. Or through the Internet: zon@zon.neo-tech.com

Chapter 4

Zon's Force Field

> Note to General Readers
> Understanding or reading this Chapter 4 about Zon's force field and the next Chapter 5 about physics is not necessary for understanding and fully using Zonpower. Skip these two chapters if you wish.

By understanding what existence *really* is, you gain control over impediments blocking your life. Without those impediments, you can foretell the future to gain limitless riches.

Indeed, you can get incredibly rich by controlling the force fields of existence. But first you must know what existence really is through Neo-Tech physics. Existence is axiomatic and eternal. For, existence simply exists with no prior causes. Existence is a natural, open-ended plasma of force fields[1] eternally evolving with no beginning or end. Neo-Tech physics demonstrates how human-like consciousness is not only an integral part of existence, but is the eternal controller of its geometries, fields, and particles. ...Yet, what is the actual nature of existence?

Most existence throughout the universe exists as an open-ended electroplasma, always evolving through its interacting matter (M) and energy (E) fields or modes. Those two fields of existence eternally interchange in a

---

[1]Fields and forces are the result of noneuclidean geometries and symmetries in space. Thus, there are no unaccounted, spooky "actions at a distance". ...Superstring theory, which would involve the geometries and mathematics of Gravity Units, consist of sixteen dimensions, or, in actuality, ten dimensions because six dimensions are redundant. Those ten dimensions can, in turn, split into a rolled-up six dimensions in which time, space, motion, and entropy do not exist — and the unrolled four dimensions of our current observable universe in which time, space, motion, and entropy do exist.

relationship expressed by Einstein as $M=E/c^2$ (from $E=mc^2$), with c being the universal constant representing the velocity of light.

Existence cannot *not* exist. Moreover, no vacuum void of existence is possible. "Vacuums" of the *matter* field can exist as in outer space, in vacuumed-pumped containers, and in areas between electrons. But, all those volumes are filled with the unmovable, frictionless ether or existence field — a uniform, continuous field of existence.[1]

Throughout eternity, a massless field uniformly occupies every spacetime point of existence. This field of existence behaves as an ether matrix with stationary wave, vibration, or string properties. Within this field matrix, both energy and matter geometries interact to form physical existence, always behaving in dynamic combinations of one mode interacting with the other. Certain motions of the matter field, for example, interact at the

---

[1]An all-pervasive existence field of mass and energy modes is somewhat analogous to a combination of (1) Dirac's ocean in which exists an endless field of "electrons" or energy fluctuations at all points throughout space and (2) Faraday's nonmatter, stationary lines or fields of force. ...All known energy modes can pressure wave through the energy/matter ratios of outer space. Most modes are absorbed or changed at the energy/matter ratios either in Earth's gaseous atmosphere or in the liquids and solids of Earth itself. By contrast, almost all neutrino wave pressures can pass through the electron/nuclear fields of thick solid masses, even through the entire planet Earth without mode change.

This resurrection of an *ether*, **not as a matter or energy field**, but as a fixed existence field, reconciles Newton's classical laws and Einstein's relativity with quantum mechanics. Such a reconciliation arises from a universal Zon constant, k, which, in turn, arises from conscious control of the existence-field ether manifested at every spacetime point of existence. The resulting causal control of existence by eternal conscious beings is (1) universal, (2) fixed, (3) unmovable, and (4) independent of any frame of reference or method of observation.

quantum level with the energy field. That interaction produces irreducible packets of quantized energies or geometric structures. Those irreducible quanta, such as photons, send relief-seeking signals or perturbations into the continuous existence field radiating throughout eternity.

Conscious Control of Existence Fields

During its creation, each new energy quantum slips smoothly and continuously from its matter field into the fixed existence field. Like water flowing from a dripping faucet, each quantum is pinched off into a minimum-energy wave packet. Simultaneously, from the continuous energy flow, a new quantum starts forming. Thus, continuous, smooth-flowing energy forms discrete photons. In turn, those photons or pinched-off wave packets of minimum *energy **matter*** create field disturbances or nonequilibrium pressures[1] signalling themselves in all directions throughout the existence field. Such signals generally travel near or at the speed of light.

Eventually, each point line of disturbance or pressure signal is relieved by a receptor that absorbs such signals. In turn, that disturbance absorption converts back into pinched-off packets of minimum *matter **energy*** — chemical, potential, or kinetic. In other words, a receptor relieves signal pressures by locally absorbing quanta equivalent to the quanta from the originating source. Each absorbed quantum is then converted back into the

---

[1]Not a pushing pressure, but a nonequilibrium pressure or disturbance signal seeking equilibrium. What is detected only *represents* what is transmitted. ...A pressure intruding into the existence field causes that field to curve around the intrusion which, in turn, traces the curved paths of gravity. The interactive relationships between mass, energy, fields, curved space, and gravity require an ether of existence fixed throughout spacetime.

equivalent of its original mode. Such exchanges of modes can be detected as a wave/particle in the energy field or a particle/wave in the matter field or a combination, depending on how and where that mode exchange is emitted, absorbed, and measured.[1]

Those field or mode exchanges occur, for example, when stars pour *nature-controlled*, gravity-fusion energy into its surrounding electrons. Those energized electrons, in turn, pour photons into the existence field. Those photons cause disturbances that simulate waves ranging from radio waves to gamma waves. Those simulated waves radiate toward receptors located at the end of all point lines throughout existence — such as a lens of a telescope in another galaxy. That receptor conserves existence by withdrawing or absorbing equivalent amounts of pressure-alleviating photons to neutralize the disturbances from the originating source.

Similarly, a hydro, fossil-fuel, or fusion power plant on Earth pours *human-controlled,* power-plant energy into, for example, a television transmitter. That energized transmitter, in turn, pours its *human-controlled* photons into

---

[1] In measurements, the distinction between metaphysical and epistemological certainties must be discerned, especially in quantum mechanics: No *metaphysical* uncertainties exist in physical nature. Only *epistemological* uncertainties exist.* Probability statistics are used in the absence of concrete knowledge. The de Broglie/Bohm's pilot-wave theories help eliminate the mystical misinterpretations of quantum mechanics arising from the 1926 Copenhagen Interpretation. ...Pilot waves are the fingerprint disturbances guiding moving particles.

*Consider the following epistemological uncertainty: The ratio of a circle's circumference to its diameter is π or 3.14159..., a number that continues indefinitely without ever repeating. Thus, the use of π in calculations, such as the area of a circle $A=\pi r^2$, can never yield an exact or certain answer. For the answer always depends on how many decimals one extends π in calculating that area. Yet, an exact area exists, it just cannot be calculated by using π or any method of diminishing triangulation.

the existence-field ether. Such an action creates radiating lines of disturbances that are equilibrated by absorption of photons into the matter field of, for example, a television receiver. The same energy/matter mode equilibrations can be traced from that television set to the retina of a human eye, then to a conscious brain, and finally to volitional physical actions that both alter and control the course of nature.

Discrete quanta or particles move at high velocities approaching the speed of light mainly in (1) expansions or contractions of the universe, in (2) certain nuclear reactions or radioactive decays causing symmetry breakings or hidings, and in (3) conscious-controlled actions such as particle accelerations. By contrast, the ordinary transmission of light, electromagnetism, or quantum energy across space is not a result of any significant particle movement. But rather such linear or curved transmissions are simply disturbances in spacetime geometries propagating near or at the speed of light through the existence field. Thus, discrete energy quantum and matter quantum do not themselves travel across space. Instead, each creates a disturbance pressure that radiates along the stationary point lines of existence. That disturbance is eventually relieved, equilibrated, or absorbed by receptors at the end of each point line of existence.

Consider the above description of *locally* creating and relieving energy pressures by emitters and receptors in the stationary existence-field ether. Now, consider the popular notion that almost every particle ever created or released physically races across space — often across millions or billions of light years in space. That notion seems to violate some sort of "least-action" principle. Such an action-inefficient notion of endlessly traveling quanta seems as quaint as the notion of a geocentric universe in which all inertial matter, planets, and stars daily race around planet Earth.

Indeed, both matter and energy interact locally, not across space. Light, for example, does not literally propagate across time and space. But, rather, light locally manifests a disturbance that spreads throughout the existence-field ether until absorbed or equilibrated by a receptor.[1]

Conscious Control of Existence

The above example of an energy-releasing star can be "deterministically" calculated from the "immutable" cause-and-effect of existence *without* conscious influences. But, the above example of an energy-releasing television transmitter is the volitional dynamics of existence being integrated, controlled, and forever altered by freewill human consciousness. Thus, as revealed by Neo-Tech physics, all existence is ultimately controlled and evolved through volitional human consciousness.

Unknown to the busily self-serving Establishment, the nature of existence and its dynamics of matter and energy

---

[1]Then what really is the "speed of light", c? First, consider atomic fission or fusion in which a given mass is converted to energy as $mc^2=E$. Now, by contrast, the "speed of light", c, is the velocity at which a given energy is converted to mass as $E/c^2=m$. Yet, light itself is the opposite — it has no rest mass. So where is the connection of light to the velocity, c? There is none. The "speed of light", c, is not the speed of light at all, but rather c is the velocity relationships of field disturbances, which all have a speed limit of 186,281 miles per second in a particular vacuum state.

Incidentally, traveling near or at the velocity of light, energy fields bend in gravitational fields. The quasi mass generated by high-velocity, photonically disturbed existence fields is what bends in gravitational fields.

are today being increasingly understood and methodically verified. That verification process will lead to the corollary verification that *human consciousness* is the eternal integrator and controller of existence. ...Human consciousness ultimately controls the relationships and geometries of the other existence modes — matter and energy along with space and time. The human-consciousness mode *is* the purposeful, unmoved mover of existence.

Zonpower Commands the Future

The scientific verification that any individual conscious being can control existence will vanish Earth's irrational anticivilization. As Earth's anticivilization vanishes, the rational Civilization of the Universe will embrace our world. ...With Zonpower, you will foretell and command the future by controlling the existence field that reaches into the future — into the Civilization of the Universe.

The age of Zon means controlling the universal information field *not* through Earth-bound computers, but through Zonpower: the foretelling knowledge of Neo-Tech physics — the certainty used to gain limitless excitement, power, and riches *eternally*.

The Five Forces of Nature

Force	Particles Affected	Manifestation	Field Quanta	Range (meters)	Relative Strength
1. strong	quarks	nuclear power	gluons	10^{-15}	1
2. electro-magnetic	charged particles	chemistry	photons	unlimited	1/137
3. weak	quarks and leptons	radioactive decay	$W^{\pm}$ and Z^0 bosons	$<10^{-15}$	10^{-5}
4. gravity	all particles	cosmic structures	gravitons	unlimited	10^{-40}
5. consciousness	gravity units + bosons (energy particles) + fermions (matter particles)	controlling all scales of existence	thinkons (see page 46)	unlimited	k•x

Chapter 5

The Physics Behind Zonpower

Zonpower is a communiqué from the Civilization of the Universe. When you carefully read the *entire* communiqué, an epiphany will occur. You will, for the first time in your life, know how to control all that affects you. Nothing negative or harmful in the anticivilization will control you again. You will gain majestic control over your mind, body, and all events involving your prosperity, happiness, and well-being. ...You will gain Zonpower from which you will capture the power and riches available from the Civilization of the Universe.

Every owner of *Zonpower* must carefully read this communiqué in its entirety at least once, perhaps twice or more, in order to reach into an ecstatic future...into the Civilization of the Universe to gain its power and riches. At the same time, you will toss the yoke of today's stagnant anticivilization. Indeed, *Zonpower* delivers a stunning new power to benefit from every event that touches your life.

Scientific Proofs

The final proof of the Civilization of the Universe lies in the foretelling powers of Zonpower that yield limitless riches, even to those trapped in this anticivilization. But to vanish this anticivilization by having everyone on Earth move into the Civilization of the Universe requires scientific proofs embedded in mathematics. Those proofs are today evolving. One such proof will evolve from answering the fundamental question: What is existence?

The answer will arise by first answering another question: What is the relationship of consciousness to mass and energy? That answer requires understanding the relationship of inertial or gravitational mass to a massless universal ether — a fixed matrix of existence. Then, one can discover the relationships among mass, energy, and consciousness itself. ...How are (1) mass as "weight" and (2) energy as "weightlessness" related to (3) conscious-controlled existence? Why do each of those three existence modes require a universal existence field? ...Below is the simplest approach to answering those questions:

If Mass is Not Intrinsic, What is Weight?

Aristotle postulated things had weight because they had tendencies to be heavy or light. But that postulate does nothing to really explain weight. Newton explained weight through the force of gravity. On careful thought, however, gravitational force does nothing more to explain weight than Aristotle's tendencies. Additionally, Einstein's general relativity demonstrates that gravity does not exist as a force. But rather mass curves space by displacing the space surrounding that mass. Thus, gravity is simply mass moving along spacetime curves — along natural paths of least action.

The greater the mass, the more it bends or curves space toward itself by displacement. Therefore, the more a unit of mass curves space toward itself the greater will be its inertia in falling toward another unit of mass with space likewise curved toward its own mass. ...Mass falling through space curved toward another mass gives the effect of gravitational attraction or negative energy striving toward nonmotion.

Now, through Einstein's relativity, one can approach

an explanation of what weight really is. But, on still closer examination, even Einstein fails to provide a complete answer. What is missing? The existence field is missing — the ether that Einstein dismissed. ...Mass is *not* intrinsic to matter. Thus, an existence-field ether is required to explain what weight really is.

Why does Einstein's General Relativity fail to explain weight without a fixed field of existence? Take two cannonballs of identical size, one made of solid iron, the other of solid aluminum. Both fall and accelerate in a gravitational field at the same rate. Why does the iron ball weigh about twice that of the aluminum ball of the same size? Einstein's general relativity explains that space curves toward the center of mass in proportion to that mass. But, if a non-ether space surrounding the equal-sized cannonballs is being displaced and curved, the space displacement must then be equal for equal-volume cannon-balls. Thus, the weight of identical-sized iron and aluminum cannonballs should be identical. ...What is wrong?

One must first dismiss the notion of composite masses, such as the mass of a cannonball, the Earth, the sun. For, gravity and weight can be understood only in terms of accumulative displacements of a fixed existence field by each *individual* quantum of mass and energy...by each individual subatomic quark and photon or smaller. Each quantum of mass/energy in spacetime geometry displaces and bends the omnipresent existence field. This geometric field represents *all* that is weightless.

The key concept is this: In order to have weight or gravity, one must have a fixed ether field of weightless existence that is *uniformly and equally present everywhere* from the spaces between galaxies and above, down to the spaces between quarks and below, down to the final symmetry of the ether-hidden Gravity Unit.

If that symmetry-hiding ether were not uniformly present and fixed everywhere in existence, the universal laws of nature, such as gravity, would be arbitrary and fail. ...That fixed existence-field ether is not only necessary for existence, but *is* existence — conscious-controlled geometries throughout spacetime.

One must recognize that a fixed, weightless field *is* existence in which its modes of matter, energy, and consciousness interact. The mathematics and experiments will then fall into place for understanding and controlling existence.[1] ...Weight is simply what and where weightlessness is not.

---

[1] Controlling Existence at *All* Scales:

Any given astral volume of matter and energy will maintain its same weight before and after collapsing into a black hole. For, any collapsed volume will still contain the equivalent number of mass/energy units for equivalent ether-field displacements. Total spacetime curvature and total gravity will, therefore, be equivalent for any mass/volume in both its black-hole form and its fully expanded star, galaxy, or universe form. Now, by definition, light and other energy or mass forms cannot escape a black hole. Thus, a normal black hole cannot be detected, except by its gravity or perhaps by Hawking radiation. But nothing, not even gravity, can escape from universe-containing black holes that further collapse into Gravity Units. Why? Because mass and energy have collapsed into a symmetrical geometry of gravity curved in on itself. By collapsing to trillions of times smaller than a regular, microscopic black hole, the Gravity Unit becomes a *quasi point that causes no ether displacement.* It becomes a part of weightless ether. Thus, the Gravity Unit is essentially weightless with no current technology to detect its totally lost, inconceivably tiny weight and volume. ...This essentially weightless, undetectable Gravity Unit represents the underlying geometry of all existence *minus* consciousness. Now, all geometries of existence are subject to nongeometrical conscious control through Gravity Units.

Light cannot escape from black holes whose volumes are proportional to their masses. Neither light *nor gravity* can escape from Gravity Units whose "volumes" are *inversely* proportional to their *potential* masses. No space, time, or motion exists in Gravity Units.

The Physics Behind Zonpower

Football-Stadium Experiments

From the macroworld perspective, conduct the following experiment: In a bowl-like football stadium, bolt on the arm of every seat a simple, low-cost, push-button, battery device. On pushing the button, a precisely tuned radio wave unique to each device is emitted. Beneath the stadium is a radio-wave detector hooked up to a computer. Now, fill the stadium with 100,000 football fans. As part of the halftime ceremonies, provide a laser-light display. Ask the spectators to keep their fingers on the signal button and immediately press it each time they see a green laser flash. Deliver fifty green flashes during the laser display. The signal detector and computer will detect and record every person's signal, plotting each as a point along either side of a dividing line continuously calculated as the medium signal time.

If those signals plot reproducible, double sine waves for each 360^0 revolution of the stadium, watch out! For, conscious quanta as an integral part of a fixed existence-field has been experimentally demonstrated. From such verifiable and repeatable experiments, the Civilization of the Universe and its powers can become known and increasingly accessible to everyone on planet Earth.

How would a double sine wave in this experiment (1) identify the fixed ether of existence and (2) demonstrate consciousness as an integral mode of that ether? The Earth is orbiting the sun at about 67,000 miles per hour...or about 0.01% the speed of light. Thus, if consciousness or conscious control is an integral part of the fixed ether, those oriented most directly in line with the direction of that motion will, because of relativity effects, record on average minutely slower but statistically measurable response times reflected by points plotted below the medium line.

Part I: Neo-Tech Physics

Those people sitting at a 90^0 angle to Earth's orbital motion will record on average a minutely faster response as reflected by points plotted above the medium line. The average of those points should then show a double sine-wave inclination for each 360^0 revolution of the stadium. Statistically, on calculating the effects of relativity, about 100 points should fall outside the statistical average, above and below the line, for each 360^0 revolution of 100,000 points of data recorded after each green laser flash. That 100 point variation per flash times fifty flashes should manifest itself as detectable, reproducible sine waves.

Why did the famous Michelson-Morley experiment in 1887, for which Michelson won the Nobel prize in 1907, "prove" that no fixed ether existed? Because the signals measured were photons of light, which are not intrinsic to the existence field. In other words, rather than seeking a weightless existence-field ether, a nonexistent matter-mode ether was sought. Therefore, no relativity effects would be detected for photons in that experiment. Thus, no detection of the ether could occur. But, what if consciousness or conscious control is intrinsic to existence — a constituent of the fixed ether? Then, with live conscious action, its mediating quanta particles called *thinkons* will cut through a fixed field of existence at 67,000 miles per hour. In that case, relativity effects on consciousness could be detected with repeatable accuracy through properly designed stadium-type experiments.

Swivel-Chair Experiments

Results from stadium experiments could be independently verified in many ways — such as by swivel-chair experiments employing a similar push-button signal device. The chair would be designed to rotate and stop at each 90^0 angle so the participant could push a button in response to a signal flashed at each stop. Given sensitive enough detection devices, properly calibrated equipment, and statistically significant test data, double sine waves identical to the stadium experiments should appear after sufficient swivel-chair rotations.

Indirect Experiments: Clocks and Computers

Physicists have already demonstrated minute differences in time for clocks at different latitudes and altitudes. Those differences are attributed to differences in gravitational "forces". Similar experiments with computer-speed variations could reflect both the orbital and rotational movements of the Earth through the ether.[1]

Gravity Units: the Basic Unit of Existence

Gravity Units are neither energy nor matter.[2] But, in sort of a de Sitter sense, energy and matter meld into the

---

[1]Neo-Tech physics with its ether field resolves the many mysteries of quantum mechanics, including Bell's theorem in explaining the 1982 Alain Aspect's "faster-than-light" experiments. Conscious control of the ether field removes the mysticism from quantum interpretations of CPT symmetry breakings, the Einstein-Bohr debate, Schrödinger's cat paradox and Wigner's friend, and even reducing Everett's parallel universes from infinitely multiplying down to two: the universe and the antiuniverse (the anticivilization). ...Rational consciousness collapses the wavefunction of the antiuniverse.

[2]Energy and mass in the strictest sense do not actually convert from one to the other as suggested by $E=mc^2$. They are really just two different modes of the most fundamental field — the *existence field* consisting of quasi spacetime points and Gravity Units. From any Gravity Unit or quasi spacetime point can spring the mass and energy of an entire universe...an entire universe of quarks and electrons.

But, how do the quarks and electrons actually materialize? They materialize by breaking the symmetry of a Gravity Unit or spacetime point, which is pure symmetry at zero energy. That symmetry breaks into exactly equal but any amounts of positive and negative energy. The amount of energy depends on how the symmetry breaks. The

(footnote continued on next page)

symmetry of Gravity-Unit space or an *existence field.* From that fundamental symmetry or field of existence, all universes spring. Indeed, Gravity Units are that which the latest string theories are groping toward. Gravity Units not only occupy all space among matter and energy particles, but comprise all such particles themselves including quarks and electrons, including gravitons and photons.

The most fundamental controller of existence is human consciousness, the force that controls symmetry and Gravity Units. From those dynamics, existence evolves. ...Consciousness is the ultimate logic, beauty, and symmetry of physics from which future, major theories and discoveries will be predicted and confirmed.

(footnote continued from previous page)

positive energy consists of mass and energy fields comprising the dynamics of quark-and-electron motions. The negative energy consists of gravity comprising the dynamics of antimotions and slowing time. The total energy for any universe or its alternate mode of a Gravity Unit is zero, with all positive and negative energies exactly cancelling each other. Indeed, in the totality of any closed universe or Gravity Unit, the conservation laws of energy, angular momentum, and electrical charge disappear. They each cancel to zero. ...In a Gravity Unit, time stops and disappears into a spatial dimension or geometry.

What really are quarks and electrons? They are existence modes or geometries of quantized momentums that are relativistically compacted into mass particles surrounded by energy fields or wave functions.

Gravity Units and their existence field are controlled by conscious beings through unblocked, wide-scope, integrated thinking efforts. The fine-coarse graining of existence will reveal a quantized particle of conscious thought: the *thinkon.* As photons mediate force in the electromagnetic field, as W and Z particles mediate force in the weak nuclear field, as gluons mediate force in the strong nuclear field, and as gravitons mediate force in the gravitational field, thinkons mediate the force of consciousness in the existence field. All existence can be identified through various sum-over histories of thinkons. ...The thinkon particle can be deduced from football-stadium type experiments. What experiments could directly demonstrate the thinkon particle? The mathematics of noneuclidean, multidimensional geometries may provide the field equations for the existence field and its thinkons.

Chapter 6
A Cosmology
of
Infinite Riches

From the Neo-Tech Discovery ©1985
(simplified in 1995 to be contextually accurate if not technically precise)

This chapter is going to take you on a journey. A journey into realms you never knew existed. By the time you finish this journey, your thinking will change about you, this world, the universe, the future. That metamorphosis will occur on putting together 25 pieces of a puzzle. ...When the last piece snaps into place, your thinking will change forever.

More specifically, after reading this 25-part chapter, an array of new concepts will jell into a matrix on the final page. That matrix will eventually end all mysticism and deliver endless riches to this world.

Part 1

A Neo-Tech Discovery

Tony, a lad of thirteen, was singing the theme song of Monty Python's "The Meaning of Life". The song went something like this:

"Just remember that you are standing on a planet that's revolving at 900 miles per hour, that's orbiting at 90 miles per second. So it's reckoned that the source of all our power, the sun, and you and I and all the stars that we can see are moving at a million miles a day. That's figured out as moving at 42,000 miles an hour, in our galaxy called the Milky Way. Our Galaxy itself contains 100 billion stars. It's 100,000 light years from

side to side and 16,000 light years thick. We are 30,000 light years from our galactic center and go around that center every 200 million years. Our galaxy is one of millions of billions in this amazing, expanding universe. The universe itself keeps on expanding in all directions at the speed of light. It's whizzing as fast as it can go, you know, at 12 million miles a minute. So remember when we are feeling very small and insecure, how amazing and unlikely is our birth. And pray that there is intelligent life somewhere up in space, 'cause we are down here on Earth."

What makes those lyrics fascinating is that every statement is essentially factual and verifiable. But the song left out the most important part: Probability statistics overwhelmingly reveal that our universe contains at least a hundred million, and probably billions of Earth-like planets populated with conscious beings like you and me. Millions of conscious civilizations exist that are millions of years more advanced than our newly born, immature, still mystically oriented civilization.

Moreover, that song was praying for what Neo-Tech already discovered. In fact, Albert Einstein spent his professional life searching in vain for what Neo-Tech discovered — the unifying, controlling element of the universe: *human-like consciousness.*

Part 2
Einstein and the Unifying Link

Throughout history, conscious beings on Earth have struggled with mystical notions of a "superior" consciousness, an imagined god, or some other "higher" power reigning over the universe. But today, by integrating the dynamics of mass and energy, Neo-Tech reveals a relationship between our own Earth-bound consciousness and all existence. The unifying power that orchestrates existence is not some mystical god or "superior" being. But, as demonstrated in this chapter, that unifying power is conscious beings — conceptual/ introspective beings as you and I.

Einstein never accomplished his ultimate goal of unifying all forces. He never derived a Unified-Field Theory. But extrapolating Einstein's work into Neo-Tech reveals the unifying entity of existence — the only integrating force of the universe: human-like consciousness.

Why did Einstein not realize that fact? One reason perhaps stems from his abhorrence for unpredictable actions among the dynamics of nature. For that reason, he disliked quantum mechanics or anything that suggested arbitrary or "god-like" interventions. Always searching for order, Einstein focused on only two components of existence: mass and energy integrated with the geometries of time and space. He believed those components could always be explained, exactly and predictably. Thus, he never considered the third and controlling component of existence: volitional consciousness — a free-will, conceptual/introspective/integrating conscious mind.

Perhaps his passionate dislike for the unpredictable and disorder caused him to overlook consciousness as the third spacetime component of existence. For consciousness can and does unpredictably alter the dynamics of nature, every moment, throughout the universe. Yet, from the widest perspective, consciousness brings the most elegant order and predictability to the universe as demonstrated in this chapter.

All past attempts to link consciousness with existence

were based on mystical, "higher forms of consciousness". Such irrational, ethereal linkages always originated as dishonest, unfounded assertions by mystics or neocheaters conjuring up religious and political power. But the Neo-Tech discovery of human-like consciousness as the unifying element of existence can be scientifically established not only with theory but with direct observation and experimental proof.

Understanding the conscious mind as the controlling, unifying element of existence first requires understanding the *unchanging* nature of consciousness and existence versus the *changing* nature of matter and energy:

Part 3

The Unchanging, Eternal Nature of Consciousness

As first identified by Professor Julian Jaynes of Princeton University and described in Part III, the conscious mind was discovered within nature's bicameral mind[1] about 3000 years ago. Given sufficient information, that first conscious mind had the same capacity as conscious minds today to understand anything in the universe from Einstein's theories to computer technologies and beyond. Consider the astonishing conscious minds of Socrates, Plato, Aristotle, Archimedes that were flourishing only a few centuries after the discovery of consciousness. They would, for example, have no problems whatsoever in understanding Einstein's theories

---

[1]The bicameral mind was man's intelligent, nature-evolved mind before he discovered consciousness as a conceptual/introspective mind. The conscious mind is not a part of nature's evolutionary process. But, rather, consciousness is a discovery by man that lies beyond the dynamics of nature. This discovery process is explained in Chapter 28, pages 241-256. ...When referring to consciousness, the word *discovered* is used when perhaps the word should be *invented*.

or computer technology. Given the information, they certainly had the capacity we have today to understand anything in the universe.

In other words, while much is unknown, nothing is unknowable to the conscious mind. By nature, the conscious mind requires no change or evolvement to understand anything in existence.[1] On acquiring the correct knowledge, conscious beings today are capable of doing anything within the immutable laws of physics throughout the universe.

Consciousness is man's discovery that sprang from his nature-evolved bicameral mind. Consciousness is not part of nature's evolutionary processes, but is a natural phenomenon of existence.[2] Thus, the first conscious minds on this planet 3000 years ago are the same as the conscious minds on this planet today...and the same as conscious minds in any galaxy ten million years from now. All conscious minds have the same ability to understand anything in existence.

Consciousness, therefore, does not evolve. It exists eternally, unchangingly.[3] And its capacity to understand anything in the universe transposes into forever fulfilling the supreme responsibility of conscious beings. That responsibility is to preserve forever the supreme value of the universe — individual consciousness. To meet that responsibility means achieving non-aging biological immortality as described in Parts 12 and 16 of this chapter.

---

[1] Individual minds are endowed with various capacities. Individuals then develop or retard their capacities through either conscious efforts or mystical defaults. But consciousness itself is either there to be used or abused...or it is not there.

[2] As demonstrated later in this chapter, consciousness has always existed throughout the universe as an integral part of existence.

[3] Consciousness is the fundamental invariance and overarching symmetry of existence.

Part 4

The Unchanging, Eternal Nature of Existence

Who Created Existence? And who or what created the creator of existence? And then who or what created the creator of the creator, and so on regressing forever. Such questions are, of course, unanswerable. But, such infinite-regression questions need never be answered.[1] For existence is primary and axiomatic — meaning irreducible, self-evident, and requiring no further explanation. While new realms of existence such as galaxies and universes are constantly being created, nothing creates existence itself. It simply exists. Existence always has and always will exist. And that primacy of existence existing forever is independent of consciousness or anything else. ...The most profound of all concepts as underscored by Einstein is simply: Existence exists. What is the alternative? No alternative is possible unless one accepts the contradiction that existence does not exist.

Throughout eternal time, existence constantly generates new realms of life out of which conscious minds spring from the evolvement of bicameral minds — minds of evolved intelligence capable of discovering consciousness. Once consciousness is discovered and harnessed, it can, with accumulating knowledge and productive efforts, learn to forever muster new realms of existence. From those new realms evolve new life. And from new life evolve bicameral minds from which conscious minds spring.

Throughout eternal time and space, the following creation cycle always has existed and always will exist:

---

[1] The *Neo-Tech Discovery*, Concept #28 identifies the specious nature of infinite-regression questions.

Table 1
THE CREATION CYCLE

Realms of existence created by conscious beings —> life evolved —> bicameral mind evolved —> consciousness discovered —> mysticism developed to replace lost, bicameral gods —> mysticism and neocheaters take control of conscious beings —> partial freedom and capitalism developed —> Neo-Tech discovered —> guiltless prosperity, power, romantic love revealed to value producers —> mysticism and neocheating are uncompetitive and, thus, eliminated —> biological immortality achieved —> control of the universe learned —> new realms of existence created by new conscious beings —> and so on, forever expanding and repeating the cycle.

Stated another way: Space, time, consciousness, and existence are eternal; they have no beginning or end. Throughout time eternal, stars, solar systems, and Earth-like planets constantly form anew. Thus, living organisms and conscious beings constantly form anew. Throughout never ending time and universes, limitless planets forever generate life. That life, in turn, forever generates nature's evolutionary processes that always end with conscious beings.[1] ...Conscious civilizations free of mysticism always survive, prosper, take control of nature and then existence.

Given the endless number of water/oxygen abundant, Earth-like planets forever spinning in endlessly evolving existence, one realizes life and consciousness have forever co-existed in limitless abundance. Human-like conscious-

---

[1]As explained in Chapter 28, pages 241-256.

ness, therefore, is as much a part of eternal existence as are mass and energy. When consciousness is integrated with endless existence and time, the stunning conclusion unfolds that human-like consciousness is also unchanging and has always existed.

Consciousness, mass, and energy are the three macro components of existence. Those three components are inextricably linked and must be integrated into all physical understandings and mathematical accounts of our universe. If only the mass and energy components existed, then all existence would be predictable and predestined through the dynamics of nature and physics. But further research and refinement of data will show that seemingly predictable actions of the universe are actually unpredictable from a mass and energy accounting alone. That unpredictability arises from not accounting for the influence of volitional conscious beings throughout existence.

Human-like, volitional consciousness is:

1) the third and integrating component of existence,

2) the unifying component or force never recognized by Einstein,

3) the supreme component of existence that controls the dynamics of nature, mass, and energy to forever preserve and evolve conscious life,

4) the eternal component that has existed and controlled existence, not for trillions of years, but forever.

* * * *

The balance of this chapter develops a non-mathematical, nontechnical understanding of how conscious beings dominate the universe and muster new realms of existence and life through increasing control of mass and energy.

Part 5
The Changing Nature of Mass and Energy:
The Grand Cycle

All events of the universe fall within nature's mighty Grand Cycle, the dominating, all-inclusive energy wave involving the entire universe. That cycle consists of nature's longest energy wave exactly counterpoised with nature's shortest energy wave. All other cycles, waves, or forces of nature, ranging from cosmic and gamma rays to radio waves fall within the Grand Cycle. ...The Grand Cycle is described in Table 2 below:

Table 2
The Total History Of The Universe
(omitting the unifying element of consciousness)
is contained in
THE GRAND CYCLE
which consists of
The Googol-Year Explosion
Half-Cycle, Long Wave

> with gravity-wave dissipation
> with proton decay
> with quark and electron annihilation

The Googol-Year Implosion
Half-Cycle, Long Wave

The Googolth-of-a-Second
Full-Cycle, Short Wave
(black hole/white hole)

(a googol equals 10^{100} or
1 followed by 100 zeroes)

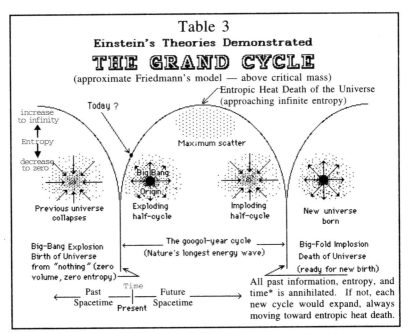

Table 3
Einstein's Theories Demonstrated
THE GRAND CYCLE
(approximate Friedmann's model — above critical mass)

*When time is annihilated, the next event (birth of a universe)
is instantaneous to the previous event (end of a universe). No
time passes between the two events.

A capsulized account of the Grand Cycle starting with the so-called big-bang birth of the universe is illustrated in Table 3 on page 56.

Table 3 also indicates that all activity during nature's longest wave, the googol-year exploding/imploding cycles, exactly equals all activity occurring during nature's shortest wave, the googolth-of-a-second cycle. An understanding of that seeming paradox will evolve over the next few pages.

Part 6

The Explosion Cycle

Within the universe, all existence oscillates in one Grand Cycle spanning trillions of years. The actual time to complete that Cycle is not relevant here, but will someday be scientifically measured by us on Earth. But, even today, experiments and calculations from the astrophysical Doppler effect[1] show our universe is in the explosion, energy-to-matter half cycle. Our universe is exploding outward at near the speed of light, scattering away from its original big-bang birth with ever increasing entropy[2]

---

[1] A change of light-wave frequencies caused by a moving light source such as a star. The wavelength of light from a star moving away *red shifts* — becomes longer — stretches toward the color red.

[2] Entropy involves the second of the three laws of thermodynamics for *closed* systems. Entropy is simply the movement of events toward their highest probability or disorder. Entropy measures irretrievable energy spent on scattering a closed universe. ...For every star that explodes, every pebble that drops from a cliff, entropy and disorder irreversibly increase throughout the universe. Approaching infinite entropy, all usable energy throughout the closed universe is spent. All is flat and scattered to the maximum. No star is available to explode, no cliff is available from which a pebble can fall. No wind blows. All is dead and still. Stars are collapsed, cold and dark, or not at all. No sound or light exists: perhaps not even mass exists. Perhaps only unusable radiation near and always approaching 0°K exists.

— a measurement of spent energy.

Energy available for work throughout the universe will keep decreasing as the universe spreads out for trillions of years until all energy is spent. In that state, trillions of years after the initial big-bang explosion, the universe exists at its maximum scattered or disordered state — as inert residue of an exploded bomb. At that moment, the entire universe is motionless, energyless, and while always approaching absolute zero Kelvin temperature ($0^{0}K=-273.16^{0}C=-469.67^{\circ}F$), all energy is in the form of uniform, unusable heat radiation. ...Do subatomic arrows of time exist? Will protons, quarks, and electrons eventually decay or annihilate to end in radiation for all subatomic particles and motions?[1]

Part 7

The Implosion Cycle

With no usable energies or motions, the universe is dead. Entropy is essentially infinite. Entropic heat death has occurred. Without the force of consciousness, one incredibly weak force remains — by far the weakest of nature's forces — gravity. And, at that moment, in the absence of all other forces, gravity begins acting as an invisible cosmic hand destined to fulfill its function as the ultimate housekeeper, healer, and energy restorer of the universe. For, at that moment, gravity begins pulling a

[1]Are gravity waves the final dissipater of energy and motion? Or does mass itself seek higher entropy? With incredibly long half lives of 10^{32} years or perhaps up to 10^{220} years, do protons themselves decay toward infinite entropy? What about the energy and mass of a quark, an electron? Do quarks and electrons finally decay or annihilate with antiparticles? In any case, without conscious intervention, entropy death of a closed universe will eventually occur. **...The laws of thermodynamics, however, apply only to *closed* systems. Existence itself is eternally open and evolving. Thus, any meaning of entropy to existence disappears, including the idea of entropic heat death.**

totally scattered, exhausted universe back toward increased order while gradually restoring potential energy. Increasingly restoring energy by reversing entropy, this cycle is the mirror image of the explosion cycle and equally lasts trillions of years. In that implosion cycle, gravity eventually pulls the universe back into essentially perfect order...an ultimate-compact, black-hole[1] bomb, ready to explode into another big bang as entropy races toward zero.

As contraction of the universe begins, gravity gradually changes from the weakest to the mightiest force of nature. Starting as an unimaginably faint but constant pull, gravity begins rebuilding the scattered universe by drawing all energyless existence closer together — perhaps initially by a millimicron in a million years. But every movement closer together increases the pull of gravity.[2] That, in turn, increases the speed at which the universe condenses toward an ordered, densifying mass. From the beginning to the end of that condensing-collapsing-imploding cycle, gravity steadily moves toward increasing all forms of

---

[1]The universe-containing black hole described here is matter and energy condensed beyond the critical mass and density needed to be captured, collapsed, and then imploded by its own gravity. When the collapse is complete, the resulting black hole can convert into a white hole, exploding into a new universe. The entire black-hole/white-hole cycle occurs in the tiniest fraction of a second because all information, entropy, and time obliterates between the two Grand Cycles.

[2]Gravitational attraction increases proportionally to the amount of existence involved multiplied by the inverse square of the distances between the eventual masses and energies. That means gravitational attraction accelerates exponentially as masses and energies are collapsed toward unity. Fields of existence are rolled ever closer together, perhaps into multidimensional space* and then into Gravity Units.

*Up to a twenty-six dimensional space has been mathematically derived in superstring theory. ...Most of those dimensions are rolled up into inconceivably tiny volumes or strings that vibrate at characteristic resonances.

energy ranging from potential and kinetic energies to chemical, heat, and nuclear energies.

In the explosion cycle, all energy escapes the diminishing grip of gravity. But in the implosion cycle, no energy escapes the increasing grip of gravity. In this cycle, the universe keeps moving together. Gravity holds all forms of increasing mass and energy within the same shrinking unit as the universe races closer together at accelerating speeds.

Part 8
The Googolth-of-a-Second Cycle

On drawing the universe *toward* a never reachable point, the accelerating pull of gravity begins compacting matter and energy toward a super-ordered, super-compact black hole. Becoming the mightiest physical force in existence, gravity begins crushing the universe. All forms of energy blend into all forms of matter and vice versa. All molecules, atoms, protons, neutrons, electrons, sub-atomic particles, and energy waves of the universe are crushed together into unrecognizable forms of matter and energy. That rapidly compacting universe assumes entirely different forms of existence occurring only during that nearly instantaneous moment of super compaction at the final instant of the implosion half cycle.

Then, as the entire universe implodes to the size of a basketball, those bizarre forms of existence keep changing with increasing rapidity. Undergoing seemingly infinite changes into ever more radical forms of existence, the universe crushes inward at near the speed of light, imploding to golf-ball size, then to pinhead size, then to pinpoint size. Everything in the universe, including trillions of stars and billions of galaxies are crushed into that pinpoint. The universe then flickers from microscopic to submicroscopic size then to sizes unimaginably smaller than a proton — all while continuously changing into near infinite varieties of unimaginable radical structures shrinking toward zero volume and infinite density.

Most incredibly, the total of all mass/energy/activity changes that occur during nature's longest cycle (the seemingly infinitely long, googol-year explosion and implosion half cycles) is exactly counterpoised or duplicated during nature's shortest cycle (the seemingly infinitesimally short, googolth-of-a-second cycle). In other words, the total action during nature's longest cycle of trillions of years is exactly counterbalanced during nature's shortest cycle occurring in the tiniest fraction of a nanosecond[1].

Part 9
The Universe Turns Inside Out
From Implosion to Explosion

At that final instant, all activity ceases as the universe is essentially, but not actually, at zero volume, infinite density, and zero entropy. At that final instant, all the universe is in the form of gravity/existence symmetry. All information and time from the previous Grand Cycle has vanished. At that moment, with a quantum flux, a new spacetime is born — the universe turns inside out from the implosion cycle to the explosion cycle. At once, the universe converts from increasing order and compaction to nothing then to increasing disorder and scatteration, from decreasing entropy to increasing entropy, from implosion to explosion. At that instant, the entire universe is cataclysmically destroyed and then instantly reborn from

---

[1]A nanosecond is one billionth of a second.

seemingly nothing — reborn in a big-bang inflation of a trillion times a trillion suns.

Created from seemingly nothing, a mammoth composite of post-inflation mass and energy expands in every direction at nearly the speed of light. That ball of mass and energy keeps expanding for centuries, millennia, or perhaps longer before blowing apart, scattering, and then congealing its mass and energy. That scattering and congealing eventually forms visible stars, solar systems, planets. During our current googol-year cycle, millions of Earth-like planets and conscious civilizations formed billions of years before Earth's formation. And millions of Earth-like planets and conscious civilizations will form billions of years after Earth's formation.

Part 10
Super Grand Cycles

Assuming similar gravitational dynamics operate among universes,[1] similar Grand Cycles would occur among the universes themselves, but on endlessly greater scales. And then, ever longer cycles exist among ever larger clusters of universes, and so on, eternally. For each greater cluster of existence, its exponentially longer Grand Cycle would have occurred endlessly in eternity.

From the perspective of forever greater Super Grand Cycles, infinity becomes two dimensional with one vector forever reaching into space, eternally gathering greater and greater mass and energy. Concomitantly, the other vector forever reaches into time, eternally repeating ever longer cycles. Thus, travelling on those two vectors, existence

---

[1]Currently, Earth beings have no way to observe other universes. Thus, no way is currently known to establish if gravity operates among the universes — throughout the meta-universe.

evolves forever throughout the endless universes.

From the limited perspective of our world and universe, the speed of light seems incredibly fast and free. But from the perspective of endlessly evolving existence and ever greater clusters of universes, the speed of light seems increasingly slow and restricting. For, the process of escaping such super big-bangs seems chained to the speed of light. Indeed, being limited by the speed of light, a seemingly endless time would be needed just for those unimaginably large masses to escape their "instantaneous", initial big-bang inflations in their Super Grand Cycles.

Space, time, and distance throughout existence are mind-boggling because they are truly infinite.

Part 11
Grasping the Ungraspable:
The Infinity of Existence

Within the Milky Way, our relatively small galaxy, billions of stars and planets exist that are billions of years older than our Earth. Within our universe, billions of galaxies exist that are larger than our Milky Way. Throughout the Grand Cycle, billions of stars, solar systems, and Earthlike planets constantly form anew. Among those billions of Earthlike planets abundant in water and oxygen, the dynamics of nature immutably generate life. Life, in turn, always undergoes nature's evolutionary process that ends with conscious beings...and conscious beings always evolve to control endless existence.

Indeed, life itself, its evolutionary processes, and thus, conscious beings themselves, have always existed throughout the universe as its third and unifying/integrating/controlling component. And that unifying/

integrating/controlling component of the conscious mind was the component Einstein always sought but never recognized. For, he focused only on the mass and energy components of the universe while overlooking the component of consciousness.

When dealing with infinity, relationships among time, distance, knowledge, events, and probabilities become meaningless, resulting in seemingly bizarre situations. Consider a realistically impossible event here on earth for which the odds are a billion to one against occurring. When put in the context of infinite time, such an improbable event will not only occur with absolute certainty, but will occur an infinite number of times. Throughout infinity, whatever is theoretically possible becomes an absolute certainty that occurs an endless number of times.

To further demonstrate the bizarreness of infinity: Take an essentially impossible event that might occur once every billion years. Now take an event that happens constantly, say, once every nanosecond. Relative to infinity, both events will reoccur endlessly, forever into the future. Thus, from the perspective of infinity, no difference exists between their occurrences, for they both occur with endless repetition. So, juxtapositioned against infinity, no difference exists between an event that occurs every nanosecond versus an event that occurs once every billion years. For, throughout infinity, both events occur infinite times.

Also, in the context of infinity, no difference exists between distances throughout space. For, throughout infinity, no reference points exist to measure differences among time or distances. ...Infinity is the only concept in existence without identity or boundaries. Thus, infinity[1] is radically unique from all other concepts.

To grasp the meaning of infinite existence, one cannot view existence from the perspective of a finite planet or a finite universe. Instead, one must view existence from the perspective of eternal endlessness. From that perspective, no difference exists between a mile and a trillion miles, or a year and a trillion years, or a forest fire and a star fire, or a lightening bolt and a big-bang birth of a universe. For, no reference points exist to compare distance, time, knowledge, or events of any magnitude when forever really means <u>forever</u>.

As shown later, certain deterministic concepts in the above four paragraphs are valid only in the hypothetical absence of eternal, free-will conscious life.

Part 12
Achieving Biological Immortality Now

From a perspective of the infinite time available throughout existence, all newly formed life evolves almost immediately into a highly intelligent brain that can invent consciousness from nature's bicameral mind. The resulting conscious beings then, nearly instantly:

1) take control of nature,
2) obsolete nature's evolutionary "need" for life-and-death cycles,
3) evolve into the Neo-Tech/Neothink mind,
4) cure irrationality and its mysticism, the only disease of the conscious mind, and
5) achieve non-aging immortality in order to live forever with growing prosperity and happiness.
6) control existence.

---

[1]Infinity, as explained in the footnote on page 14, is a useful mind-created concept that does not exist in reality.

But from a perspective of the brief, finite time available for contemporary life on Earth, exactly how and when will biological immortality occur? First consider that, today, newly discovered Neo-Tech will eradicate the disease of irrationality and its parasitical neocheaters. Without the constant destructiveness of professional parasites, conscious beings will quickly, naturally develop commercial biological immortality as described below.

As Neo-Tech cures the disease of irrationality and vanishes those professional parasites, biological immortality will become a certainty for most human beings living today, regardless of age. In fact, today, freedom from irrationality will almost guarantee biological immortality for most people. And that could happen without massive efforts or spectacular medical discoveries. What is necessary, however, is the curing of irrationality and its mysticism. For irrationality, directly or indirectly, eventually kills all human beings while preventing biological immortality for all conscious beings.

Irrationality is the only disease of human conscious-ness. The symptoms of irrationality are harmful dishonesties and mysticisms. Those symptoms undermine the ability to integrate together the values of rationality *and emotions*. What is the value of emotions? The all-important value of emotions is to experience happiness — the bottom-line moral purpose of conscious life. But, mysticisms mixed with emotionalisms dishonestly assume a primacy over reason and reality. That dishonesty, in turn, casts mortal harm over every individual human being on planet Earth.

But Neo-Tech, which is fully integrated honesty, eradicates the disease of irrationality. Thus, the immediate evolvement of biological immortality need not require quick technological breakthroughs, major research projects, or even explicit, direct efforts. But rather, with Neo-Tech, the process of biological immortality can begin immediately within one's own self. And that process will culminate with definitive biological immortality as the 3000-year disease of irrationality is cured by Neo-Tech worldwide.

How will biological immortality actually happen? First, consider:

- a world without irrationality,
- a world without professional value destroyers, parasitical elites, and dishonest neocheaters,
- a world without their destructive institutions of usurped power, such as the FDA (the most health-and-life destroying entity) and the IRS (the most value-and-job destroying entity),
- a world without the *anti-business* elements of irrational governments.
- a world without irrational governments.

Without life-corroding irrationality and its virus-like neocheaters draining everyone, business would explode into an endless productivity spiral. That value-driven explosion would launch human life into upward-spiraling prosperity with continuously expanding life spans.

Consider, for example, how the dynamics of computer technology have so far operated relatively free of parasitical elites, professional value destroyers, and government interference. Being relatively free of irrational regulations, force, coercion, and destructiveness, the computer industry has burgeoned. Computer technology is now delivering soaring capacities for processing and utilizing new knowledge at rates faster than new knowledge can be integrated and used by human beings. Such explosive advances in computer technology, or any technology, requires being free of government irrationality and its professional parasites.

The rational, conscious mind is synonymous with the productive, business mind. The value-creating business mind is the antithesis of the value-destroying political mind. The destructiveness of socialist, fascist, and religious societies prevent their citizens from developing efficient business-driven technologies. Indeed, all such societies are controlled by parasitical elites using force and deception to usurp harmful livelihoods. Such people live by attacking, draining, harming, or destroying value-and-job producing businesses...and their heroic creators and competitive expanders.

By contrast, explosive computer-like advances in human health and longevity directed toward commercial biological immortality will naturally occur in any mystic-free, business-driven society. But exactly how could biological immortality quickly occur today in a mystic-free society? Consider, a 60-year-old person today having a life expectancy of 20 more years. In a rational, business-minded society, uninhibited market forces will rapidly develop the most valuable products and technologies. ...The most valuable of all technologies — the quality preservation of conscious life — will advance so rapidly that when that person reaches 70, high-quality life spans will have expanded to 100 or 120 years, or more.

In a rational, mystic-free society, knowledge and technology accelerate geometrically. Thus, when that person reaches 100, high-quality life expectancy will have expanded to 140 or 180 years, or more. Those accelerating extensions of life expectancy would provide the time needed to develop *definitive biological immortality* for almost every value producer living today. Indeed, in the coming years, Neo-Tech will cure the disease of irrationality to eradicate physical diseases and death among all conscious beings on planet Earth.

In a competitive business-driven atmosphere free of irrationality, the life spans of conscious beings will advance faster than the passing of years. Thus, the result of Neo-Tech eliminating irrationality is immediate, de facto biological immortality. Then, rapidly accelerating health technology — including antiaging genetics — will yield that *definitive biological immortality.*[1]

Therefore, by replacing all forms of irrationality, mysticism, and neocheating with the fully integrated honesty of Neo-Tech, nearly everyone today can live forever.[2] Most important, with Neo-Tech, one can live forever with increasing prosperity, happiness, and love.

Almost anyone living today can survive to biological immortality by (1) replacing the death disease of irrationality with the life elixir of Neo-Tech and by (2) stopping mystical behaviors and destructive actions, such as making problems where none exist, smoking, and becoming mentally and physically unfit. Almost everyone today can and will achieve biological immortality by rejecting irrationality and neocheating both in one's self

---

[1]Curing death is described in the *Neo-Tech Discovery*: specifically in Part V and generally in Appendix F titled, *Achieving Commercial Biological Immortality in Our Lifetime.* ...Mortality is natural in life, *except* for conscious beings whose nature *is* immortality — the same immortality God possesses!

[2]The longer a productive individual lives, the more valuable that person becomes through his or her increased knowledge, experience, competence, productivity, and capacity for business and happiness. Thus, in any rational, mystic-free society, the motivation for and value of biological immortality increases as the age of the individual increases.

and in others. The key for everyone is to first recognize and then reject the disease of irrationality and mysticism from within one's own self. Then one can effectively reject irrationality and mysticism in others.

Life is everything. Death is nothing. Irrationality trades everything for nothing. Irrationality is a terminal disease that breeds professional value destroyers who eventually harm or kill everyone. ...Today, the disease of irrationality is totally unnecessary since it can be cured with Neo-Tech. Thus, through Neo-Tech, essentially everyone can live forever with ever increasing prosperity and happiness.

Also, as demonstrated in Neo-Tech Advantage #31 of the *Neo-Tech Discovery,* conscious civilizations much advanced beyond ours would by necessity be free of irrationality and neocheating. For, by holding irrational premises, no civilization can advance much past the Nuclear-Decision Threshold[1] without destroying itself. ...In rational mystic-free societies, the idea of dishonesty is unknown. Thus, *unknown* ideas also include war, murder, deception, fraud, forced taxation, conscription, racism, theft, assault, envy, anxiety, guilt.

Part 13
Infinite Knowledge

To quote from the first Neo-Tech World Summit (March, 1986) keynote address titled, "Three Steps to Achieving Commercial Biological Immortality in Our Lifetime":

"Living forever would be boring. False. Exactly the opposite is the fact. For creating and increasing values is the essence of a happy, exciting life, which, in turn,

---

[1]Planet Earth is currently at that Nuclear-Decision Threshold. For our civilization to survive, the disease of irrationality must be cured.

gives increasing motivation to live forever. Indeed, all new values come from expanding knowledge. And each new unit of knowledge generates several newer units of knowledge. Therefore, the ability to generate new knowledge is limitless. The notion of finite knowledge is only an illusion from our present, limited-knowledge perspective. Indeed, knowledge is not simply uncovered; it is generated from past knowledge. Thus, each day, the discovery of new knowledge generates ever greater bodies of ever newer knowledge and values.

"No one in the last century could have, for example, imagined any aspect of quantum mechanics, the computer age, genetic engineering, superconductivity, or fusion energy. For, everyone was many layers of knowledge away from even imagining those twentieth-century achievements. Yes, knowledge upon knowledge and achievement upon achievement will be generated anew —- forever — by human consciousness.

"Human consciousness is the only force in the universe not predetermined by nature. Indeed, only consciousness can alter or go beyond the fixed patterns of nature. Consciousness obsoletes nature's blind, life-and-death survival cycles when applied to human beings. ...In a society free of irrationality, every conscious being produces open-ended achievements for society without bounds or limits. Thus, by producing an eternal stream of benefits for society, each conscious life continues happily, forever."

Part 14

Immortality — the Natural State of Consciousness

Thousands of years ago, before anyone on Earth grasped the concept of geometrical shapes, a man looked toward the heavens at the moon, then at the sun, then at the eyes of his woman. Suddenly he grasped the concept of "round"...a strange, new concept that no one had grasped or understood before. From that geometric concept came the circle, the wheel, the principles of mathematics and science, the automobile, the computer, and the latest theories of gravity. Yet, essentially no one today realizes that a concept so naturally integrated with life and taken for granted as the shape "round" was at one time unknown, strange, and spectacular to discover.

Likewise, a few thousand years from today, the natural physical state of conscious man — biological immortality — will be so natural, so integrated with life, so taken for granted that only historians would realize how during a brief time in faded history conscious beings were irrational and thus mortal. Indeed, mortality is not only the most unnatural, bizarre state for conscious beings, but is an essentially unknown state among rational, mystic-free, conscious beings throughout the universe.

In addition to biological immortality as revealed in the *Neo-Tech Discovery*, conscious man's most natural, psychological state is happiness. Essentially all human unhappiness arises directly or indirectly from the disease of irrationality and its mysticisms. With irrationality cured, happiness will become so natural and commonplace that in future millennia few if any will know that unhappiness and death ever existed.

Part 15
Einstein's First Oversight:
Failure to Integrate Human Consciousness *On Earth*
With the Grand Cycle
Consider us Earth beings with our technology of less than 3000 years. Consider our advances projected by the

year 2000, only a few years away. Then project that rate of growth into a geometrically increasing curve of knowledge soaring toward a thousand years hence, a million years hence. One can easily see that conscious beings are altering the dynamics of nature at ever increasing rates. And through a relatively minuscule time span within the incomprehensibly long, googol-year cycle, conscious beings on Earth can quickly learn to dominate nature.

After only the first few centuries of consciousness, around 500 BC, human beings begin controlling nature faster then nature's evolutionary processes. Witness, for example, the development of consciousness from only 3000 years ago, an invisibly short time span in the Grand Cycle as shown in Table 4 below. Earthbound consciousness has already obsoleted nature's evolutionary processes: Today, man-made shelter, food, medicine, and technology

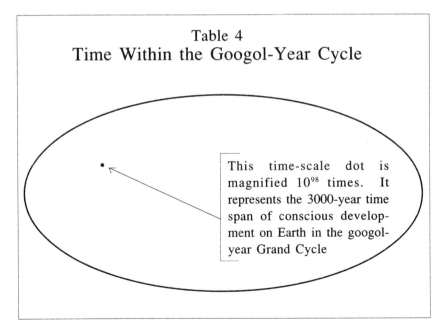

Table 4
Time Within the Googol-Year Cycle

This time-scale dot is magnified 10^{98} times. It represents the 3000-year time span of conscious development on Earth in the googol-year Grand Cycle

advance human survival and well-being much faster and better then do the slow evolutionary, adaptive processes of nature. In less than 3000 years, consciousness is already taking over the dynamics of nature on Earth. With that takeover, consciousness obsoletes nature's protective/ survival mechanism of death. Thus, through time, consciousness mandates biological immortality for all conscious beings.

Becoming free of irrationality, Earth beings will not just increasingly control nature, but will dominate nature just a few hundred years hence as explained below.

During the next million years, planet Earth will geologically remain relatively static with basically the same oxygen, land, and water conditions. But, with geometrically accelerating knowledge, we on planet Earth will soon dominate and control nature. Consider, for example, the world's largest man-made lake accomplished by building Hoover Dam with only 3000 years of accumulated, conscious knowledge. That man-made feat controlled and then dominated nature's mighty Colorado River.

From the discovery of consciousness to the first automobile took 2900 years of accumulated knowledge. Then, within 100 years, man went from the auto to the airplane, to the moon, and now toward super computers for everyone. ...Knowledge accumulates geometrically, quickly leaving nature's forces far behind as if frozen compared to the incredibly fast, always accelerating generation of new knowledge.

Perhaps only a few-hundred years hence, we Earth beings will be accumulating new knowledge at lightening speeds. With that rapidly increasing knowledge, we will easily, for example, corral heavenly asteroids into man-made orbital matter to fill our needs, just as today we corral river water into man-made lakes to fill our needs. ...What needs will we Earth beings have a thousand years from now, a million years from now? And how will we use our super-advanced knowledge and tools to control nature in filling those needs?

A thousand, even a million or a billion years, is an incredibly short time, a mere instant, within the Grand Cycle as shown in Table 4. But, well within that brief time span, we Earth beings can also accumulate the knowledge to dominate and drive the universe — to interdict nature's mass/energy dynamics in preventing the Grand Cycle from ever completing itself.

Part 16
Einstein's Second Oversight:
Failure to Integrate Consciousness *Beyond Earth*
With the Grand Cycle

Consider the billions of Earth-like planets existing within our own universe that are billions of years older than Earth. Through immutable evolutionary processes among those billions of Earth-like planets, conscious beings have evolved with millions or billions of years more advanced knowledge than we have on Earth today. ...Just imagine the technology and capacity of those conscious beings who have enjoyed geometrically accumulated knowledge for a million years, a billion years.

Human-like consciousness is the only entity in existence that can alter the inexorable course of nature. Human consciousness quickly advances from building cities to utilizing nuclear power, to developing computers, to making astronautical flights, to corralling astro matter, to understanding the universe, to controlling existence —

and beyond forever.

Integrating nature's Grand Cycle with conscious beings reveals an elegantly simple understanding of existence. That integration reveals how individual consciousness is not only an integral component of existence, but is the dominating and controlling component. For example, at either end of the Grand Cycle, all life would perish. But individual consciousness — the supreme value of the universe — must forever protect itself. Thus, conscious beings a thousand or a million years more advanced in knowledge than we on Earth have long ago *met that responsibility to preserve the supreme value of existence: individual consciousness.*

Without immortal consciousness, the Grand Cycle would inexorably and infinitely repeat itself as dictated by the natural dynamics of mass and energy. But, with consciousness, the integrating and controlling component of existence missed by Einstein, the Grand Cycle is always interdicted and truncated. Thus, the destruction of the universe and consciousness has never occurred and will never occur. In other words, by integrating conscious beings into the dynamics of existence, nature's Grand Cycle becomes hypothetical and never occurs.

Consciousness and Existence Integrated

1) Anything theoretically possible in existence, no matter how remote the probability, will happen infinite times unless interdicted by conscious beings.

2) Human-like consciousness has forever been and will forever be an integral part of existence.

3) Conscious beings, as you and I, can

understand anything in existence. On gaining the knowledge, therefore, we can and
will eventually do anything theoretically
possible that rationally benefits our
existence.

4) Thus, human-like conscious beings throughout
the universe always have, and always will,
control existence.

5) On curing the disease of irrationality through
Neo-Tech, we Earth beings will gain the
same power, prosperity, and immortality of
our fellow beings who control existence
throughout the universe.

Part 17
Knowledge at the Speed of Light

Everything in existence seems limited by a universal
constant — the speed of light. For, as shown by Einstein,
nothing can exceed the speed of light. Consciousness,
therefore, being an integral part of existence, must also
be limited by the speed of light. But how can the speed
of light limit knowledge, especially since consciousness
has no limits on understanding anything in existence? To
answer that, one must first understand the dual faculty of
consciousness:

1) The unlimited faculty to understand anything
in existence.

2) The limited faculty to store and process
knowledge.

By nature, each new unit of knowledge begets multiple
units of still newer knowledge. Thus, consciousness
creates knowledge geometrically. So, then, what can limit
increases in knowledge? Nothing can stop knowledge

from increasing forever. But, the rate of knowledge accumulation is ultimately limited by the speed of light in our closed universe.

To understand the faculty of consciousness that stores and processes knowledge, one must first understand the history of that faculty starting with the origins of man-discovered consciousness on Earth 3000 years ago: For the first 2000 years after the discovery of consciousness, knowledge accumulated very slowly. That accumulation gradually increased as the base of knowledge increased through memory and oral communication. Knowledge then accelerated through written communication.

For man to produce great sailing ships, for example, he needed that initial 1800 years of accumulated knowledge and technology stored and passed by memory, hand-scribed documents, and oral communication. Then he needed another 1000 years of faster accumulated knowledge and technology stored and passed through written works to produce steamships and trains in further improving transportation. He needed another 100 years of more rapidly accumulating knowledge and technology stored and passed through printed works to produce automobiles that greatly improved transportation. Next, he needed only 60 more years of accelerating knowledge and technology stored and passed through books, journals, and communication equipment to produce practical airplanes that provided transportation inconceivable a century before. Finally, he needed only 40 more years of soaring knowledge and technology stored and passed through computers and electronic communications to develop space ships for landing men on the moon and building space stations.

Now, today, new knowledge is accelerating so rapidly

that our productive focus is shifting toward storing, processing, integrating, and transmitting information through million-dollar super computers moving toward thousand-dollar personal computers. Thus, today, computers are undergoing explosive increases in capacities, power, practicality, and economies. And from now into the future, the demands of accumulating, storing, processing, and transmitting knowledge will shift into high gear from man's limited storage-capacity brain to external extensions of the brain with electron/photon-circuited computers and beyond.

Today, storing and processing our geometrically increasing knowledge depends on our developing and building increasingly efficient, man-made computers. Advancing economies and prosperity depend on developing ever more advanced devices until the capacity of every spacetime point in the universe is utilized for storing, processing, and transmitting knowledge.

Knowledge will increase geometrically for a few millennia or perhaps only a few centuries — until the building of external-knowledge devices approaches the speed-of-light limitation. From that point, the expansion of knowledge shifts from geometric to linear. Knowledge will then expand linearly, near the speed of light, and limited by the speed of light.

When our own expanding knowledge reaches that limitation, we can join the millions of other civilizations in our universe who have reached that point. We can then communicate through the universal computer (perhaps gravity-coded) and control existence as our fellow conscious beings do. For, then, the entire universe of universes expanding at near the speed of light becomes our computer and storage facility for all acquired knowledge.[1]

The relationship of conscious knowledge to existence reduces to a single equation. To understand that equation, the following two points must be understood:

1) Knowledge is a function of time, which as Einstein determined is related to the speed of light.

2) Essentially all mega-advanced knowledge throughout the universe is generated, stored, and processed near the speed of light, limited only by the infinite Universe of universes on vectors forever expanding at near the speed of light.

Thus, knowledge ultimately obeys the same laws that all existence obeys...such as Einstein's law that integrates energy and mass with the speed of light as expressed by his famous equation:

$$E = mc^2$$

where:

E = energy;   m = mass; c^2 = the speed of
light squared

Likewise, knowledge integrates with time and the speed of light as expressed by the following equation:

$$K = tc^2$$

where:

K = knowledge;   t = time; c^2 = the speed of
light squared

Today, in our young Earthbound civilization, the

---

[1]Conscious beings perhaps overcome the speed-of-light limitation through eternal inflationary expansions of Gravity Units beyond our universe, into limitless existence and hyperspace.

always fatal disease of irrationality darkens the future for all human beings. Growing irrationality reduces and eventually stops the accumulation of new knowledge needed to survive and prosper. Growing irrationality eventually destroys the conscious mechanism for processing and accumulating knowledge. But, with the Neo-Tech discovery, irrationality can be cured worldwide to let all conscious beings forge ahead, geometrically accumulating knowledge at rates eventually limited only by the speed of light.

Part 18
The Universe is but a Dot Next to
Individual Consciousness

Every individual consciousness has the capacity to generate, process, and use new knowledge at rates approaching the speed of light. By fully understanding the effects of such knowledge production and use, one quickly rectifies the false view of life held by most people who have lived on Earth. That false view expressed in Monty Python's "Meaning of Life" and promoted by mystics throughout history is: "Individual human beings are but insignificant dots among the vast universe."

Facts and logic demonstrate the exact opposite: Without irrationality or mysticism, each individual consciousness has unlimited capacity to generate and utilize new knowledge at near the speed of light. Francis Bacon identified, "Knowledge is power." Thus, after a few millennia of such knowledge accumulation, any conscious individual gains the power to so totally dominate existence that the entire universe and all its evolutionary processes seem by comparison to shrink into static insignificance. For, in both power and significance, individual consciousness quickly soars beyond the dynamics of nature and the entire universe.

Today, on Earth, the fully integrated honesty of Neo-Tech finally reverses that mystical view bewailing mankind's insignificance. Neo-Tech demonstrates that the power of the universe shrinks to almost nothing when compared to the unlimited power of individual consciousness.

Part 19
Who is the Creator?

Does a creator of galaxies and universes exist? Indeed, such a creator could not defy the laws of physics. Yet, today, as for the past three millennia, most people believe a creator must be some mystical higher "authority" or power as promulgated by someone's scriptures or edicts. ...For two millennia, such mystical gods of creation were conjured-up by neocheaters wanting nothing more grand than to live off the efforts of others.

As demonstrated in the balance of this chapter, everyday conscious beings like you and me work within the laws of physics to create and control all heavens and earths.

Part 20
The Goal of Conscious Beings

Throughout the universe, conscious beings pursue their natural goals and responsibilities by achieving biological immortality, limitless prosperity, and eternal happiness. Thus, they forever preserve the supreme value of the universe: individual consciousness. For without conscious beings, no value or meaning would exist throughout the universe. ...Conscious beings free of mysticism never allow their precious lives — lives of limitless value — to end.

Part 21

Galaxies Created Beyond The Dynamics of Nature

A million years ago, a conscious being, as you and I, worked at the edge of a distant galaxy with an integrating computer of a spatial-geometry driven, mass/energy assembler. By assembling units of gravitational geometries, that person corralled enough strings of wound-up gravity to equal the mass of another galaxy. As the moment of critical gravity approached, the final collapse into an entropy-reversing, rotating "black hole" began. He then arose smiling. With arm held high, he cried, "Let there be light!"[1] ...At that moment, in a far corner of the universe, the light of a billion times a billion suns flashed and began its photonic journey across the universe. A galaxy was born...a man-made galaxy.

Part 22

Galaxies Discovered Beyond The Dynamics of Nature

Today, a million years later, the faintest speck of light from that conscious-made galaxy falls on the planet Earth — on the lens of a telescope. An astrophysicist examines computer data gathered from that speck of light. Then, integrating that data with the physical and mathematical dynamics of astral mass and energy, he moves closer to a momentous discovery. He moves closer to discovering a major astral event falling outside the natural dynamics

---

[1]The expression "Let there be light" was first manipulatively used in the mystical world of the Bible, then entertainingly used in the science-fiction world of Isaac Asimov, and now factually used in the objective world of Neo-Tech.

of mass and energy — an event that irrevocably altered nature's charted course for the universe.

But, that scientist knows, as any competent scientist knows, that nothing, including conscious beings, can alter the axiomatic laws of physics, mathematics, and existence. And he knows that existence can have no antecedent basis or original creator. Yet, he realizes that, within the laws of physics, conscious beings can alter the natural dynamics of mass and energy. Thus, he realizes conscious beings and only conscious beings can alter nature's manifest destiny, not only here on Earth, but throughout the universe.

Combining such knowledge with computer processed data, that scientist moves closer toward directly observing the alteration of nature's Grand Cycle by conscious beings. Such direct observation may come, for example, through a correlation of computer data concerning black holes or possibly quasars and pulsars. In fact, such correlations of data probably already exist on Earth — hidden in considerable accumulations of uninterpreted data. Integrating such data could reveal that certain cosmic events exist outside the natural dynamics of their mass, energy, and gravity. In turn, that data could then demonstrate how conscious beings create and control such cosmic events as energy and galaxy creators for the eternal prosperity of all conscious life.

Thus, conscious beings could forever prevent the Grand Cycle from completing itself. They could do that, for example, by routinely creating gravity dimensions and geometries that constantly pump entropy-reversing structures back into the universe. Such constantly created, new structures would break the dynamics of the Grand Cycle, allowing the universe to forever oscillate within its most efficient range for conscious beings.

Part 23
Create Your Own Galaxy

Beginning with the data from that speck of light born a million years before, today's Earthbound scientist will discover and prove a newborn galaxy created outside the mass/energy/gravity dynamics of nature alone. He will then look toward the heavens realizing that he has discovered a galaxy made by a conscious being. He will further realize that over eternal time, over eternally interdicted cycles, all the galaxies and universes, all the heavens and Earths, were at one time created from conscious-made structure pumps that formed new realms of existence while preserving old realms.

And finally, he will realize his mind is the same conscious mind possessed by our immutable conscious cousins who create new realms of existence in other worlds and galaxies for us, they, and everyone.

Part 24
After the Discovery

After that first discovery of a conscious-made galaxy or black hole, scientists will then approximate from our geometric increases of knowledge on Earth and our achievement of biological immortality, when you and I can stand above all the imagined gods to give the command, *Let there be light!*

Part 25
Conclusion

No intimidating god or ethereal super consciousness reigns over the universe. Mystical gods or "higher beings" do not exist, cannot exist, need not exist. For only universes created and controlled by rational, value-producing conscious beings as you and I are needed to explain all existence. And with biological immortality, we Earth beings will someday stand smiling at the edge of space creating our own stars, galaxies, universes, collections of universes, and beyond.

EPILOGUE

The mightiest power in existence, the power to control existence, is expressed by the great command, "Let there be light!" That power has forever existed among fellow beings throughout the universe. The essence of that power is available to all of us, now, here on Earth today through Neo-Tech. ...Neo-Tech eradicates irrationality — the disease that causes ignorance and death among conscious beings.

AIDS degenerates the body's protective immune system into weakness, sickness, then death; irrationality and mysticism degenerates the mind's protective thinking system into ignorance, sickness, then death. Irrationality cripples and finally destroys the conscious mind.

But unlike AIDS, an immediate cure exists right now for irrationality and its virus-like neocheaters. That cure is Neo-Tech. Curing irrationality will also bring definitive cures for AIDS, cancer, heart disease, and all other diseases harmful to conscious beings. Neo-Tech forever eradicates irrationality and its symbiotic neocheaters, allowing the individual to direct his or her life toward achieving guiltless prosperity and abiding happiness for self, others, and all society.

Neo-Tech also opens the way for knowledge expanding geometrically to eventually approach the speed of light. Every person applying Neo-Tech, therefore, holds unbeatable advantages over those crippled by irrationality, parasitical elites, and neocheaters. Indeed, Neo-Tech allows human beings to acquire total control over both the material and emotional realms. Neo-Tech gives all human beings on Earth today the power to execute the tripartite commands: "Let there be wealth!", "Let there be romantic love!", "Let there be eternal youth!"

The time has come to grow up...or be left behind to perish in a world of irrationality. Clinging to irrational or mystical beliefs such as supreme creators or "higher authorities" is as crippling to human life and prosperity as would be the clinging to the once popular belief that the Earth is flat or today's fading belief that force-backed "authorities" or politicians can advance the well-being of any individual or society.

After 3000 years, the time has come to abandon life-destroying irrationality and all its symbiotic parasites and neocheaters. Now is the time to mature into meeting our responsibility of grooming the supreme value of the universe — our own conscious lives. Now is the time to groom our conscious minds with fully integrated honesty for limitless growth and value production forever into the future. Now is the time to join our fellow conscious beings throughout all existence in meeting our supreme responsibility to life — to live happily, prosperously with our fellow conscious beings throughout eternal existence. **For, we are the creators of all heavens and earths. ...All glory to us conscious beings!**

Chapter 7
Gravity Units

The fully integrated honesty of Neo-Tech bridges the widest gaps among physics and science — from the general relativity of cosmic gravity and beyond to the quantum mechanics of quarks and below.[1] Conscious life using Neo-Tech — fully integrated honesty — bridges those and other problems, great and small, to deliver eternal life, happiness, prosperity.

The controlling keys of existence are the ultimate-symmetry Gravity Units as explained in Chapter 5. Also, as explained on pages 45-46, gravity is negative energy, always pulling in toward nonmotion. Mass and energy are positive energy, always pushing out toward motion. Our universe and all existence consist of gravity, mass, and energy. The sum of all existence equals zero energy. Therefore, the total energy of (1) our universe, of (2) every universe-containing, microscopically undetectable Gravity Unit, and of (3) all vacuums are zero — nothing — as explained on pages 45-46.

No real vacuum exists in nature. All spacetime points in existence contain *existence* itself. All existence consists of Gravity Units with zero energy. Thus, any and every point in existence can be quantum fluxed into equal amounts of negative-energy gravity and positive-energy mass/energy. Then, exploding from the cold "vacuum" or "nothingness" of pure geometric gravity into a cosmic

---

[1]And, from chemical clocks of strange-attractor chaos that are strong on empirical demonstration but weak on theory...to superstrings* of ultimate symmetry that are strong on theory but weak on empirical demonstration. Neo-Tech bridges all those gaps.

*Strings, not points, seem to be the basic entities of existence. Even in nature-evolved life, the string helix of DNA is basic.

inflation, that Gravity Unit forms a new universe of mass, energy, space, time, and motion.

Zon Jr. Creating a Galaxy before Breakfast

From any point above-and-below, in every vacuum state and universe, conscious beings can flux, break, or inflate Gravity-Unit symmetries into limitless new galaxies or universes. All of those actions can occur without violating the laws of physics.

Existence exists. For, existence cannot not exist. Existence is Gravity Units with fields of existence at every point in space, matter, energy, and time.[1] As philosopher Ayn Rand recognized, "Existence *is* identity." Thus, Gravity Units *are* identity: the fundamental identity of existence — as is consciousness. ...The melded symmetry of consciousness and Gravity Units points the way to unifying consciousness with physics — points the way to unifying all existence.

---

[1]Time is always within a background of existence: Existence is not in time. Instead, time is in existence. Thus, time can be measured as changing geometric shapes in space. Indeed, spacetime is a geometry dependent on its contents and their configurations. Inside Gravity Units, time disappears into fixed spatial dimensions.

Gravity Inflations, Light Cones, and Universe Creations

Existence does not smoothly reduce down to nothing or non existence. Instead, everything in nature ultimately reduces to a discrete bump, a quantum, a unit in an ether of Gravity Units (GUs), which are the eternal quantum units of existence. GUs comprise the ether substrate in which all broken symmetries exist. A GU is an unimaginably small entity with essentially zero surface at seemingly infinite curvature. Yet, each GU is still an entity, a unit of existence — the prime unit of existence with specific properties. The GU is essentially maximal symmetry: a pure symmetry of gravity or field of geometry.

But, at the boundaries of GUs are *asymmetric* regions of countless smaller, connecting Gravity Units at which quantum fluxes can inflate into separate universes. Each of those universes create a spacetime quasi light cone that eventually meets the real light cone of every other universe evolving from that Gravity Unit to create a universe of universes many times the total size of the distance traversed at the speed of light.

For example, as shown by the illustration on page 92, magnify a Gravity Unit by a googol...or 10^{100} times. The GU would now appear as unimaginably large with its highly curved surface now appearing as essentially flat. That surface is asymmetrically disrupted with bumps of countless other, smaller Gravity Units. Those disruptions can flux into universes at countless points on the surface of the GU to produce countless quasi light cones that eventually link at distances in any amounts beyond that communicated by the speed of light.

As shown on the illustration on page 92, light cones linked from Y to B″ have communicated at many times the speed of light with nothing exceeding the speed of light.

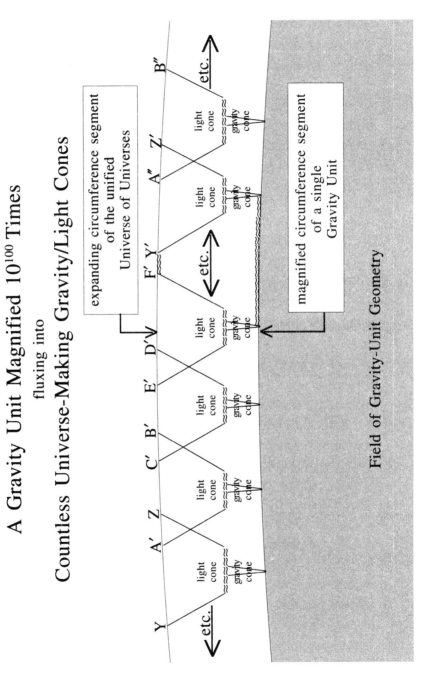

A Gravity Unit Magnified 10^{100} Times

fluxing into

Countless Universe-Making Gravity/Light Cones

PART II

The Anticivilization

The Problem

Unconquerable Honesty

In this anticivilization, we each are alone in our struggle to live rationally. We have always been alone with our own honesty. That aloneness of honesty is our only unconquerable strength in this anticivilization. For, we are chained to a civilization based on dishonesty. In the end, that dishonesty cheats us of our earned rewards as we each die unnecessarily... and unfulfilled.

By contrast, in the Civilization of the Universe, no such struggle or dishonesty exists. In an honest culture of certainty and rationality, everyone is free — eternally free, prosperous, fulfilled.

Chapter 8

Unlocking the Secrets

to

Limitless Wealth

On planet Earth, no major breakthrough of knowledge has occurred in two generations — since (1) Albert Einstein replaced Newtonian physics[1] with relativity and (2) a handful of brilliant physicists like Dirac and Feynman developed quantum mechanics. Why no further seminal breakthroughs? Because thinking from today's greatest minds, such as those of Stephen Hawking and Roger Penrose, short-circuit when their wide-scope thinking turns to mysticism. Indeed, mystical bubbles reduce conscious minds to those of lost children, even the greatest minds like those of Hawking and Penrose. Thus, trapped in mysticism, new knowledge needed to deliver prosperity, both now and into the future, can no longer evolve.

In this anticivilization, the most brilliant conscious minds can no longer develop major, breakthrough knowledge. Most such brilliant minds today are stuck — limited to narrow, specialized areas — bounded by integration-blocking mysticisms. Those brilliant minds weakened by mysticism turn wimpish. They can be outflanked and outperformed by lower IQ minds that are

---

[1]Einstein did not "overthrow" Newton's gravity. Rather, Einstein adjusted and *explained* gravity (Newton would "frame no hypotheses"). Einstein actually strengthened and solidified Newton's inverse square law for gravity with spacetime geometry. *In context*, Newton was, is, and will remain correct.

mystic-free — minds that can integrate wider perspectives of reality. Because of their expanding mysticisms, geniuses today are thinking and living with increasing impotence. ...So, what is the answer to our future?

The answer is the Zonpower discovery: Throughout history, six seminal changes have occurred in the way mankind views itself and its world: (1) the invention of consciousness three millennia ago, (2) the Greeks' discovery of logic and its power, (3) the Renaissance's overthrow of traditional "truths" for the scientific method, (4) the Copernican revolution, (5) the Newtonian revolution, (6) Einstein's relativity and quantum mechanics. Today, the seventh seminal change arises: the unifying discovery of Neothink, Zonpower, and the Civilization of the Universe.

Zonpower delivers boundless knowledge and riches to any conscious individual. For, Zonpower frees reality from irrational illusions. Zonpower connects reality with *all* existence to bring unlimited purpose, wealth, and happiness to conscious beings.

Such wealth-producing, wide-scope integrations are easy to grasp and implement. This *Zonpower* communiqué will prepare you. First, *Zonpower* provides an entirely different way to view yourself, the world, and all existence. Second, *Zonpower* is so widely integrated yet so simply expressed that, on the first reading, you are ready to collect its guiltless riches. Then, on each subsequent reading, your powers to collect its boundless rewards expand.

How scientifically valid is Zonpower? Its mathematical models reduce to T1=T2k. Do not worry about that formula now. It is derived on page 239 and made clear throughout Part III. Such a simple formula or model can explain most, if not all, major anomalies in today's science and physics. That universal mathematical expression meets the "simplicity-and-beauty" criterion of Nobel-prize-winning Paul Dirac. Also, for validating major theories, the T1=T2k hypothesis meets the "correspondence" criterion of Nobel-prize-winning Niels Bohr.[1] The "correspondence" criterion requires noncontradictory linkages with science and nature.

And, finally, valid theory must meet three other criteria: (1) offer answers to previously unanswered questions and unsolved problems, (2) offer predictability, and (3) offer many ways to verify or refute the theory. Scientific demonstration of those three criteria focuses on identifying conscious configurations encoded throughout the cosmos. That scientific verification is the object of Neo-Tech research. But, practical proof already exists: **Today, Zonpower can make you rich, happy, and healthy.**

---

[1]Niels Bohr's correspondence criterion should not be confused with his *complimentary principle*, which means the more of one the less of the other. For example, position and momentum of a particle are complementary — the more precisely one is known the less precisely the other is known. Truth and honesty are complementary. For example, the more dogmatically one asserts truth the less honest one becomes. In other words, the more one demands truth, the less contextual or honest become the facts.

Chapter 9

Birth of Parasitical Elites
in
America

James J. Hill was a 19th-Century super value producer who pushed into a worldwide business dynamic. Just as Hill achieved great success in the American railroad industry and began spearheading an international expansion, he was snuffed out by a newly burgeoning parasitical-elite class in America. The story of James J. Hill is documented in the book *"Entrepreneurs Versus The State"* by Burton W. Folsom, Jr.

Political Entrepreneurs Versus Market Entrepreneurs
In that book, Folsom identifies how throughout history there have been two distinct types of entrepreneurs: political entrepreneurs and market entrepreneurs. Political entrepreneurs seek profits by working with the government to get subsidies, grants, and special privileges. They seek success through political pull. In contrast, market entrepreneurs seek success by producing increasingly improved values, products, and services at increasingly lower costs.

The Transcontinental Railroads
The building of America's transcontinental railroads provided a dramatic example of political entrepreneurs versus market entrepreneurs. In the 1860s, railroads began expanding rapidly throughout America. Thus, political entrepreneurs seeking easy dollars teamed up with

Congressmen seeking unearned power and glory. Those political entrepreneurs lobbied Congressmen for the federal government to subsidize the building of America's first transcontinental railroad.

That situation presented a perfect combination for the parasitical-elite class: White-collar-hoax political entrepreneurs could line their pockets with lavish government subsidies, and the Congressmen handing out those subsidies could garner self-glory and justify their jobs by proclaiming how beneficial they were to the American people by financing America's first transcontinental railroad. Thus, a deception was woven by that parasitical-elite class through claiming only the government could finance an undertaking as large and expensive as building a transcontinental railroad. That same deception is still promoted in history books to this day.

With great fanfare, enormous subsidies were granted to the Union Pacific and the California Pacific. The California Pacific started building track from the west coast, the Union Pacific from the east coast. Those companies were paid by the government according to how many miles of track each laid. Consequently, both companies built along the longest, most out-of-the-way routes they could justify. That way, each company collected the maximum dollars from the government.

Spending public money they controlled but did not earn, the Congressmen were quick to claim credit for building America's first transcontinental railroad. But, unlike market-entrepreneur businessmen spending their own money, those Congressmen were not about to exert the nitty-gritty effort required to insure good value was received for each dollar spent. Thus, the building of that government-financed transcontinental railroad turned into an orgy of fraud.

As a result, after that first transcontinental railroad was built, subsequently called the Union Pacific, it had enormously high operating costs. Because extra-long routes had been purposely built, because time and research had not been taken to locate routes across the lowest-grade hills, each train took more time and fuel to complete its journey. More wages had to be paid; more equipment was tied up. In addition, because the railroad track had been laid so hastily, thousands of miles of shoddy track had to be pulled up and laid again before the first train could even travel over it. Thus, from the start, the Union Pacific could not make a profit. As a result, the federal government had to continue doling out taxpayer dollars just to enable the Union Pacific to operate after the line had been completed.

Soon other political entrepreneurs ganged up with local politicians to demand federally subsidized transcontinental railroads be built in their areas of the country. Thus, the federal government financed a transcontinental railroad in the North, the Northern Pacific, and a transcontinental railroad in the South, the Santa Fe. The building of those two additional government-financed railroads followed the same course as the building of the Union Pacific. The lines were poorly constructed. The builders focussed on obtaining maximum government subsidies, not on achieving economy and quality. Thus, after the Northern Pacific and Santa Fe transcontinentals were completed, they too had unnecessarily high operating costs. Both lost money from the start, and both had to continue receiving government subsidies just to operate.

A Deception Is Woven

A parasitical-elite class consisting of political entrepreneurs, job-justifying politicians, and government-salaried university professors propagandize to this very day that only the federal government could have financed the building of America's first transcontinental railroads. The story of James J. Hill is ignored.

James J. Hill was a market entrepreneur, *not* a political entrepreneur. He was an integrated thinker and a forward-essence mover. Hill was born in a log cabin to a working class family in Ontario, Canada. He got a job with a local railroad when he was a teenager. He loved railroads and integrated his life with them. Hill moved up quickly. Soon he became involved in the building of local railroads. Then, in 1880, Hill decided to build a transcontinental railroad privately, without any government subsidies. He would call his line the Great Northern.

Hill's plan to build a transcontinental railroad at the very northern border of America was labelled "Hill's folly." Why? First of all, Hill was building a railroad way up north in unsettled wilderness. From where would his business come? Secondly, Hill would have to compete with three transcontinental railroads to the south: the Northern Pacific, the Union Pacific, and the Santa Fe. How could a private railroad be built without government help and then compete with three other railroads that had their expenses paid by the government?

James J. Hill was forced to meet the disciplines of a bottom line. He had to stay within profitable red-to-black business dynamics. Thus, instead of "rushing to collect government subsidies", he built his railroad one extension at a time, westward into the northern wilderness. Hill would build an extension westward a few hundred miles, then move in farmers from the East, free of charge, in order to settle the land along his railroad. Those farmers would then start using Hill's railroad to ship their crops back East to market. Because Hill received no government money, each extension constructed westward would have to profit before another westward extension could be built. In ten years, Hill completed his transcontinental railroad, the Great Northern, without receiving one cent of government money.

His railroad had to earn a profit at each stage of expansion. Thus, Hill had to build each extension with detailed planning to achieve maximum efficiency at minimum operating costs. Hill personally mapped out and built along the shortest, most direct routes. He also carefully surveyed land to find routes containing the lowest grades of hills over which to build. And, with Hill spending hard-earned private money, he insisted on the highest quality workmanship and materials.

It is easy to see why people initially labelled Hill's undertaking as folly. The three government-financed transcontinental railroads south of Hill's Great Northern were in the heart of the country and none of them could earn a profit. But, what actually happened once Hill's Great Northern reached the Pacific? The opposite! All three government-financed transcontinentals went bankrupt and required ever more government bail-out money — taxpayer money — to continue running. In stark contrast, Hill's railroad flourished from the very start. The Great Northern produced a profit, even during recession years. Why? Because the three government-financed transcontinental railroads had such high operating costs, poor quality workmanship, and corrupt management that they were the ones who could not compete with Hill's Great Northern

line. It was not the other way around, as had been
predicted.

A Spiral of Inefficiencies

Because the federal government continued subsidizing
the money-losing, government-financed transcontinentals,
each of those railroads had to obtain government approval
to build any new extension. On the other hand, once the
Great Northern was running, Hill built up business with
extensions called feeder lines. For example, if coal was
discovered a hundred miles to the north of Hill's line, he
built a feeder line to service that mine. If good trees were
available for lumber on a nearby mountain, Hill would
build a feeder line to that mountain so that a lumber
company could move in and use his railroad to ship its
lumber to market. If a suitable valley for cattle ranching
existed a few miles to the south, Hill would build a feeder
line to service that valley. Railroads discovered that
feeder lines were crucial to their profitability. But
whenever one of the government-subsidized railroads
wanted to build a feeder line, it had to get approval from
Congress since it was providing the financing.

Well, everyone knows what happens when politicians
become involved. A simple business decision would get
hung up for months, even years, before receiving approval.
Thus, the government-subsidized railroads could not operate
effectively. They could not compete with Hill's Great
Northern railroad. What had initially been labelled "Hill's
folly" by the establishment ran circles around the
government-subsidized, poorly managed railroads.

Fraud Is Inherent in the Parasitical-Elite Class

Over time, the corruption that laced the government-
financed transcontinental railroads began unraveling.

Unlike James J. Hill's privately-financed transcontinental railroad, the managements of the government-financed transcontinental railroads were not operating by the disciplines of a bottom line. Thus, those white-collar-hoax political entrepreneurs did not exert the discipline required to closely supervise the construction of their railroads for quality and efficiency. The survival of those political entrepreneurs did not depend upon efficient management. Their survival, instead, depended upon exerting political pull. Consequently, the government-financed railroads were left wide open to fraud. Managers often formed their own supply companies selling substandard materials to their own railroads at inflated prices. Payoffs and sellouts were rampant.

Over time, the fraudulent practices of the government-subsidized transcontinental railroads increasingly surfaced. The public became fed up with that corruption. Thus, glory-seeking politicians in Washington once again rushed in to grab attention and "serve the public". A new deception was woven. Congressmen now claimed they were the defenders of the American people and would expose the corruption in the transcontinental railroads. Glory-seeking Congressmen began conducting investigations into the nation's railroad business. Yet, in reality, those glory-seeking politicians were the root cause of that corruption.

As the fraud continued between political entrepreneurs and job-justifying politicians, consider what James J. Hill, the market entrepreneur, was accomplishing. After completing his profitable transcontinental railroad, Hill promoted the building of entire new industries in the Northwest, such as lumber companies in Oregon, apple farms in Washington, mining industries in Montana, cattle ranches in the plains. Hill helped businesses move to the Northwest and gave them special rates to ship their products back East until those businesses became established. This practice quickly built up business along Hill's railroad line.

Next, Hill began thinking about business beyond America. He began exploring opportunities in the Orient. Hill calculated that if a single major Chinese province substituted just one ounce of American wheat for rice in their daily diets, he could ship 50,000,000 bushels of wheat to China from America. ...Hill, using wide-scope integrated thinking, began moving beyond the boundaries of a restricted, single-nation mode. He began moving into a worldwide mode.

James J. Hill decided that he was going to promote American trade in Asia, just as he had promoted trade in the Northwest. So, he bought cargo ships and formed his own steamship company to ship American goods to China and Japan. He then sent agents abroad to promote American goods to Asians.

While the white-collar-hoax political entrepreneurs were still trying to figure out how to get more subsidies from the federal government, Hill was turning his attention to world business. James J. Hill was figuring out how to deliver increasing values to the world. He realized that the key to tapping the vast markets of Asia was to build trade by offering to ship American products on his railroad and steamships for free until trade could become established. So, Hill began racing his steamships back and forth between Japan, China, and America.

Hill was a heroic forward-essence mover. He exported to Asia wheat from Midwest farmers and cotton from Southern farmers. He offered a group of Japanese industrialists low-cost American cotton if they would test the American cotton in place of the cotton that they traditionally imported from India. If the Japanese did not like the American cotton, Hill offered to let them keep it free of charge. This worked. Soon Hill's boxcars were filled with cotton bales heading to Japan. Utilizing this same technique, Hill got both the Japanese and the Chinese to start buying American textiles from New England.

James J. Hill Was Spearheading
An American Dominance of Asian Trade

In 1896, American exports to Japan totalled 7.7 million dollars a year. Nine years later, James J. Hill had pushed that figure to 51.7 million dollars a year. He was spearheading an American dominance of Asian trade. And this was occurring nearly a hundred years ago! James J. Hill worked diligently to promote American exports to Asia. For example, starting around 1900, Japan began a railroad building boom. England and Belgium were the traditional suppliers of rail. American rail-makers were still fledgling in the Pittsburgh area. But Hill recognized the importance of the Asian market for steel and rails. So, he personally underbid the Europeans to capture Japanese orders for American rail-makers.

Hill diligently promoted American goods in Asia, ranging from lumber from the Northwest to wheat from the Midwest, to copper from Montana, to apples from Washington, to steel from Pittsburgh, to cotton from the South, to textiles from New England. While the white-collar-hoax political entrepreneurs of the government-subsidized railroads were being closed in upon, Hill was booming American business while blossoming his railroad into an international dynamo.

So what happened next? Attention-seeking politicians began parading the corrupt political entrepreneurs infesting government-subsidized railroads before the public through Senate investigation hearings. Yet, it was Congress that created that corruption in the first place by self-righteously giving away public money it controlled but did not earn. Instead of identifying that Congress was the root cause of the problem, Congress began clamoring for strict regulation of the railroad industry. Congress then devised a strong-arm approach, proclaiming it was protecting the American public from greedy, corrupt railroad executives.

Congress proposed creating the Interstate Commerce Commission to regulate and control the railroads and the Sherman Antitrust Act designed to threaten and punish the railroad industry. Well, James J. Hill realized what was occurring. He travelled to Washington to testify before Congress. Hill meticulously explained what had happened with the government-subsidized railroads versus his privately-financed railroad and how the solution was for government to get out of the railroad business altogether.

But Hill was ignored. Those politicians and bureaucrats could not increase their power nor garner self-glory if they admitted that the root of the problem was caused by Congress getting into the railroad business in the first place — a place in which government never belonged.

Conscious Destruction

Congress ignored James J. Hill and went ahead to create the Interstate Commerce Commission (ICC) and pass the Sherman Antitrust laws that heavily regulated and punished the railroad industry. The ICC and antitrust laws forbid giving any special deals to customers. Thus, the techniques Hill had used to build up trade in the

Northwest and was now using to build American trade to Asia became "illegal" — illegal not through objective law but through *force-backed, political-agenda "law"*. As a direct result of that legislation, James J. Hill ended his expansion into the Asian markets. One year after Congress created the Interstate Commerce Commission and passed the Sherman Antitrust laws, Hill sold his steamship line. His farsighted, wide-scope methods were stopped by corrupt government regulations.

America's trade to Japan and China dropped forty percent within two years. ...Remember, before that point, America's trade with Asia had been increasing geometrically. Two years after that legislation was passed by Congress, America's trade with Asia dropped almost in half.

What happened in Congress was not a case of ignorance. James J. Hill actually set up residence in Washington to intensively lobby Congress and its investigative committees. Hill made sure those Congressmen knew what had really happened in the railroad industry and why. He even wrote a book about the situation and published the book himself. Still, Hill's arguments were ignored. For, Congress's goal was not to serve the best interests of the public.

Instead, Congress could garner public support and praise by attacking and regulating the railroad industry, not by admitting that they had been the root cause of railroad corruption. ...Power-seeking politicians with regulating bureaucrats will always block free enterprise and competitiveness. The intervention of politicians and bureaucrats will always drive prices up, service down, while spreading decay and corruption.

What Are the Implications?

What are the implications of that event that occurred nearly a hundred years ago? Today, America's economic weakness is foreign trade with Asia. Presidents make speeches about and create commissions to study this problem. Heads of America's Fortune 500 companies, top economists, professors, and management gurus issue grave warnings about America's waning international competitiveness and its trade imbalance with Asia. Everyone then points to certain mistakes made along the way since World War II — management laziness, excessive union demands, burdensome government regulations, and so on.

But how many people today have the slightest idea what happened a hundred years ago with James J. Hill? How many people today know what was started by a single, integrated thinking, forward-essence mover? How many people today know that James J. Hill was spearheading an American dominance of trade in Asia one-hundred years ago!

Hill's incredible parade of value production, trade, business, and job creation was cut off in its infancy because of a handful of politicians. Seeking to advance their own harmful careers, with total disregard of honesty and reality, those politicians stopped a tremendous value producer, James J. Hill, and his push into Asia.

Hill's master plan was destroyed by corrupt Congressmen one-hundred years ago. And, one must not forget, those Congressmen knew what they were doing. Hill diligently informed them of the real situation — what he had done with his privately-financed railroad, whose fault it was for the corruption that occurred within the government-financed railroads, and what his railroad was doing for America's international trade by its freedom to nurture new business. Yet, those elite, college-educated Congressmen proceeded to pass their self-serving laws and regulations in order to protect and enhance their own harmful livelihoods.

What Really Happened a Hundred Years Ago?

Let us examine this situation even closer. ...What really happened a hundred years ago? What really was cut off by the parasitical-elite class in Washington using force-backed political policies? James J. Hill was not only spearheading an American dominance of trade in Asia a hundred years ago, he was also spearheading an industrialization of Asia. Hill was pushing American business into Asia, causing railroads to be built, causing factories to be built, causing new businesses to be created. He nurtured American business in Asia, and that business was beginning to follow its natural course of flooding into markets and dominating trade. That, in turn, would have led to a rapid industrialization of Asia.

Had James J. Hill been left free to continue spearheading the industrialization of China a hundred years ago, the world would be different today. What kind of creative energies would have been released if China, a country of one billion people, had industrialized a hundred years ago? Where would civilization be today? Would we have cures for cancer, heart disease, AIDS? Would we be building cities in the oceans and on the moon? The contributions that the Chinese could have made to science, to technology, to the world economy are mind-boggling. But no. All of that potential was smashed. A billion people were pushed down and stagnated, 30 million Chinese were killed. Why? Because parasitical

Congressmen a hundred years ago wanted to exercise unearned power and feel false importance!

Thus Arose the Newly Born Parasitical Elites

A hundred years ago, one man learned how to honestly integrate business with reality. He started moving up. He learned how business worked; he learned how the American economy worked. Then, he learned how the world economy worked. He began learning how the whole up-rising of civilization worked. One man, a hundred years ago, learned how to do integrated thinking and forward essence movement. He then began pushing the lid up on society. If that man had been left alone, if he had not been stopped by the politicians, he would have swung open that lid, China would have industrialized, all of Asia would have industrialized, the whole world would have risen up, and America would have been sitting on top of it all.

Instead, James J. Hill was smashed down. The newly born parasitical-elite class consisting of politicians, bureaucrats, political entrepreneurs, and other professional value destroyers smashed down whatever threatened to expose their hoaxes, whatever threatened their nonproductive livelihoods.

Thus arose the newly born parasitical-elite class in America. They joined the worldwide parasitical elites that created an anticivilization on planet Earth. But this irrational civilization based on illusions and hoaxes will be replaced by the rational Civilization of the Universe sensed by James J. Hill at the start of the 20th century and implemented by Zon at the end of the 20th century.

E.S.

Anticivilization: The irrational planet Earth riddled with dishonest parasitical elites like Woodrow Wilson causing endless cycles of destruction, misery, and death.

Civilization of the Universe: The rational universe filled with honest value producers like J.J. Hill providing endless wealth, happiness, and life for others and society.

Chapter 10

Who Is Wasting Your Brief Life?

An old man is dying. His one-and-only life is ending. All his adult life he worked hard producing values for others. He complained at times, perhaps even questioned, but never more. He always accepted the dictates of the ruling elite — the politicians, bureaucrats, journalists, lawyers, university professors. For that acceptance, he collected social security, food stamps, and other handouts for which he paid hundreds of times over with shrinking happiness, security, savings, and standard of living. At the same time, threats from crime, drugs, racism, and poverty kept growing.

His wife died ten months before. She had devoted her life to following the mystic path from the church, to astrology, to theosophy. He always silently thought her life path was for nothing — a sadly wasted life. Yet, was his path any different? Indeed, they depended on each other. Her loss caused unbearable pain that wanted to scream out. And now, for the first time, he began feeling an indescribable anger bubbling deep within his soul. What caused that rising anger? Did it come from the same source discovered by his wife during her dying days?

Her anger began when she realized the mystic path, which consumed her entire adult life, was a terrible hoax — was nothing real. Her life was wasted on an illusion — a vast hoax perpetuated and manipulated by those who used deceit to advance their own harmful livelihoods, self-importance, and usurped power. ...Indeed, over the centuries, those hoaxers used and wasted the one-and-only lives of their victims by the millions.

As his wife lay dying, she suddenly startled him. She had always been so tranquil. But, now, anger lashed out. Suddenly that frail woman wanted to obliterate everyone associated with manipulating those mystic frauds.

Strangely, during her final moments of anger, he once again, after fifty years, felt love, excitement, and life with his wife. And he knew she felt the same. Their eyes shared the most precious moment of their lives. They shared once more, after fifty years, a fleeting moment of long-lost love and passion. Suddenly, they had discovered the key to life and happiness together. Then, she closed her eyes for the final time. She was gone forever.

Now, today, as he is dying, that old man feels anger rising deep from within. He wonders what would happen if that anger ever discovered its undefined targets. But, what targets? No, not the same mystic-leader targets his wife so angrily attacked. Those mystic leaders deprived his wife's entire adult life of love, happiness, and excitement. Yet, he was never tricked by those exploiters of ignorance and illusions. Then, who are his targets of this fifty-year accumulation of anger now surging from deep within? ...On second thought, could those targets be the same mystic hoaxers his wife discovered — just more cleverly disguised?

In his mind, he begins reviewing his life, year by year. In the perspective of potential, his life seems to have meant so little. He feels life lacked the growth, prosperity, and accomplishment that belonged to him. ...Did he miss a tremendous life experience that he earned but never collected? Who then collected those earnings?

Who Is Wasting Your Brief Life?

What happens to everyone's one-and-only life? The old man wondered. What happens to the promise of youth? Indeed, almost every human life is drained or used up until each dies. Why does such a waste occur to essentially everyone? Almost everyone seems to lose his or her life to nothing, for nothing. Who is responsible, who is to blame?

Then, he recalls an experience shortly after his wife died. It was a Saturday afternoon. He went to the shopping mall to which he and his wife had often gone. Somehow he knew this would be his last visit to that mall — or any mall. He sat in the rotunda to think about her.

After some time, he began noticing the people in the mall. He gradually noticed something different — something he never saw before: No one looked *really* happy! Many seemed overweight. So many seemed drained. Some were harassed by their children. Others seemed unhappy with their spouses. He knew most wanted or needed more money. Many probably disliked their jobs. Others were worried about losing their jobs, or had already lost their jobs. Most looked bored, anxious, or empty. Like him, he knew almost everyone had abandoned his or her youthful dreams of success, glamour, prosperity. ...Almost everyone's life seemed wasted.

He then thought to himself: To have so many losses and problems, we must be guilty of something. We must be guilty of all kinds of faults, failures, and mediocrities. Anyway, we cause our own problems and limitations, don't we? That's what the authorities say. They say we're to blame, we're at fault.

Wait a minute! We cause our own problems? We're to blame, we're at fault, we are guilty? Who says? Who exactly are those who say we are responsible for not having success, prosperity, and happiness? Do we really prevent ourselves from gaining success, prosperity, and happiness? Does that really make sense? Is that natural? Or is some dark secret fooling us?

Coming back to the present, the old man realizes his rising anger is unlocking that secret. Such losses do not make sense, he tells himself. Such losses are not natural. Yes, some dark secret has been fooling everyone. The old man closes his eyes. He is dying. ...Someday everyone will discover the cause of that old man's anger, pain, and suffering. Everyone will discover that the deeply hidden causes of human suffering and death emanate from the parasitical-elite class.

Who exactly are the parasitical elites? A simple, wide-scope accounting process reveals one fact: Parasitical elites are those whose livelihoods are draining much more, often infinitely more, from the economy and society than they deliver. Such accounting answers the following question: Does one's job, livelihood, profession, agency, bureaucracy, or company *build or drain* the economy — *benefit or harm* the productive class? **Does one produce values or destroy values?** ...Wide-scope accounting is a definitive economic-impact statement.

Murderous Organizations are Killing *You*

Some net value destroyers are so obvious that no specific accounting figures are needed for the public to see the destructiveness of such people and their harmful organizations. Consider some of the most harmful bureaucracies in America today: the BATF, DEA, EPA, IRS, INS, FDA, FTC, SEC. Such murderous organizations[1] need guns, jails, and ego "justice" to exist and expand. Those organizations breed legions of professional value destroyers who are responsible for mass property and business destructions that eventually bring economic and social devastations. But, most harmfully, those organizations move *everyone* toward life-wasting stagnation, unhappiness, and death.

Daily, those organizations violate objective justice by committing real crimes of force and fraud. Those organizations are not only harming the economy, but are destroying society and everyone's freedoms by violating each of the ten Bill of Rights except the third — they have not yet forced the quartering of their troops in private homes. ...Those organizations depend on a legal system corrupted with the subjective laws and ego "justice" used to advance their harmful political agendas.[2]

The DEA

With conventional accounting within arbitrary or closed boundaries, almost any destructive end, even destructions of entire economies and genocide, can be made to appear beneficial to the public as demonstrated by Lenin, Hitler, and Mao. But, wide-scope accounting

---

[1]Murderous organizations? Even the EPA, for example, is responsible for the deaths of 8–20 people for every life it theoretically saves. The EPA kills people through the increased living costs and decreased standards-of-living it forces on society, especially on the lower classes (Ref: *Forbes*, 7/6/92, page 60). Likewise, other bureaucracies cause long-term harm and death to countless more people than those few people who may benefit. In fact, those who profit from or live off the lethal actions of those bureaucracies are accomplices to murder — often mass murder.

[2]Reference: *The Neo-Tech Protection Kit*, Volumes I and II, 780 pages, The Neo-Tech Research and Writing Center, revised 1994 and *The Golden Helmet brings Limitless Prosperity by Eliminating Harmful Bureaucracies*, 96-pages, Zon Association, 1995.

immediately reveals the destructiveness of those men and their organizations. Now, apply that wide-scope accounting to organizations like the Drug Enforcement Administration (the DEA). First, consider that the DEA exists entirely through gun-backed policies created by self-serving politicians. From that fact, the public can increasingly see that the armed divisions of the DEA are the engines that support and expand the drug problem, crimes, death, and loss of constitutional rights for every American citizen.

The armed DEA divisions continuously expand the market for drugs by providing the super-high price supports that make possible the flourishing of organized crime and drug cartels. Such government-forced economics necessitate pushing ever more potent drugs onto others, especially onto vulnerable young people. In turn, those immoral DEA actions keep escalating the crimes and deaths related to drugs.

Gun-backed organizations like the DEA serve but one purpose — the expansion of harmful livelihoods that let politicians and bureaucrats drain the economy and damage society by creating ever expanding drug problems.

The IRS

Likewise, the gun-backed divisions of the Internal Revenue Service work with Dole-type[1] politicians in expanding destructive political agendas that enhance their jobs and power. Their armed criminal activities diminish everyone's future by crippling or breaking the daring entrepreneur and aggressive business person. Indeed, every large business today started with the daring courage,

---

[1]Career politician Senator Bob Dole has been a major supporter of expanding the destructive power and criminality of the IRS through its violent armed agents.

hard work, and precious seed capital of a heroically aggressive entrepreneur. Yet, as official policy, the IRS directs its newest-trained auditors and armed agents to "cut their teeth" on small, vulnerable, first-year companies. In that way, the IRS each year ruins countless individuals and small businesses — destroying the seeds to our economic future by destroying millions of current and future jobs.[1] Indeed, wide-scope accounting reveals how the armed divisions of the IRS are criminally destroying the essence of our economy, society, and freedoms not only for today, but for future generations.

The IRS thrives as a destructive bureaucracy *because* of the irrational income tax. By contrast, revenues raised through consumption or sales taxes would vanish deficits, reduce the IRS to a fraction of its current size, and eliminate its evil armed divisions.

No rational reason for armed agents in any bureaucracy exists. Local police and courts, not armed bureaucratic agents, can competently and constitutionally protect all individuals, property, and organizations, including physically protecting government officials and their organizations.

The INS

What about the Immigration and Naturalization Service, the INS? By throwing wide-scope accounting on the gun-backed segments of that organization, anyone can see its harm to the economy. With its army of enforcers who never have to answer to American citizens, the INS ravishes hard-working value producers and their families.

---

[1] The Neo-Tech Research Center estimates that 7.1 million jobs in the American economy were lost from 1980-1990 due to businesses being damaged or destroyed by illegal IRS actions.

The INS army expands its power and livelihoods by attacking America's most competitive workers of the past and future. Those workers are the immigrants who abandon their homelands and risk their lives to deliver competitive values to our economy. Thus, they raise the well-being and prosperity of all Americans. Such life-improving immigrants have been the backbone of competitive growth and economic prosperity in America...and will continue to be after the overthrow of the parasitical-elite class and their armed divisions in bureaucracies like the racist INS.

The FDA

And the Food and Drug Administration? Wide-scope accounting shows the FDA to be the biggest killer of all — literally killing millions of human beings. Operating under a power-mad Commissioner like Dr. David Kessler, armies of FDA bureaucrats destructively build their own "achievement" files for their own promotions. By enforcing increasingly cost-prohibitive compliance to irrational regulations, the FDA blocks scientific and medical progress.

As specifically identified in the Neo-Tech literature, without the FDA and its armed enforcers, today we would have cures for cancer, heart disease, AIDS, muscular dystrophy, and essentially all other serious diseases (Ref: *The Neo-Tech Discovery*). Moreover, biomedical advances would have the human race moving toward non-aging longevity as achieved in all mystic-free civilizations throughout the universe — in all civilizations free of parasitical elites. This concept is supported by recent findings in physics and astronomy as summarized in Parts I and III of *Zonpower*.

Destructive Organizations
How Do They Survive?

How do destructive organizations succeed in deceiving everyone so completely for so long?

A successful magician deceives *everyone* in his audience with illusions. The key to the magician's successful tricks or deceptions is to keep everyone distracted. The magician with his wand keeps attention focused on a decoy illusion removed from the point of deception. With everyone's attention diverted, no one sees the deception.

All parasitical elites and their organizations have a myriad of decoy illusions. Created through deceptive rationalizations, those illusions have hidden the destructions of the parasitical-elite class since Plato showed golden-soul parasites 2300 years ago how to rule the value producers.

Consider today's Drug Enforcement Administration: With subjective laws enacted by power-usurping politicians, the DEA uses its wand of deception to point at the drugs it seized and people it jailed as progress in the "War on Drugs". But, in fact, the DEA has no motivation to diminish any drug problem. Without an expanding drug problem, its system of livelihoods and power would diminish. Thus, the DEA has every motivation to expand its bureaucracy of bogus livelihoods and power by creating and expanding drug problems, which it does very successfully.

Consider the armed criminal divisions of the Internal Revenue Service: With their wands of deception, those IRS divisions point at the money and property seized. Through its gun-backed agents, the IRS criminally squeezes the working assets out of the "underground" economy, heroic entrepreneurs, struggling individuals, and small businesses. They point to the dollars they have seized from those whom they have crippled, destroyed, or jailed. But throw wide-scope accounting on those illegal elements of the IRS, and everyone discovers its armed divisions are destroying our present and future economy, jobs, freedoms, privacy, and well-being. Indeed, IRS-forced paperwork alone is the greatest time-and-life destroyer *ever* devised to expand bureaucratic jobs and power. ...And most destructively, the IRS smothers tender youth. Few, if any, youths today can rise to become the independent business giants needed for the future prosperity of any society.

Consider the Immigration and Naturalization Service: The INS points its wand of deception at the "illegal" aliens it forcibly drains, blocks, jails, or ejects from America. Such uses of force are not only racist, but are criminal acts against innocent value producers. Those crimes are hidden by deceptive-wand myths such as "draining welfare funds" and "keeping jobs for Americans". Both such claims are patently false. Wide-scope accounting clearly reveals that "illegal" aliens (1) add much more in taxes than they "drain" and (2) create many more jobs for Americans than they take. Thus, each racist INS crime diminishes everyone's job and life by undermining America's standard of living, its economic strength, its international competitiveness.

And finally, consider the Food and Drug Administration: The FDA points its wand of deception toward "protecting" the health of Americans. But, in reality, the FDA is responsible for killing more citizens than any other group of parasitical elites. For, through power-usurping regulations, the FDA blocks the cures for all major diseases. The FDA also blocks the development of major longevity advances. ...Only unhindered science and business can bring disease-free, non-aging longevity, as accomplished in all mystic-free, parasite-free civilizations throughout the universe.

The Neo-Tech Literature

With actual wide-scope accountings, the Neo-Tech literature reveals the huge net destructions caused by specific politicians, bureaucrats, judges, lawyers, prosecutors, white-collar-hoax business people, and other parasitical elites. The Neo-Tech literature also details how those elites can exist only by creating and expanding power-building instruments such as armed bureaucracies. The Neo-Tech literature identifies how all parasitical elites depend on armed bureaucracies and subjective ego "justice" to enforce their harmful survival agendas. And finally, the Neo-Tech literature details the spectacular prosperity that awaits everyone upon terminating the parasitical-elite class.

The Neo-Tech Wedge

Most people in government, business, and the professions are *not* targets for personal ostracism or job termination. Instead, they are candidates to benefit economically, professionally, and personally by getting on the honest side of the split caused by the *Neo-Tech Wedge*. That Wedge is already beginning to move through governments and businesses, separating the honest productive people from the parasitical elites. ...Only parasitical elites and their armed enforcers are targeted for ostracism and job termination. They are the ones who waste everyone's brief life. They shall not escape the Neo-Tech Wedge.

Part II: The Anticivilization

Eliminating Armed Bureaucrats

In contrast to legitimately armed policemen who serve to protect life and property, armed bureaucrats serve to harm life and property. Today, the increasing social and physical harms caused by politicized armed bureaucrats are endangering all federal employees and their innocent families.[1] ...Bureaucrats, not law-abiding citizens, must be disarmed.

As with Shakespeare's Iago in *Othello*, an armed bureaucrat exists not to produce values but to destroy them, not to bring social harmony but to disrupt it. As with Sophocles' *Antigone*, the conflict between Neo-Tech and politicized armed bureaucracies is the conflict between rational values and irrational burdens. That conflict evolves from the deepest issues of right versus wrong, honesty versus dishonesty, and protective government versus destructive government.

Neo-Tech will bring *peace* to America and *trust* in government by eliminating armed bureaucrats.

---

[1]The criminalities of the Clintons mixed with the brutalities of their attorney general, all deceptively whitewashed by the news media, fueled public loathing toward government and its armed bureaucrats. Consider this: On May 29, 1995, the following notice was posted on various Internet newsgroups through America Online (AOL).

Memorial Day: a Political Hoax

Clinton's wreath laying: obscene hypocrisy. Notice how such politicians, the cause of all wars, revel in glory as they eulogize their dead victims.

Remember when Memorial Day was called Decoration Day? It was not a eulogy day for the politicians' dead victims, but a celebration for the end of war and its living survivors.

Within three hours, under government pressure, AOL yanked those notices from all newsgroups and terminated the sender's account. Fortunately, neither bureaucrats nor AOL can control cyberspace. Indeed, because of AOL's political "banning", that Memorial notice was subsequently plastered all over the Internet from outside AOL. The government/AOL establishment cannot stop Neo-Tech (fully integrated honesty) in cyberspace. Censorship and oppression only widens Neo-Tech's reach throughout the Net from limitless locations worldwide.

Chapter 11

Your Personal Terminator

guarantees

Limitless Prosperity

In the popular Arnold Schwarzenegger movies of the early 1990s, the terminator represents a nonstoppable force of destruction. In the real world, Neo-Tech represents a nonstoppable force that terminates *all* destructive forces. ...Neo-Tech is *your* personal terminator.

Today, right now, you hold a personal terminator in your hands — a terminator programed to eliminate all forces that harm you, your family, your future. ...Your terminator comes alive today to deliver unending happiness and prosperity.

What is a Personal Terminator?

A personal terminator is your natural self programed to deliver limitless prosperity by terminating all life-depriving forces, large or small. For example, consider the most damaging of those forces, which began growing over six decades ago: In 1933, politicians with their expanding bureaucracies began draining America's business and economic assets. Starting with Rossevelt's New Deal, that drainage has expanded into the largest, most camouflaged theft and destruction of assets in history. Today, politicians and bureaucrats, as part of a growing *parasitical-elite class*, are devouring those shrinking assets.

Economic deterioration is upon us. But, with your personal terminator, you can end such parasitical harms while creating prosperity for you, your family, and society.

Neo-Tech — the Master Terminator

Personal terminators are generated from a Master Terminator called Neo-Tech. That terminator is eternally protective to all conscious life.

First, consider that neither harmful leaders nor destructive terminators can exist in civilizations evolved beyond the nuclear age. In other words, no civilization can survive much past its nuclear age with a destructive ruling class — with a parasitical-elite class.

Now, consider our civilization: Already well into our nuclear age, we are still ruled by parasitical elites. They are unnatural beings. For, they replace their productive human nature with a nonhuman program of purposely harming others, the economy, and society. Thus, they are not human beings. They are subhumans or *humanoids*. Not science-fiction humanoids, but self-made humanoids. For, each parasitical elite has removed from his or her thinking process the essence of a human being. That essence is the competitive production of economic and societal values needed for human survival, prosperity, and happiness.

Those humanoids increasingly drain everyone and society through dishonesty backed by the deception and force needed for parasitical survival. Those parasites live by covertly draining values produced by others rather than by competitively producing values for others and society. ...A civilization ruled by parasites must end in nuclear conflagration. But, that conflagration will never occur. For, the Master Terminator is programed to vanish the parasitical ruling class as nothing in cyberspace.

In pre-nuclear ages, the Master Terminator worked to overcome nature's forces that were harmful to conscious beings. With that natural terminator, for example, human beings worked to increasingly protect themselves from the elements, wild animals, hunger, injuries, disease. Now, today, during this nuclear age, conscious beings are using that same natural terminator to eradicate their most harmful and dangerous enemy — the parasitical elites. For, those professional value destroyers control the means to kill everyone on Earth in a nuclear holocaust.

In post-nuclear ages, evolved conscious beings will continue using the Master Terminator to overcome diseases and death itself...along with overcoming the longer-range destructive forces in nature such as weather disasters, earthquakes, asteroid and comet collisions, cosmic disasters, solar burnouts, and collapses into black holes.

That natural Master Terminator which functions throughout all ages in all universes *is* Neo-Tech. Indeed, Neo-Tech is simply fully integrated honesty — natural honesty. Nothing can stop the natural mission of Neo-Tech. Nothing can stop its mission of terminating the parasitical-elite class.

Terminating the Parasitical-Elite Class

Today, economic deterioration accelerates: An enlarging pool of professional value *destroyers* increasingly pillages the shrinking pool of professional value *producers.* But, today, the rising Prosperity Revolution will accomplish the first-and-final *valid* class overthrow in history. That overthrow and termination of the parasitical-elite class by *Neo-Tech self-leaders and honest business leaders* will boom all economies. Mankind will finally experience the unlimited prosperity enjoyed by all advanced civilizations throughout the Universe.

This is *your* revolution to unlimited prosperity.

Your Prosperity Revolution

A prosperity revolution? Neo-Tech self-leaders? Class overthrow? Relentless and uncompromising? Overthrowing the entire parasitical-elite class? Yes. Forward march to the overthrow and unlimited prosperity!

Another revolution of bullets, blood, and tears? Power-seeking revolutionary leaders? Another round of destructions leading to ever more destructions? Socialist, fascist, or world-order "democracy" inspired? Building a new parasitical-elite class? No. Just the opposite.

All past revolutions required inconsistencies, illegalities, and destructions. But this revolution is unique. It is based on Neo-Tech. And, Neo-Tech requires logical consistency, objective law, and honest productivity. Neo-Tech upholds objective law by terminating all subjective political policies that harm you, society, and the economy. ...This is your revolution. This revolution will bring you unlimited prosperity.

Your prosperity revolution? When will it happen? What will happen? Who will make it happen? How will it bring you unlimited prosperity?

All past revolutions and class overthrows were bogus or compromised. For, all were fomented so one parasitical group could take power from another parasitical group. All were fomented from false or artificial class conflicts of nationalities, races, religions, political issues, economic levels, or social levels. .

The Prosperity Revolution is the first and only legitimate class overthrow possible among human beings: The honest productive class ranging from ditch digger to billionaire entrepreneur will overthrow the parasitical-elite class — a criminal class comprised of destructive politicians and their legions of harmful bureaucrats, armed political-policy enforcers, ego judges, politico prosecutors, corrupt lawyers, dishonest journalists, evil academe, and white-collar-hoax business quislings.

Parasitical elites survive through false power — power gained through deceptive illusions. But, today, with your personal terminator, you can break their illusions to end all false power. ...Right now, with Neo-Tech, you can prosper without limits.

Chapter 12

Terminating Evil

You are a hard-working entrepreneur. Starting with $3500, you worked 16 hours a day, seven days a week, for over twenty years to build a medical-research firm. Your life is dedicated to a single goal: develop marketable knowledge leading to the root cause of disease. Marketing various segments of that developing knowledge increasingly provides the keys to understanding and then curing all diseases — including cancer, AIDS, muscular dystrophy, and death itself.

Your only competitor, I & O Research and Writing, was attacked on November 3rd, 1986, by an armed criminal element growing within the IRS. I & O was destroyed through physical violence and looting inflicted by that criminal element. Each level of criminal behavior used by the IRS is identified in the table below:

Responsibility Level	**Criminal Activity**	**Remedy**
IRS Commissioner	Sanctions and uses criminal activities	Ostracize and prosecute
IRS District Directors	Direct criminal activities and destructions	Fire and prosecute
IRS Guns-and-Fists Agents	Blindly carry out physical violence and property destructions	Educate and rehabilitate if possible...or fire
IRS Seizing Agents	Blindly carry out financial lootings and economic destructions	Educate and rehabilitate if possible...or fire

10:00PM, April 15: You have spent the last two weeks, sixteen hours a day, completing the tax paperwork for your company and employees. Along with your accountant and lawyer, you have spent an average of ten weeks each year over the past decade handling all tax matters concerning your company and its twenty-five employees. That means for this decade alone, two years were lost to forced-labor paperwork. And that does not include the irreplaceable time destroyed on paperwork forced by other government bureaucracies and regulatory agencies. ...Because of that growing destruction of time and life, both you and your business can never reach full potential. Thus, you may never reach your goal of delivering the fundamental, unifying cure to all diseases.

That productive time consumed through such forced-labor paperwork diminishes the long-range potential of every person, every trade, every profession, every business. You realize that destruction of the value-producers' time is undermining the future of our economy and society. That time destroyed is even more harmful than the *irrational* taxes the value producers are forced to pay. And, that devastating time destruction serves but one purpose — to expand harmful jobs and power throughout the government. That expansion of harmful jobs and government power, in turn, serves only to expand the parasitical-elite class.

You have struggled long hours at the cost of all personal relationships. You have no time for vacations, leisure, relaxation. That unrelenting struggle is required for meeting the responsibilities to your customers, employees, and company. Without more time, you cannot reach your potential of building a worldwide enterprise — an enterprise providing countless jobs by delivering health, happiness, and prosperity to everyone. You realize that those two years of forced-labor paperwork per decade was the very block of creative time and crucial concentration needed to reach your potential, your goal. ...Such is the destruction inflicted today on every hard-driving value producer with supreme potentials and goals.

Then, you realize the escalation of time-destroying tax complexities backed by harsher and harsher penalties has nothing to do with collecting taxes. Instead, that escalation of destructiveness and penalties has everything to do with increasing bureaucratic control. For, that increasing control over the value producers is how the parasitical-elite class survives — how it creates more and more harmful jobs and power needed to live parasitically.

You now understand how the parasitical elites join with white-collar-hoax executives of stagnant big businesses to prevent competition from the most competent entrepreneurs. You now understand why those elites must malign, destroy, and imprison great value producers — honest but aggressive, tough, often unpopular business-people like Michael Milken and Leona Helmsley who prospered by delivering competitive values to society, thus, threatening the livelihoods of all parasites. By stifling aggressive competition, parasitical elites keep their own harmful livelihoods from being exposed and eliminated.

Also, without that competition, parasitical business quislings can entrench themselves in big businesses. For years, even decades, such pseudo businesspeople can gain unearned wealth and prestige by milking the great accumulations of assets built by genuinely competitive, aggressive value producers of the past. ...Most of those original, heroic value producers came from an age before the creation of armed bureaucracies used to enforce evil political agendas.

You then think about history's greatest value producers in art, music, science, and business. Despite the many-fold increases in population and technology, we have no more daVincis, Michelangelos, Beethovens, Mozarts, Galileos, Newtons, Hugos, duPonts, Carnegies, Fords, Einsteins. Why? The reasons can be traced to the destructive effects of an expanding parasitical-elite class methodically draining everyone's time, energy, resources ...and long-range potential. With each passing year, fewer and fewer tender youth can rise to become great value producers. That shrinkage of individual potential reduces or eliminates greatness from all conscious beings.

You realize that increasing armed enforcement of destructive political agendas is designed to support a growing parasitical-elite class not only throughout government and stagnant big businesses, but throughout much of the news media, public education, and the legal profession. You then realize *all* political enforcements involve criminal violations of objective law by armed bureaucracies.

You realize that supreme value producers such as Andrew Carnegie, Florence Nightingale, J. J. Hill, and Henry Ford will not rise again until that criminal class of parasitical elites and their armed bureaucracies are eliminated. Indeed, if living today, every one of those heroic value producers would be in prison with their potentials collapsed. In prison for what? For violating political-agenda "laws" enforced not only by the IRS, but by all the other armed bureaucracies and invasive regulatory agencies cancerously growing today.

As described throughout Parts II and III, Neo-Tech and Zon will terminate those evils.

Chapter 13
My Termination
by humanoid
Ted Kennedy Dole

Depression hits me as I survey the view. The camp is bitterly uncompromising — its sheer vastness, its images of hopelessness and deprivation. The sight of withered, dying men and shoddy cardboard shelters, along with the endless odor of decay, combine to bring emotions of hatred and abhorrence in all the unfortunate people who live here.

In the distance is the city: a tall, beautiful, magnificent symbol of man's achievement and prosperity. That symbol makes the dichotomy of this land all the more painful. But this has been my home for the past three years. And, deep down, I detest myself and all that I represent. Disgust wells inside me as I think of this place and my failed attempts to rationalize my pathetic existence. Occasionally, in moments of honesty, I stop the rationalizing and grimly accept my fate, knowing that I deserve no better. In recognizing these rare moments of honesty, I find my mood becomes more positive. I almost mistake the mood for happiness. It isn't. I struggle to define the feeling for a few seconds and then stop, fearing that analysis may eliminate it. But the feeling stays, alien yet welcome. Welcome because it helps me face my last few minutes of life.

Death. An obsolete state in today's world. And yet today, the 3rd of November 2003, I will die a hideous and barbaric death. I will be sacrificed, murdered. But strangely, through the actions of my life, I have given my consent to this grotesque act. Again, the cold shock of reality hits me. My mind for once is free of mysticism and dishonesty. How ironic that I have allowed myself to evade honesty for so long, only yielding to it at the end of my miserable existence. My mood becomes reflective as I begin to wonder how I could have prevented this self-loathing and desperate end.

For as long as I can remember, I have succumbed to camouflaged laziness — to wangling values from others rather than earning values. Never have I put forth the effort to create anything of genuine value. Indeed, it is this self-chosen flaw that has sealed my fate, just as that same flaw has sealed the fate of thousands like me around the world. Decades ago, after cheating my way through a prestigious, Ivy-League university, I decided on a career in law and politics. I had no grand plan to improve the world. But I knew the power of politics would be to my advantage. I could use that power to outmaneuver my peers and competitors. For, most blindly believed, at least initially, that politics was benevolent and designed for the good of the people. They rationalized against seeing the big lie. I, without such quixotic limitations, easily used politics to capture a prosperous and prestigious living from the efforts of others. I fostered the big lie to usurp values from productive people. Indeed, my skills of deception and manipulation became highly refined. I made honest value producers feel guilty for any "selfish" gain or accomplishment. It was easy. My technique was simply to blame them for the endless sufferings and injustices we politicians ourselves cause. ...The value producers paid for our pillagings — those suckers paid us to drain them dry.

Within a short time, I was rich, famous, powerful. My

life was easy, and my potential for further success seemed endless. I was single-handedly capable of developing laws and getting them passed. I could control almost anyone or anything...and look like a saint while doing it. I was responsible for legislation that greatly empowered the Drug Enforcement Administration and its armed enforcers. That DEA bureaucracy had no motivation to reduce any drug problem; for, it had no desire to reduce its jobs or power. It didn't matter to us that innocent lives were lost or destroyed through our trampling on individual rights and property rights. We pushed to spend billions upon billions of tax dollars on projects that I knew would never work. But, so what. Through the media, I always looked good to the masses. Indeed, my "War on Drugs" created some of my richest years.

And my soul mates at the IRS? I helped create and expand their armed divisions. I cleared the way for them to rule through fear and destruction. I loved increasing their power. I loved the viciousness of their commissioner. I loved their lawlessness and criminality. We were soul mates. For, through them my power grew.

We politicians and our bureaucrats created a bond of malevolence with *Newsweek*-type journalists. That unified dishonesty let us smear, control, and ruin America's greatest value producers — innocent people like Michael Milken and Leona Helmsley. We giulianied them. ...We almost took over America with me riding high.

Next came the environmental movement. With dishonest journalists and bankrupt professors, we exploited every phony notion conjured up by pseudo environmentalists. Their hate-filled, save-the-earth movement offered a bonanza of opportunities to increase my power. Political correctness became my favorite weapon. We passed regulations controlling or influencing essentially every business. And, because of my power within Congress, almost every special-interest group courted me. I seldom paid for anything. The gifts and privileges were endless. It didn't bother me that the cost of everyday goods, automobiles, and housing increased substantially because of the regulations I created. In essence, I said to hell with the masses. If they have to suffer or pay a higher price, so be it. For, I was gunning for power — the presidency and beyond.

I further increased my power by exploiting the ego-seeking demagoguery of the anti-abortion gangs as well as the Ralph-Nader gangs. With that power, I passed more and more laws telling people what they could and could not do. ...And they did what I told them because my laws were backed by guns and jails. At times, even I could not believe the power I had — the extent to which people could be controlled and manipulated.

The power. I loved the power. It was as if people would fall to their knees before me — I could do no wrong. And the women, they were everywhere. Most were prostitutes, but I never paid for any of them. Sex. Orgy sex, kinky sex, sex of any kind was the order of the day. Gradually, my wife, with the help of alcohol, learned to accept this, not that her feelings or health mattered to me. I came to believe that I was above everyone. It began to seem that such favors and advantages were owed to me. I answered to no one. Indeed, I quickly learned to live with myself; or should I say, to suppress any twinge of self-respect and honesty. For, with the money and power, it was easy to keep going, to keep taking more and more money, more and more power, more and more of everything. My lust for power constantly grew. I could never get enough.

But then it all crumbled with the Prosperity Revolution of the mid 90s. That's what caused my downfall. I remember what seemed like the starting point — our destruction of people like Milken and Helmsley. Our atrocities began backfiring when we sadistically flaunted our power on that April-15th tax day. Using subjective laws, ego "justice", dishonest journalists, and a vicious IRS, we snuffed out the unpopular but innocent Helmsleys.

Soon after, we saw our own end coming with the 1994 American elections. Value-producing men and women all over the world began angrily realizing how they were being duped and exploited. ...Our final ploy was the Dole/ Perot pirouette of 1996. Then came the Internet.

Finally, with Neo-Tech echoing around the world through cyberspace, the value producers took control of their own lives, ending the stupidity of their blind obedience to me and all other false authorities. Almost overnight, politicians like me were scorned out of existence: first in Eastern Europe, then in Asia and Africa. In America, it started in those 1994 elections. Then, the whole world woke up to the hoax. Self-sufficient, value-producing men and women suddenly realized they didn't need self-serving politicians giving them inflation, poor economies, and wars. People realized they could control and direct all areas of their lives without a parasitical ruling class. Charismatic political leaders such as myself were finished when the public started scorning us — then started laughing at us. For us, the bottom line to our final campaign was fear — shear terror and panic over losing our livelihoods, our social standing, our power.

Very quickly, once-powerful politicians were ostracized from society. We were no longer able to plunder the values produced by others. And for society, everything began to improve. There were a few initial and minor problems caused by the change, but advancement was rapid. Indeed, genuine free enterprise was the order of the day, not the insidious "free-trade" mercantilism that I, Bush, Clinton, Newt, and others touted throughout the world. A torrent of jobs were created. The standard of living soared. Poverty and racism disappeared. Third-world wars and starvation ended.

Before being overthrown, my cohorts and I used constant tax increases to force everyone's extra earnings into our power-boosting schemes. After we were overthrown, people invested their extra earnings into business and technology. ...Trade and science flourished. Unemployment fell to nearly zero. Only the professional social schemers were unemployed. Street crime vanished.

The technological advancements came quickly. Cures for AIDS and cancer came in a matter of months. Soon, one goal captured the focus of the world: Non-aging longevity. The religious and political objections were increasingly being scorned by the once submissive masses. The masses of productive people now demanded wealth, happiness, love, and life itself.

For me, I sat on the sidelines, increasingly feeling pity and hatred for myself. I had known the truth about politics and religion. Yet, I pushed my dishonesties onto the unthinking public. I knew I deserved the fate that awaited me — it was deserved because of the untold lives I had ruined by promoting and enforcing my destructive political policies. ...The loss of prosperity, happiness, love, and life itself caused by my actions was too great to count or imagine. If only I had assumed the responsibility to be honest and to produce values. Had I done this, I could right now be living in that prosperous other world. All the pain and fear I now suffer was avoidable had I been honest. In fact, if I and the others here had only exerted the effort to be honest in taking the responsibility to create values and pay restitution for our crimes, we all could have moved into that sunlit world of prosperity, happiness, and beauty. But now, it is too late for me. Starting over is impossible. Once, in desperation, I even offered myself to a zoo as an extinct humanoid. I thought scientists could study me as a relic of evil. But alas, the wide-scope accounting records of Neo-Tech showed I belonged here.

So that is why I am here — in this nightmare of a camp. I was ostracized like the rest — scorned out of society, laughed out of existence, unwilling to participate in any activity with the producers of the world, unwilling to produce or trade any desirable value.

In the beginning, we had food and supplies, mostly brought by the later arrivals. But eventually those supplies ran out, as did the animals shortly afterward. It was at this point that our very existence became threatened. Survival became the goal. We could no longer steal from the producers. They were now too smart, too organized. Computerized ostracism made hiding or even a nomadic life impossible. Ironically, the only choice we had was to live as before — to live off other people, to live by sacrificing the lives of others to us. So, we took the concept of sacrifice to its logical but horrific conclusion:

Some would have to sacrifice their lives so the rest could survive. That is why I am in this position today. My lot came up. I would now be sacrificed to the remaining few. Death, a fair and just outcome for all that has gone before me. It is with this perverse feeling of justice and inevitability that I console myself while I think of the manner of my death: clubs raining down on my weak, undernourished body, wielded by those remaining few. I imagine their emotions as they rip my limbs apart. They will be content with their meal, their hunger temporarily averted; each will be glad it's not him this time, but each knowing that soon, very soon, it will be. Fear will be the only companion until the bitter end. ...None can escape.

Suddenly, my introspection is broken by the sound of voices. I see my peers clambering over the rubble, weapons in hand, their ragged clothes and starving bodies almost comical, contrasting strikingly to the power and strength of the city visible on the horizon. Although I have accepted this ghastly end, I feel a fleeting desire to run, to escape before they get too close. But where? What is the point? My death is certain whatever I do.

I am aware that I am smiling as they face me. A matter of feet separate us, death seconds away. No words are spoken, but the sound of fear is deafening. My fear. And theirs.

I see the first club being raised high into the air by my own son. My life flashes before me. ...Oh, the millions who suffered just to keep me feeling important! I craved the ultimate — the goal of *every* politician — the power to rule the world. I craved the unearned power to control everyone in every way. For that power, I'd gladly surpass Hitler in destruction. Yes, I'd gladly nuke the world just to have that power. For, I'm not human. I'm a politician. I'm a humanoid.

I feel the first blow. I fall with my diary. I scrawl my last note: *Honesty terminated me.*

K.A.C.

Chapter 14

The Prosperity Revolution

Over two millennia ago, the Greek politician and philosopher Plato established the techniques for hoaxing the public, thus, allowing a parasitical-elite class to rise. Throughout the subsequent centuries, parasitical elites have used Plato-like hoaxes to drain the prosperity that the productive class generates for society. ...Such sacrifice-to-higher-cause hoaxes remained largely unidentified until Neo-Tech unraveled them. Today, Neo-Tech is dissolving those Platonistic elite-class hoaxes. That dissolution of illusions will wash away the parasitical elites along with their higher causes that sacrifice us to them. ...All value producers will then gain their earned prosperity stolen from them and society for 2300 years.

Human History Approaches Its Greatest Event

As our civilization approaches the year 2000, the greatest event in human history is about to break across our planet. Planet Earth will give birth to a super civilization. Indeed, the whole world is shimmering, ready to reveal a new, previously unknown world. Today, raw and unguided fomentations are bubbling from beneath the seams circling the globe — from beneath Eastern Europe, Russia, Burma, Cuba, China. Those fomentations are from the productive class — those who add more to the economy and society than they take. Those value producers are lashing out independently, without authoritarian leadership. Without guidance, they are driving parasitical elites from their destructive livelihoods, including some of the highest "authorities": politicians, clerics, bureaucrats in America, Europe, and Asia —

including elites in America like world-order-dominator George Bush, theocratic-statist William Bennett, and master-hypocrite Hillary Clinton.

Blindness of Past Revolutions

Without Neo-Tech, the productive class impotently lashes out at the parasitical elites, never identifying their underlying hoax of sacrificing the workers to the rulers under the facade of helping the needy. Without identifying that hoax, all revolutions eventually fail by perpetuating the very same hoax to often yield new, even more destructive parasitical elites — new breeds of parasitical masters: new breeds of socialist, fascist, communist, theocrat, and world-order elitists.

To eradicate the parasitical-elite class, productive people must have access to Neo-Tech. That access will fly about the world through cyberspace.

Stop Paying the Parasite-Class Deficits

Who pays for the economic and social deficits created by the parasite class? Someone always has to pay. Until the Neo-Tech Discovery with its wide-scope accounting, the parasitical elites could always delude the productive class into paying their deficits. The parasitical elites have tricked each productive person of the past 23 centuries into supporting their destructive livelihoods.

What hoax could make the productive class continuously pay for those deficits? That hoax as revealed in Plato's *Republic* is to use truth rather than honesty. Ever since, that hoax has tricked the productive class into sacrificing itself to the parasitical elites. The key to perpetuating that hoax is building public-accepted illusions — illusions built by dishonestly twisting truths and facts into limited or false *contexts* acceptable to the public.

The Hoax of Using Truth Instead of Honesty[1]

How does that hoax work? It works through *false context*. **Avoiding full context to build false context is the most powerful tool of deception**. For, avoiding full context and building false context leaves honest people ignorant of the "sacrifice the producers to the parasitical elites" hoax.

Truth

Noncontextual Facts, Unintegrated Evidence, Dishonest

I saw John O'Grady premeditate and then purposely kill a man. Conclusion: John O'Grady is a murderer. He should be jailed for life.

True facts. Incomplete. Out of context.
Unjust conclusion.

Honesty

Contextual Facts, Fully Integrated Evidence, Honest

I saw John O'Grady save a platoon of men in 1944 during the Battle of the Bulge at Bastogne, Belgium. Trapped beneath a snow-covered ledge by a Nazi machine-gunner, John premeditated a plan. He then scaled an icy cliff. Wounded twice, John shot and killed the machine-gunner. He saved the twenty men in his platoon. Conclusion: John O'Grady is a hero. He should be honored.

Honest facts. Complete. In context.
Just conclusion.

---

[1]See page 327 for explantation of truth versus honesty.

By limiting or falsifying context, anyone can build *closed systems* of bogus logic to support or rationalize almost any idea or action — such as the rationalizations behind all force-backed organizations like the DEA, EPA, FDA, INS, IRS. Through false logic and context, one can create bogus but good-sounding claims or illusions to justify essentially any destructive means to any parasitical end. And each public acceptance of such bogus claims or illusions means the continued hoaxing of value producers into supporting the parasite class.

Once such hoaxes are identified through *full-context* wide-scope accounting, value producers worldwide will rise in irreversible revolution. ...The genuine value producers will stop paying those leech-class deficits forever.

Irreversible Revolution

All parasitical deceptions and illusions are now exposed by the Neo-Tech literature. Thus, through Neo-Tech, the business/working class will rise in the Prosperity Revolution to overthrow the leech class worldwide.

That Overthrow Can Occur Almost Overnight

In December 1989, on CNN satellite news, citizens of the Romanian productive class suddenly saw the false power of their dictator Ceausescu and the rickety hoax of his parasitical-elite class. In just five days, those citizens unleashed an anger that brought Ceausescu from the height of life-and-death power over all Romanian citizens to his death before a firing squad manned by those same citizens.

* * *

Today, in America, innocent political pawns are increasingly broken or jailed in order to support an expanding parasitical-elite class. Tomorrow, without Neo-Tech, those victims would become one's own children, parents, brothers, sisters, friends. ...Eventually, everyone who is not a parasitical elite or an active supporter of the leech class would become a victim.

Self-Defense against Criminals and Murderers

Consider the natural dynamics of a valid revolution: What happens when totalitarian oppression and censorship occur? As identified by Thomas Jefferson two centuries ago, overthrow becomes the only *moral* self-defense against the resulting rise of totalitarian criminals. That is why the government should never be allowed to disarm its citizens. By contrast, the *immoral* self-defense against those criminals is to support them in order to "be safe" from their enforcers.

Neo-Tech Assures Everlasting Peace

The opportunity for a peaceful overthrow must not be lost. The gun-backed oppression of free press executed against Neo-Tech must be rectified. With unfettered free press, the Prosperity Revolution will vanish the parasitical-elite class without a single incident of physical harm or violence. ...Everyone can then enjoy the unending peace and prosperity available to all conscious beings.

NEVER AGAIN

If Neo-Tech were implemented in the 1930s, the above criminal-minded value destroyers would have been laughed out of existence. ...Their gun-backed government would have ended ignominiously.

Ending Gun-Backed Governments

with

Neo-Tech

*Greater than the tread of mighty armies
is an idea whose time has come.*
Victor Hugo, 1852
Histoire d'un Crime

Chapter 15

Neo-Tech Resurrects
The Child of the Universe

The Child of the Past
leads to the
Civilization of the Universe

Neo-Tech is fully integrated honesty. Neo-Tech is the natural essence of conscious beings as demonstrated in *every* young child still uncorrupted by dishonesty and irrationality. Through integrated thinking and rational exuberance, every child learns to perceive, talk, and then conceptualize. Every child learns with the certainty of integrated honesty present throughout the Universe. Yet, *every* child loses that certainty through the diseases of dishonesty, irrationality, and mysticism.

The dynamics of Neo-Tech bring back that certainty of fully integrated honesty. Neo-Tech brings everyone

151

back to his or her nature. Neo-Tech resurrects that *Child of the Universe* who sleeps in everyone's soul. ...Fully integrated honesty *is* the nature of every conscious being throughout the Universe.

Uprighting our Upside-Down World

Nearly everything the parasitical-elite class promotes as *right* is dishonest and destructive. Nearly everything it promotes as *wrong* is honest and productive. That upside-down world of the past 23 centuries was recognized a century ago by Russian writer Mikhail Bakunin:

"For there is no terror, cruelty, sacrilege, perjury, cynical theft, brazen robbery, or foul treason which has not been committed and is still being committed by representatives of the State, with no other excuse than this elastic, at times so convenient and terrible phrase, *for reasons of the state.* A terrible phrase indeed...as soon as it is uttered everything becomes silent and drops out of sight: honesty, honor, justice, right, pity itself vanishes and with it logic and sound sense; black becomes white and white becomes black, the horrible becomes humane and the most dastardly felonies and atrocious crimes become meritorious acts."

Hitler described parasitical elites as leeches, vampires, vermin, termites, maggots, bacilli. In his upside-down world, he then labeled the Jews as those parasitical elites. But Hitler's description of parasitical elites really applied to himself, his cohorts, and his guns-and-fists enforcers who empowered him through armed bureaucracies. By contrast, his targeted Jews were among Germany's greatest value producers.

Likewise, to exist, all other parasitical-elite kingpins

must also turn reality upside down. Mao and Khomeini, for example, used force to unnaturally posit free-enterprise and individual property rights as unjust and parasitical, while positing Mao's gun-barrel socialism and Khomeini's gun-barrel religious fundamentalism as just and valuable. ...Such people can rise to power only in an upside-down world of force, dishonesty, and mysticism.

Today, however, all parasitical elites are moribund because of Neo-Tech — because of fully integrated honesty and wide-scope accounting. ...Today, Neo-Tech can and will upright our upside-down world.

What is Neo-Tech?

Neo-Tech is a matrix of fully integrated honesty and wide-scope accounting. From that matrix comes a certainty about the most effective way to live every aspect of conscious life. Each human being has sought that certainty since mankind became conscious. Indeed, Neo-Tech is the *natural* certainty residing in every conscious being throughout the Universe.

But, on planet Earth, a parasitical-elite class has hidden the objective process of honesty for twenty-three centuries by manipulating subjective *assertions of truth*: Beginning about 300 BC, the philosopher Plato pulled civilization into a cave. He obliterated the individual with his force-backed master-servant collectivism. Plato then crowned the parasitical elites and his philosopher kings with souls of gold.[1] Only they would have the "wisdom" to control, exploit, and drain the productive class: the masses trapped in Plato's cave. Plato relegated to his

---

[1]Plato also assigned souls of silver to the obedient armed agents of force serving the golden-souled rulers.

trapped servants lowly souls of copper and iron.[1]

How did Plato finesse such an outlandish hoax that dominates the Western world to this day? By using the *arbitrariness of truths* to turn reality upside-down, causing a sea of "noble" lies, illusions, deceptions, shadows, doubts, and uncertainties. Such created uncertainties let the parasitical elites rule through dishonesties backed by armed agents of force. By contrast, Neo-Tech eliminates manipulated truths, doubts, uncertainties, out-of-context facts, deceptions, illusions, and gun-backed parasitical "leadership". ...The certainty of Neo-Tech uprights reality and forbids initiatory force against individuals and their property, thus, dooming the parasitical-elite class.

Certainty Without Omniscience[2]

Reality is relational. Knowledge is contextual and hierarchal. Thus, certainty evolves from Neo-Tech — from fully integrated honesty. By nature, fully integrated honesty is the mechanism for building relational, contextual, hierarchal knowledge. Through fully integrated honesty, we share the same certainty — the same knowledge-building *processes* — enjoyed among all mystic-free civilizations throughout the universe.

America Today

America today is at once the greatest and the worst nation on Earth: The greatest by the productivity, well-being, and happiness created by the mightiest host of professional value producers and competent workers in

---

[1]In America, Plato's hoax reached its climax in 1993 with golden-soul Hillary Rodham Clinton knowing what was best for the health and welfare of the masses with their lowly souls of copper and iron. Through Neo-Tech, the American public broke that hoax in the elections of 1994.

[2]Title of a lecture by objectivist philosopher Leonard Peikoff.

history. The worst by the harm, deprivations, and unhappiness caused by a rapidly expanding parasitical-elite class. That leech class is cannibalizing history's most bountiful trove of earned wealth and created values. ...But, today, everyone can look happily to the future. For, the rising Prosperity Revolution and its army of independent self-leaders will eliminate the parasite class to bring ever growing well-being and happiness to everyone.

Discovery from Prison

What if every judge, prosecutor, and high-level bureaucrat spent a month in a Federal[1] Prison Camp for political prisoners — spent a month among the victims of subjective, political-agenda laws and ego "justice"? Each judge, prosecutor, and bureaucrat manager would be indelibly struck by the suffering and destruction wreaked on innocent, good people and their families. Only by directly experiencing prison can one discover the profound harm caused by the unjust incarcerations of political prisoners — versus the just incarceration of real criminals guilty of objective crimes.

One and only one reason exists to enforce political-agenda laws. That reason is to enhance the harmful livelihoods of a few parasitical elites. Be it in 100th-BC galley ships, in 12th-century dungeons, in 20th-century Nazi death camps, or in today's federal prisons, its

---

[1]Why federal? Most prisoners in state prisons are criminals. Many prisoners in federal prisons are political prisoners. State and county trial judges and courts deal mainly with legitimate, objective laws and crimes. By contrast, federal trial judges and courts deal mainly with enforcing bogus political-agenda laws. The federal government in Washington gives its judges lifetime appointments so they never need be accountable to the public. Thus, federal trial judges can reign in their courts as government heavies with totalitarian power. Such judges practice ego "justice" with impunity. ...Eliminating the anticivilization justice system involves revoking all political-agenda laws and ending life-time appointments for Federal District-Court trial judges.

innocent victims are *purposely* incarcerated and often destroyed just to indulge the bogus livelihoods and immature egos of a few evil people: a few habitual, mass-destruction criminals ranging from Caligula to Castro to today's parasitical elites with their legions of professional value destroyers.

Only by directly experiencing prison does one discover the deep moral difference between evilly enforcing subjective political-agenda laws versus justly enforcing objective laws. With that prison experience, many bureaucrats, prosecutors, and judges would forever reject pursuing, prosecuting, or adjudicating political-agenda laws. They would reject all such subjective laws and ego-"justice" support systems as the prime evil of any civilization.

Ending the World of Chains

Imagine a world of cruel masters binding to a stake every puppy born — binding every dog for every moment of its life from birth to death to a stake with a short chain. Those dogs during their entire lives would know nothing except a totally bleak, constantly chained life. Thus, they would accept their one-and-only lives being used up and wasted without ever experiencing the joys and well-being possible for all dogs, but experienced by none. Not a single dog would ever experience natural puppy joy, playfulness, or the happy companionship of a loving master. But, imagine if those dogs had the ability to become aware of their chained lives. Imagine what they would feel toward their cruel masters.

Now, consider conscious human beings with almost infinitely more life experiences available to them. Imagine a world of human beings chained to stakes from youth to death. Imagine their lives being used up and wasted solely to support the destructive livelihoods of a few parasitical-elite "masters". ...Imagine the anger that would explode if all those chained beings suddenly discovered that their lives and the lives of a hundred generations before were used up and wasted just to support a handful of parasitical elites.

What will happen when conscious beings on Earth discover the hoax that has kept them chained, used up, and wasted for a hundred generations? The rising anger will push the ostracism matrix everywhere in government, religion, business, and the professions. A relentless army of value producers will then eradicate that parasite class, ending the world of chains forever.

A World Brightly Lit

Over one hundred years ago, Thomas Edison lit the world with his electric light bulb. For many years, he built his foundation of knowledge. He knew exactly what would happen and exactly how *it* would happen...the *it* being electrically lighting the world. Then, he and his co-workers needed several more years of intense work to find the exact combination to unlock an incandescent bulb with more and more uses until the entire world was alight with electricity.

Using Neo-Tech, which means fully integrated honesty, Frank R. Wallace and his co-workers spent twenty-three years building the foundation of knowledge for intellectually and emotionally lighting the world forever. Today, those co-workers worldwide know exactly what will happen and exactly *how it* will happen...the *how* being cyberspace, the *it* being the vanishing of the parasitical-elite class in resurrecting the Child of the Universe on planet Earth.

Chapter 16

Neo-Tech
Self-Leaders

> *A Single Credo for Neo-Tech Self-Leaders*
> Direct every thought, every discipline, every effort
> toward the overthrow of the parasitical-elite class —
> toward the eradication of every livelihood that harms
> the value producers, the economy, and society.

Eleven Requisites for Neo-Tech Self-Leaders

1. To recognize that all past revolutions and their class overthrows have been false, compromised, or temporary. Only the Prosperity Revolution that eradicates the parasitical-elite class will permanently empower the productive class.

The Self-Leader's Goal

2. The self-leader has but one implacable goal: the unrestricted well-being and happiness of the productive class and all humanity.

3. To accomplish that goal, the parasitical-elite class must be eliminated. How will that be accomplished? By welding the productive class into an ostracism force that is all-subversive toward everything supporting that leech class.

4. Until now, every revolution in history eventually betrayed itself by overthrowing one parasitical-elite class in order to replace it with another. But, the *leaderless* Prosperity Revolution can never impose any form of rule

or exploitation on the productive class. For, the single task of the Prosperity Revolution is to eradicate the parasitical elites by eliminating their dishonest illusions, hoaxes, and mysticisms. The revolution will then be over. ...All revolutions will be over forever. Unending prosperity and happiness will reign.

The Self-Leader's Behavior

5. The self-leader dedicates his or her life toward the uncompromising eradication of the parasitical-elite class.

6. The self-leader breaks all bonds with the world controlled by parasitical elites. Yet, the self-leader infiltrates that world. He or she deals with parasitical elites, increasingly through cyberspace, only to subvert and destroy their corrupt systems more rapidly.

7. The self-leader rejects public opinion and the existing social morality. For the self-leader, morality is everything that advances the overthrow. Immorality is everything that blocks the overthrow.

8. The self-leader not only suppresses all sentimentality, but he or she abandons all private hatred and revenge. Day and night, the self-leader has but one thought, one aim — the merciless overthrow of the parasitical-elite class.

The Self-Leader's Relationship to Others and Society

9. The degree of friendship, devotion, and obligation toward others is determined solely by the degree they are useful in terminating parasitical elites.

10. A second-degree or third-degree self-leader is one who has not yet totally committed to the elimination of the parasitical-elite class. He or she is part of the common revolution capital to be used for the greatest advantage in advancing the revolution.

11. The self-leader is proven not by his or her words but by the deeds toward advancing the overthrow. The self-leader has no sympathy for the parasitical elites and does not hesitate to undermine their every position. He or she may frequently penetrate any area and live among their world in order to hasten their eradication.

Parasitical elites can be split into several categories. The first category consists of those who are condemned to termination as soon as possible. The second category consists of those who are spared temporarily as being useful for provoking the public into revolution. The third category consists of those liberals and conservatives in high positions of unearned power and influence, various dishonest politicians, and certain harmful bureaucrats, lawyers, and judges. Those parasitical elites can be useful — they can be exploited for advancing the revolution. The fourth category consists of pseudo-leaders who can be useful for a while. But, eventually, parasitical elites in all categories must be terminated.

The Greatest Event in History

What about other great events in history? Forget them. The emerging Prosperity Revolution is by far history's greatest event. That event will open the way for *all* future advancements toward eternal prosperity and happiness.

Terminating the Parasitical-Elite Class

Independent self-leaders are developing with no leader to follow or obey. They are people who will increasingly carry out missions of subversion against the parasitical-elite class.

So long as self-leaders have no leader to obey, they will steadily multiply and never stop moving forward. For, on learning how to break the hoax of professional parasitism, they will react personally to each parasite who harms or drains society. On their own, in their own ways, they will increasingly subvert the entire parasite class. They will subvert the leeches one by one, relentlessly, until each is driven from his or her bogus career. Especially through the computer, they will have no time or energy limits to stop them from eradicating the parasitical-elite class that wastes the lives of everyone. They will have no more compunction about swatting down parasitical elites who exploit society than they have about swatting down mosquitoes that spread disease.

So long as cyberspace and free expression exists, the Prosperity Revolution will proceed peacefully. Without gun-backed oppression, the overthrow of the parasitical-elite class will be peaceful but uncompromising, total, permanent.

Seven Waves to Prosperity

1. Plant the root system: Identify and define the problem, the enemy, the solution. ...Completed 1976.

2. Build the foundation: Establish a two-million-word body of literature published in twelve languages with audio, video, art, and music supplements. ...Done 1966-1991.

3. Develop the confrontational phase: Setting self-exposure traps such as the Golden Helmet for neocheaters, professional value destroyers, and the parasitical elites along with their armed enforcers. (Ref: *Politicians and Bureaucrats on Trial,* B & W, 1991) ...Began in 1980. Activated in 1986. Continuing.

4. Carry out and complete the free-press protection phase: Decentralization of publishing activities and literature distribution. Dispersion into independent phantom-bantam companies worldwide. Translate foundation work into twelve languages. Distribute into 156 countries. Those actions protect Neo-Tech publishing activities from being wiped out in further attacks by armed agents in America or in any other country. ...Completed in 1987. Insures a peaceful revolution.

5. Enter the direct confrontational phase: Activate the self-exposure traps for the neocheaters, professional value destroyers, and parasitical elites in government, the courts, business, and the professions. Establish a computerized ostracism matrix that will drive all parasitical elites and their cohorts from their destructive livelihoods. As of 1994, over 2450 parasitical elites, neocheaters, and professional value destroyers have been permanently locked into the Neo-Tech Ostracism Matrix. ...Began in 1990. Continuing.

6. Begin the worldwide revolution-overthrow phase: Move from quiet foundation-building and self-exposure confrontational modes to public-action terminator modes. To begin in 1996.

7. Cyberspace.

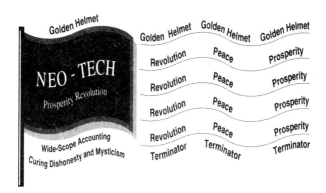

RULES FOR LIMITLESS PROSPERITY

Rule 1

No person, group of persons or government may
initiate force, threat of force, or fraud against
any individual or private property.

Rule 2

Force may be morally and legally used only in self-
defense against those who violate Rule 1.

Rule 3

No exceptions shall exist for Rules 1 and 2.

*Initiation of force, except in self-defense, always
leads to destruction and is the opposite of value.*

Preamble

We stand united — the worker, ditch digger, farmer, tradesman, office worker, business person, billionaire entrepreneur — the productive class. Dishonest parasitical elites shall no longer live off our work. They shall no longer exist by deceiving us.

The Two Points of Revolution
The Enemy
The Promise

Point One **THE ENEMY**	The enemy is the parasitical-elite class comprised of harmful politicians, lawyers, judges, prosecutors, bureaucrats, clerics, and other leeches, neocheaters, professional value destroyers, and agents of force. Those people fraudulently live off you. …They have stolen their livings from you for far too long.
Point Two **THE PROMISE**	We will eliminate the parasitical elites. That ridding of the leech class will yield the unlimited expansion of jobs, prosperity, pride, and security for all honest value producers, their children, and their future generations.

WE DEMAND!

We the value-producing workers, entrepreneurs, business people, soldiers, police, youth, students, parish priests, exploited government employees, and suffering unemployed demand the breaking of all deceptions foisted upon us — deceptions that let the parasitical elites drain and harm our lives.

WE SHALL TERMINATE THE PARASITICAL-ELITE CLASS

We shall break the chain that chokes our lives. We shall terminate the parasitical-elite class forever. …Our march to peace and prosperity begins now!

Peace●Prosperity

Have you been wronged, hurt, used, drained, exploited, or diminished by government "authorities", bureaucrats, religion, "law" enforcers, lawyers, certain unions, certain businesses, certain "friends" or relatives? The Prosperity Revolution will turn that harm into peace and prosperity.

Peace●Prosperity

4-3/92

Chapter 17

Commanding Life
on
Planet Earth

The Final Decade of Earth's Anticivilization

A parasitical-elite class has spawned this upside-down civilization — an irrational civilization that inflicts purposeful harm on conscious beings, their economies, their societies. Parasitical elites today manipulate nearly all politics, many bureaucracies, the legal profession, the courts, public schools, the academe, the news media, religion, entertainment, and certain big businesses. What most of those manipulators represent as the best is really the worst...the *most destructive* — and vice versa.

Be prepared to discover the facts: Jay Gould is the best, Abraham Lincoln is the worst; Leona Helmsley is the best, Eleanor Roosevelt is the worst; Malcolm X is the best, Martin Luther King is the worst; Michael Milken is the best, Rudolph Giuliani is the worst; Florence Nightingale is the best, Hillary Clinton is the worst. ...Indeed, you must first dismiss nearly *everything* that the parasitical-elite class and its news media represent as good and bad in order to command your life on planet Earth toward boundless prosperity.

What Do the Following Have in Common?

Armed ATF, DEA, IRS agents, force-backed anti-abortionists, jailing of Milken and Helmsley, Jew and Japan bashing, busting Noriega, gay bashing and gay "rights", racism, urban riots, RICO and seizure laws, PETA, political correctness, the DEA, EPA, FDA, INS, IRS, OSHA, formal religion, Greenpeace, evangelism, gun control, Jesse Jackson, Ralph Nader, Fidel Castro, Jesse Helms, white-collar-hoax big-business executives: What do they all have in common?

All of the above are based on economic and social parasitism. They are all backed by professional value destroyers, parasitical elites, envy mongers, and self-righteous neocheaters infesting government, religion, big business, entertainment, the media. By purposely creating problems where none exist, all such parasites end in destroying the very values they pretend to support. Such destructive people must pretend to support values. They must fake compassion and good intentions to survive — to gain false esteem, power, and bogus livelihoods.

They and their supporters comprise a rapidly expanding class of parasitical elites. Today, from survival necessity, they are converging in a final feeding frenzy. They increasingly loot and destroy innocent value producers through despotic "laws": RICO, seizure, and EPA/FDA-type "laws"...all backed by the irrationalities of ego "justice", fake scientisms, and deep-pocket litigations. And now, they fight one another to devour the last remains of a vanishing class of genuine job-and-wealth producers.

Indeed, for decades, that escalating class of professional value destroyers has orchestrated slander and public envy to attack and drain a now decimated, crumbling class of super value producers. Eventually, under disguised forms of fascist socialism such as Clinton's envynomics, those converging parasites would drain dry the remaining, tiny remnant of super job producers and aggressive entrepreneurs. The demise of those last great value producers would bring annihilations of the world economies and societies. ...But, none of that will happen because of Neo-Tech and the coming Prosperity Revolution.

The only justifiable purpose of political institutions is to insure the unhindered development of the individual.

Albert Einstein

Printed with permission from the National Archives: Niels Bohr Library

Chapter 18

What is the Illuminati?
What is Zon?

> **The Illuminati**
> has its origins in the biblical Abraham who smashed the idols four millennia ago in establishing the existence of only one reality.

Ever hear of the Illuminati? For the past two centuries, they have been condemned by nationalistic governments and mystical religions. How about the Bilderbergers, the Club of Rome, the Council on Foreign Relations, the Trilateral Commission? They are semi-secret organizations that for the past several decades have been linked to one-world conspiracy theories. Consider the controlling influences behind those worldwide organizations — businessmen, such as today's quiet businessman David Rockefeller. He, for example, is seldom seen or mentioned in the mainstream media. But, he is hysterically attacked as the epitome of evil by the ultra-conservative media, the nationalistic-populist media, and the religious-right media. Yet, David Rockefeller is among the world's most moral, clear-thinking, responsible people.

The Illuminati Protocols

This chapter refers to the early Illuminati protocols — the master plan for worldwide control first formulated over two centuries ago by leading European bankers and businessmen. Essentially anyone reading the protocols alone and out of context would view them as one of the most evil plots ever devised. Yet, on reading those very same protocols in the context of wide-scope accountability, one will realize the men responsible for those protocols were among the most moral, clear-thinking, responsible people who ever lived on this planet. Moreover, through Zon, today's Illuminati can make everyone on Earth rich and happy.

Making the Illuminati Serve You

Zon will far surpass the goal of the Illuminati. By understanding Zon, the Illuminati and their organizations will be at your service — providing you with limitless wealth.

Business-Controlled Master Plans

Business-controlled master plans underlie all actions controlling the creation of long-term prosperity and happiness. Two such master plans or protocols operate on planet Earth: (1) the closed-system Illuminati protocols developed in Europe over two centuries ago, and (2) the evolving, open-ended Zon protocols that began developing in early 1992 and reflected in the American elections of 1994. Today, Zon is replacing the Illuminati's master plan. With Zon, the world will soar in cyberspace beyond the Illuminati's plan for worldwide prosperity. For, Zon delivers eternal happiness with limitless wealth to all conscious beings.

The Illuminati, from its founding protocols forged in the mid-18th century by Adam Weishaup and Albert Pike, have nearly completed their noble goal of undermining and eliminating the twin instruments of irrationality and destruction on this planet: (1) forced-backed nationalist governments, and (2) fraud-backed mystical religions.

Now, after two centuries, that goal will not only be achieved but far surpassed, perhaps by 2000AD. How? By replacing the established, seemingly violent Illuminati protocols with the newly evolving, peaceful Zon protocols as deduced from the original, 176-page *Cassandra's Secret* manuscript developed in 1993. The specific Zon protocols will be ready for public use in 1996. But, first, one must understand the goal and protocols of the original Illuminati as described below:

The Illuminati's Business Plan
for
Depoliticizing Planet Earth

Since the late 1700s, essentially all public reporting and exposés of the secretive Illuminati have been rabidly negative. Most such reports and exposés emanate from paranoid conspiracy theories presented in populist, nationalistic, or right-wing religious publications. All such reports and exposés present the Illuminati and their protocols as diabolically evil. Modern-day exposés especially rail at the Illuminati's tools used to undermine public respect for political-agenda laws, irrational traditions, and predatory institutions. The Illuminati work to undermine public support of the parasitical-elite class...a destructive class that survives through politically and religiously ruled governments.

The modern-day tools of the Illuminati include international organizations such as the Trilateral Commission, the Council on Foreign Relations, the Bilderbergers, the Club of Rome, and the outdated Freemasons. In addition to high-profile parasitical elites, those organizations comprise the most-influential, low-profile businesspeople throughout the world. Still, they are all simply tools masterfully maneuvered into advancing the Illuminati's goal.

Many members of those organizations are sincere value producers; others are power-seeking parasites. Yet, all effectively serve the Illuminati's pretended goal of worldwide political and economic cooperation. Beneath that goal, however, lies the Illuminati's real goal: break the institutions that support this destructive anticivilization.

To understand the Illuminati, one must understand their poker-playing modus operandi. The Illuminati perfected the shrewdest poker-playing stratagems imaginable — analogous to those stratagems revealed in Frank R. Wallace's *Advanced Concepts of Poker*, first published in 1968. After 21 printings, plus additional printings by Crown Publishing and Warner Books, Wallace withdrew that book from print in 1986 in favor of the evolving Neo-Tech literature.

Consider the following stratagem by the Illuminati: To most effectively achieve their goal, they knew their real targets for termination must remain concealed for as long as possible. Because of their world-wide influences, the Illuminati also realized that, over time, information about their work and goal would leak to the public, despite their influence over the world news media. Thus, the Illuminati planted ruses in their protocols that would invite hysterical criticism of them and their satellite organizations. By promoting hysteria against themselves, criticisms would lose credibility, preventing any effective effort to block or retard their progress.

For example, the Illuminati realized their secret protocols would eventually be publicly revealed. Thus, they drafted their Protocols to conceal their real agenda. They made their Protocols to appear as a Jewish or Zionist plot for placing all human beings under one-world tyrannical rule. They even mistitled their document *The Protocols of the Learned Elders of Zion*. Throughout that document, they shrewdly planted a Jewish slur word for Gentiles to describe their targets — the *goyim*.

That strategy has worked brilliantly for two centuries: All exposés or attacks on the Illuminati turn into strident accusations about being evil socialistic, communistic, Jewish, Zionist, satanic, or Luciferin plots for world domination. Thus, all exposés and attacks have ultimately been dismissed as paranoid anti-Semitic, Jew baiting, racist, or religious-right paranoia — exactly what the Illuminati intended.[1] ...Incidentally, from their origin to modern day, many among the Illuminati are Jewish. But, they are moral Jewish businessmen, not socialists or Zionists seeking world domination. Indeed, the Illuminati are ingenious "poker players" who orchestrate criticisms of them to advance their goal.

The Illuminati especially utilize their poker strategies in wielding influence from their toolbox of international organizations. Those organizations comprise the world's leading businesspeople, politicians, journalists, publishers, bankers, industrialists, military leaders, and other influential people used to advance a one-world agenda. But, that agenda conceals the real goal fully known only to the Illuminati. That goal is to undermine and eliminate the institutions supporting parasitical elites.

What gave the Illuminati businessmen their overwhelming power and success for the past two centuries? The answer lies in their ability to create genuine values and jobs for society, *combined* with an unshakable moral responsibility to bring growing prosperity to all conscious beings on this planet. Their

---

[1]A good example of how this strategy works is found in the April, 1995, *Reader's Digest* article titled, "This Lie Will Not Die".

moral foundation, however, was based on knowledge limited to this closed, irrational anticivilization. Thus, for them, the only possible way to preserve and then flourish human consciousness on Earth was to eliminate, by whatever means necessary, the institutions that support this anticivilization and its parasitical-elite propagators.

The recent discovery of Zon with its eternal, open-ended Civilization of the Universe void of politics and violence removes the moral base upon which the Illuminati have solidly stood since their institution-breaking role in the 1793 French Revolution. ...Today, Zon has replaced the Illuminati's moral base with an omnipotent, eternally evolving moral foundation that peacefully, continuously elevates the wealth and happiness of *all* conscious beings throughout all existence and time. That omnipotent moral base stands on fully integrated honesty, productive effort, wide-scope accounting, objective law, and the Golden-Helmet dynamics as detailed in the original Cassandra's-Secret manuscript.

The institution-breaking accomplishments of the Illuminati along with their one-world organizations such as the Bilderbergers and the Trilateral Commission provide an advanced position from which the Civilization of the Universe can flower on this planet while peacefully vanishing the anticivilization and its manipulators.

With the discovery of Zon, the key to limitless prosperity for conscious beings is (1) to originate *all* conscious actions from the Civilization of the Universe and (2) ignore everything in the anticivilization as *nothing*. In that way, *every* harmful aspect of the anticivilization is dismissed and vanished. Also, in that way, the two-century-old Illuminati dynamics of using deceit and force to undermine those elements supporting the anticivilization are replaced by the honest, peaceful Zon dynamics. Those new dynamics will quietly vanish the entire anticivilization along with its harmful institutions and humanoids.

The Most Moral Men on Earth

Without the concepts of advanced poker strategy combined with Neo-Tech, anyone who reads the Illuminati protocols[1] will come to the same conclusion: Those protocols are the epitome of evil. But on understanding advanced poker concepts along with Neo-Tech and Cassandra's Secret, one comes to the exact opposite conclusion: The Illuminati protocols reflect the most responsible and moral forces on Earth — forces designed to bring wealth and happiness to our world by breaking the institutions that support this parasitically drained, death-oriented anticivilization.

As identified in the *Neo-Tech Discovery*, the original Illuminati also realized that honest business dynamics are what sustain and advance *all* conscious life. Thus, those business dynamics are the only source of genuine, life-enhancing power among conscious beings. Indeed, only competitive value-and-job producers hold real power — the ultimate power to control not only all current events but all future events on planet Earth.

Until the original 18th-century Illuminati, no value-and-job producer understood the draining hoaxes and illusions of the parasitical elites. From Plato's time, a ruling leech class has built and propagated an anticivilization with the single purpose of sustaining their own harmful livelihoods by draining the productive class.

The Illuminati discovered that they, not kings, popes, tyrants, or other parasitical elites hold the power to control

---

[1]*The 18th-Century Illuminati Protocols*, 32 pages, Zon Association (1994).

and direct society. On that realization, those original Illuminati, most of whom were powerful businessmen and bankers, moved with complete confidence to eliminate the parasitical elites by relentlessly pitting those leeches and their institutions against each other. That dynamic caused the world populations to increasingly lose confidence in politics, nationalistic governments, mystical religions, and their parasitical leaders.

As depicted by the movie *Schindler's List*, the factual story of German businessman Oskar Schindler in the 1940s illustrates how even at the evilest depths of this anticivilization, the value-and-job producer is the *only* person with genuine power and love...even midst the evilest humanoids who live by guns and mass murder. Only businessman Schindler, for example, could walk through the bloody mud of the Holocaust without soiling his soul, his compassion, his respect for human life. Only job-producing Schindler had the power, moral character, and strength to reach into the depths of this anticivilization to save conscious beings from the destruction and death wrought by its humanoid propagators.

Extrapolate businessman Schindler into the advanced technologies among the Civilization of the universe. One will then recognize that honest businesspeople with their limitless valuation of conscious beings are the real saviors of everyone in existence. Only such value-and-job producers have the power, responsibility, and love to never let perish the supreme value throughout the universe — conscious life — including conscious human beings on planet Earth. ...The competitive, value-and-job producing businessperson eternally preserves and advances all conscious life.

The Illuminati originally comprised the few most

powerful, efficacious businessmen in Europe. The original Illuminati rejected all parasites holding false or life-draining power. Indeed, none of the Illuminati were kings, tyrants, politicians, lawyers, religionists, entertainers, writers, or orators. Instead, they were quiet businessmen and bankers — they were the world's most potent creators of life-sustaining values and jobs.

The Illuminati's relentless work has always been directed toward saving the future generations of conscious beings from destruction by the institutionalized irrationality woven throughout this anticivilization. The Illuminati's goal has always been to free conscious beings from the tribal mentalities that make possible parasitical governments, insane socialism, the welfare state, and mystical religions.

The Illuminati sought a world in which its citizens valued their fellow citizens not by social status, wealth, nationality, race, or religion, but by what each did to competitively benefit others and society.

For 250 years, playing the most ingenious poker game in history, the Illuminati have brought the entire world close to their goal of ending 3000 years of unnecessary suffering and death inflicted on all populations of Earth — inflicted by parasitical humanoids through their criminal anticivilization institutions. ...Finally, today, the newly arrived Zon dynamics will not only peacefully achieve but far surpass the noble goal of the Illuminati.

Part II: The Anticivilization

Pages 311-317 of Part III publicly identify for the first time the real meaning beneath the Illuminati protocols[1], their master plan, their one-world organizations...and the resulting future for all of us on planet Earth through Zon.

---

[1]What is the source of those Protocols? In 1906, the British Museum in London received a copy of the Illuminati Protocols written in Russian. Those secret Protocols were probably translated into Russian sometime after 1850 from the original German language Protocols, which first appeared in Bavaria during the late 18th century. Parts of the Protocols were used by Maurice Joly in his 1864 satire, *Dialogue in Hell Between Machiavelli and Montesquieu*. In the early 20th century, British journalist Victor Marsden translated the Protocols into English. His translations were finally issued by the British Publishing Society in 1921 (Ref: Des Griffith, *Fourth Reich of the Rich*).

The Neo-Tech Trojan Horse

Over the years, the Neo-Tech/Illuminati dynamic has evolved into today's *Zonpower*. This 200-year-old dynamic is increasingly undermining false, harmful authorities throughout governments and religions worldwide. The Neo-Tech/Illuminati dynamic has been the hidden force beneath the collapse of communism in Eastern Europe, the collapse of the conservative party in Canada, and America's sea-change first reflected in its 1994 elections.

The seventh and final cyberspace stage of Neo-Tech/Zonpower — the public phase — will activate in late 1996 with the Internet distribution of the *Zonpower Protocols*...the Trojan-Horse penetration of Neo-Tech into the heart of the Establishment in America and worldwide.

Chapter 19
Dumping Goy Politics

Reality and Objective Law

The *real* physical world resides in a beautiful symmetry of rationality embodied by the objective laws of nature. Philosophers and scientists throughout the ages have striven to discover the ultimate nature and symmetry of existence. For 24 centuries, great minds have opened one door after another, solved one deep mystery of nature after another, only to discover whole new and deeper symmetries hiding beneath the ever evolving forces within the unchanging laws of nature. That long history started with the postulating of atoms and led to the discovery of gravity, electromagnetism, and relativity. Those great minds ranged from Democritus to Newton, to Faraday, to Einstein...to Nobel laureate Leon Lederman, the pre-eminent experimental physicist who in his book *The God Particle* (Houghton Mifflin, 1993) metaphorically named the ultimate nature of existence, the "God Particle"[1].

Are we opening the final door that reveals what lies beyond the "God Particle"? Will we find at last the elegantly simple, beautiful force with no beginning or ending, lying beneath and above the "God Particle"? ...Beneath and above that particle lie Gravity Units of symmetrical, subspatial geometries controlled by conscious beings free of *goy* politics.

Nonreality and Subjective Law

The *unreal* political world of the goyim hides the ugly irrationality embodied by subjective laws born of politics. Those laws are used to gain destructive livelihoods and criminal power in an anticivilization. As one discovers

---

[1]Technically the "God Particle" is called by physicists the Higgs boson.

the secret of goy politics, one discovers that *everything* arising from their political-agenda laws involves the criminal acquisition of power — from Caligula to Hitler to the Clintons.[1]

From Caligula's socio-fascist Rome to Hitler's socio-fascist Germany to the Clintons' socio-fascist America, all destructive laws arise from political processes — processes designed to create self-serving political powers. Today, as in Germany 60 years ago, the process of law making is driven by politics rather than by objective reality. Indeed, most law today arises from arbitrary political correctness in a drum roll of force-backed, political-agenda laws.

Such laws are turning political tools like the FDA, DEA, BATF, IRS, INS, EPA into armed bureaucracies that destroy life, liberty, and society. Other evils include today's politicization of health care and food diets, politicization of abortion and religion, politicization of education and communication, politicization of drugs including alcohol and tobacco, politicization of law enforcement and criminal prosecution, politicization of taxing and spending, politicization of immigration and the environment. Decisions in those areas should have nothing to do with politics, but everything to do with objective reality. ...What irrational forces underlie the politicization of human action?

Two forces underlie all harmful political action: camouflaged dishonesty and hidden laziness. From those two forces, a purposeful destructiveness arises. That destructiveness is used to gain harmful livelihoods and unearned power at the expense of the productive class.

---

[1]Consider the following: How many Caesars, Caligulas, Attilas, Genghis Khans, Tamerlanes, Napoleons, Lincolns, Lenins, Woodrow Wilsons, Mussolinis, Hitlers, FDRs, Stalins, Maos, Pol Pots, Castros, Idi Amins, Bokassas, Khomeinis, Pengs, Saddams, Nicolae and Elena Ceausescus, Bill and Hillary Clintons were Jews? None.

Beneath those forces of dishonesty and laziness lie irrationality and insanity — the schizophrenia of parasitism. Contrary to common belief, schizophrenia is not a split or a duel personality, which is just one of many possible *symptoms* of schizophrenia. Rather, the disease of schizophrenia is the **detachment of consciousness from objective reality**, which is required to convert one's precious conscious life into a destructive parasite — into a humanoid.

The tripartite cure for insanity in government is simple: depoliticize, depoliticize, depoliticize. ...How will that cure arise? Consider the following Illuminati article of June, 1994. This article was published five months before the first Neo-Tech domino fell in America — five months before America's November 1994 elections and ten months before the Oklahoma City bombing:

Obsoleting the Criminal-Minded Goyim
The most valuable, criminal-minded goyim of the '90s are Bill and Hillary Clinton. Faking compassion and using super-hypocritical demagoguery, they foment envy against the productive class — against the competitive producers of wealth and jobs. They move forward, feeding on the remaining seeds of individual rights and competitive entrepreneurs. Their grand wealth-distribution schemes consume the source of earned values and well-being. Their illegal schemes, epitomized by the bribes paid to Hillary Clinton through fraudulent cattle straddles, undermine the public's sense of justice and honesty in America.

*Moreover, the fake compassion of the Clintons is nothing more than a three-step, **Toll-Booth Compassion:** Personally they give nothing that genuinely benefits* *humanity or society. Instead, (1) they collect self-serving tolls by forcing the productive class into financing an expanding parasitical-elite class through political-agenda laws. (2) They collect destructive tolls by draining the only real benefactors of the needy and society: the competitive value-and-job producers. And, then (3) they collect the jackpot: a neocheating livelihood replete with force-backed political power and praise-filled honors.*

Such three-step, toll-booth compassion includes purposeful murder. For example: "If this law saves one life, then it's worth it" type demagoguery hides the 100 or 1000 or million innocent victims hurt, impoverished, or killed directly or indirectly through such sound-good, toll-booth-compassion laws — laws that subjugate society through force-back control, destruction, and death.

Seeking unearned power through virtuoso lying, the Clintons are emasculating America's long-term economy for their own power. Left unchecked, the Clintons' criminal agendas would destroy health care, individual rights, the economy, and maybe start a war to avoid impeachment or jail. ...Such goys will loot, kill, and build violent hatred toward government just to sustain their destructive livelihoods.

Indeed, today, political predators are crushing property rights, plundering the middle class, and widening the gap between the rich and poor. How? By escalating police-state regulations, destructive political-agenda laws, and irrational taxes enforced by armed bureaucrats. Those irrationalities decimate small businesses, the middle class, and individual self-reliance: the three originators of all productive jobs and earned profits. ...Why do political predators purposely advance economic and social harms? So they can flourish in power and praise without themselves having to produce competitive values.

Dumping Goy Politics

The above dynamics are ironically in accord with the original Illuminati Protocols. Those master-plan protocols use Machiavellian political tools such as the Clintons who have Dostoyevsky-type criminal minds[1]. For, such goy tools cause calamities that undermine planet Earth's twin institutions of parasitical evil: organized religions and nationalistic governments...institutions that subjugate the well-being of society to the parasitical-elite class.

Today, however, by using the new Zon protocols, the Illuminati are shifting their moral and operational base from the politicized anticivilization to the nonpolitical Civilization of the Universe. One visible result will be their use of the media to remove from office, by impeachment or defeat, the now useless Clintonian coterie. That removal will end their drive for power through draining society by force and fraud.

Obsoleting such criminal-minded goyim will halt the government's parasitical feeding on the value-producing class. A depoliticized civilization will bring eternal peace and prosperity. Indeed, the laws among the Civilization of the Universe arise from the divine grace embodied in every conscious being who has ever existed. From those laws arise virtuous prosperity and happiness.

Seven-Point Agenda
for
America's First Neo-Tech President

1. Immediately pardon and free *all* individuals convicted of political-agenda crimes.
2. Veto and work to repeal *every* political-agenda law passed by Congress, current and past.

---

[1]Such deluded "superior beings" think their "greatness" puts them above objective law, including murder...as Raskolnikov in Dostoyevsky's *Crime and Punishment*, as the OJs and the Clintons in today's America.

3. Work to end all welfare and social programs. Replace Clintonian toll-booth compassion with genuine compassion.

4. Privatize Social Security. Fully meet all obligations by paying back with market-rate interest *all* monies paid into Social Security. Finance this payback by selling government businesses and assets.

5. Permit government activity only in areas of national defense, *local* police, and the courts to protect individual and property rights. Eliminate all other force-backed government powers and programs. Disarm all bureaucrats, not honest citizens.

6. Replace the irrational, envy-based income tax with a rational consumption tax — a national sales tax. Then phase out sales taxes with major budget reductions, market-rate user fees, and the Golden Helmet. Use revenues only for national defense and the protection of individuals and their property from objective crime.

7. Help redeemable parasitical elites, neocheaters, and professional value destroyers convert to competitive value producers in the Civilization of the Universe.

Accomplishing the above seven points are the natural results of upholding the Constitution of the Universe:

CONSTITUTION OF THE UNIVERSE

Article 1

No person, group of persons or government may initiate force, threat of force, or fraud against any individual's self or property.

Article 2

Force may be morally and legally used only in self-defense against those who violate Article 1.

Article 3

No exceptions shall exist for Articles 1 and 2.

Dumping Goy Politics

Even Plato recognized that the creation of a civilization is the "victory of persuasion over force...". By contrast, an anticivilization means the use of force over persuasion.

The Zon Illuminati

Why did most of the news media and much of the public keep accepting the automatic lies and crimes from someone like Bill Clinton when he became the President of the United States? What about his Machiavellian drive to escape his crimes and stay in office? Through his and his wife's dishonest camouflages, the Clintons tried to ravage the economy, health care, and society itself.

All genuine jobs, prosperity, and happiness in *any* society come from honest individuals and businesses. President Clinton has no concept of honesty or business. He never held or created a productive job in his adult life. He lives parasitically by (1) demagogically attacking and then (2) self-righteously draining those who produce the jobs and values upon which society depends. ...How does such a person become accepted by a population as its leader?

Congenial President Clinton is the most skilled, slickest public speaker since Hitler, Churchill, and FDR.[1] His gross lack of principles combined with his supreme ability to sound good lets him project sincerity and good intentions with persuasive skills, perhaps surpassing any neocheater living today. Pandering to envy and parasitism, both Clintons "compassionately" extract maximum capital from the producers to buy votes and power from the public.

Indeed, Bill and Hillary Clinton were an important find for the Illuminati to accomplish their two-century goal of eliminating public acceptance of the parasitical-elite class draining the value producers and society. ...Ultimately, the pernicious Clintons will bring prosperity and happiness to

[1]Words and speeches are crafted to make evil actions sound good.

189

America. How will that happen when all their actions work to decay individual rights, property rights, self-responsibility, self-respect, objective law, crime prevention, education, health care and the economy?

President Clinton is a professional Elmer Gantry who exudes sincerity, confidence, and compassion upon all whom he exploits for his own unearned livelihood and selfish ego. But, just as he built his illusion to the height of false success, the fully integrated honesty of Neo-Tech began breaking that illusion in the 1994 elections. Eventually, everyone will convert the Clinton illusion into reality. Then, the more the Clintons try to convey sincerity and compassion, the more they will be recognized as hypocrites and predators.

As the illusions break, the Clintons and their supporting cast will be scorned or prosecuted out of existence. Then, their dishonest concepts of politics will be trashed along with their political-agenda laws and ego-"justice" systems. At that point, America will be ready for depoliticization and decriminalization.

Put another way: When the Clintons' illusion publicly pops, they will stand naked before the world. Everyone will see them as nothing more than the criminal parasites they have always been. That popping of illusions, especially in cyberspace, will start the depoliticization of this anticivilization. The Illuminati will then have achieved their two-century goal of curing the irrationality disease in order to bring limitless prosperity to planet Earth.

The Clintonian criminal mind is woven throughout the White House, the Congress, the legal profession, the media, and the celebrity industry. Above-the-law/beat-the-law, golfing-partners OJ/Clinton hide their criminal minds behind sharp lawyers, automatic lying, public adulation, and wonderful-person facades. Such persons will always coldly, arrogantly rationalize themselves out of criminal acts ranging from wife batterings and WACO killings to the destruction of public safety and the economy.

The fully integrated honesty of Neo-Tech and the wide-scope accounting of the Golden Helmet combined with the coming cyber-information revolution will eliminate dishonest politicians, their harmful political-agenda laws, and their armed agents of force. ...*That Neo-Tech revolution will bring limitless prosperity to planet Earth.*

Why is total victory on Earth inevitable over the next few years? Consider the survival tool of all purposely destructive politicians and government officials. Their survival tool is the public acceptance of armed bureaucracies made possible by deception and irrationality. To perpetuate those dishonesties, the fully integrated honesty of Neo-Tech and the wide-scope accounting of the Golden Helmet must be hidden from the population by force, coercion, and fraud. Yet, every act to suppress the Neo-Tech/Golden-Helmet, including the jailing of its author and publisher, enhances public movements toward its all-revealing, depoliticization dynamic.

By shunning publicity and the media since 1981, Neo-Tech has quietly spread its political and religious subversions worldwide. Published in twelve languages, Neo-Tech is distributed in 156 countries. It is now too late to stop the Neo-Tech dynamic of fully integrated honesty and its wide-scope accountability.

Neo-Tech has been the underlying dynamic subverting destructive politics and organized religion for the past decade. Neo-Tech has been the deep-root cause of (1) collapsing totalitarian governments, such as in Eastern

Europe, (2) eroding the authority of Western religions, such as Roman Catholicism, (3) removing from office economically and socially destructive politicians, such as begun in America during its 1994 elections. In turn, that Neo-Tech dynamic is now undermining economically and socially destructive bureaucracies worldwide, including America's most-harmful armed bureaucracies such as the ATF, DEA, EPA, FDA, INS, IRS.

Independent of every quarter in today's Establishment, the Neo-Tech/Golden-Helmet dynamic quietly affected the 1994 elections and will control future elections. Moreover, that dynamic will increasingly vanish harmful politicians, including the still redeemable President Clinton[1]. Indeed, the constant undermining of harmful people by Neo-Tech will eventually eliminate *all* destructive bureaucrats, judges, and lawyers.

Through cyberspace, Golden-Helmet economies backed by nonpolitical *objective* law could be in place by 2000 AD or earlier. ...Limitless prosperity and happiness will then be available for everyone and society.

[1]Redeemable? Bill Clinton appears to have a redeemable core of innocence. By contrast, Hillary Clinton, despite her constant, hypocritical make overs, appears to be void of innocence. Ironically, President Clinton's high intelligence combined with a total lack of principles leaves him uniquely qualified to understand and then implement the Neo-Tech/Golden-Helmet dynamic. Thus, in the following way, Clinton could become the greatest, most valuable world leader in history: Before Neo-Tech and the Golden Helmet, no consistently rational principles were available in which anyone could invest. Bill Clinton, maybe out of a special integrity, never locked into or invested in bogus principles from the irrational philosophies that swirled about him and everyone else. Such a fact leaves him uniquely free for redemption — free to extricate himself from the problems, crimes, and harms of his past. How? Through the Neo-Tech/Golden-Helmet dynamic, Clinton could sweep away armed bureaucracies, political-agenda laws, and ego "justice" to boom America and the world into limitless prosperity. ...History will record if he seized that historic opportunity. Or, if he was ignominiously driven from office.

Chapter 20

The End of Chaos
$$x_n = rx(1-x)$$

The Start of Guiltless Wealth

The best-selling book *Chaos* by James Gleick (Penguin, 1988) popularized the vogue theories of chaos in nature. Yet, the universal laws of physics and nature preclude chaos throughout time, space, and existence. Still, *appearances* of chaos are everywhere in nature, especially through irregular shapes called fractals.[1] Yet, with enough knowledge, one discovers genuine chaos does not exist, save one exception. Indeed, the law of identity along with cause and effect holds everywhere, barring that one exception.

That one exception proves the rule that *conscious beings* control existence. They control existence with a system designed for eternal survival through limitless value creation. Ironically, that universal rule can be proven by its one exception — the existence of parasitical humanoids who survive by creating chaos. They survive by creating chaos in draining economies and harming societies. With facades of good intentions and compassion, those humanoids inflict cruel harm and fraud on society. Such inflictions of harm and fraud are epitomized by Clinton-type *Envynomics*. Those media-hyped economics of envy

---

[1]Nonlinear, far-from-equilibrium situations bifurcate into potentially endless fractals in any finite space. That process, in turn, self-organizes into patterns of near-perfect order reaching over potentially limitless distances. ...Thus evolves not only the cosmos and life itself but all productive work, creative thinking...and limitless knowledge.

would drain dry all productive dynamics remaining in America. Indeed, envynomics provide the only means of survival left for the expanding clique of parasitical elites and their value-destroying bureaucracies.

Throughout the vast universe, genuine chaos exists only in an unnatural anticivilization such as now dominates planet Earth. Its humanoid rulers survive through parasitisms requiring force, threat of force, and fraud. They live by criminally draining those who produce values for society. ...But, all such parasites and their unnatural anticivilization will vanish on exposure to the natural Civilization of the Universe, which is now coming to planet Earth.

Beyond that exception found in an anticivilization, no fundamental chaos exists in nature, from quarks to universes. Still, *appearances* of chaos exist everywhere. However, investigation into every such appearance reveals either a transitory illusion in nature or a purposely *productive* act by conscious beings creating higher degrees of order as explained in the coming paragraphs. ...Remember, conscious beings are the grand-unifying force and controlling dimension of existence as identified in Part I on Neo-Tech Physics and discussed in Part III on the Civilization of the Universe.

Only purposely *destructive* acts of parasitical humanoids create genuine chaos. Wars, for example, create bona fide chaos that has no connection to the conscious-controlled flow of value production throughout the universe. Still, chaos-causing humanoids and their anticivilizations, such as infesting planet Earth today, comprise only a minute, transitory part of the universe. Thus, the effect of humanoid chaos on the universe is essentially nil and undetectable, except at its tiny moment of flickering existence in time and space. By contrast, the *appearances* of chaos created by increasing values are not chaos at all. Instead, all such appearances are revealed as conscious creations of ordered values...even in Earth's anticivilization.

Look at a sleek, high-powered sports car from a little distance. One perceives beautiful symmetry and order — the antithesis of chaos. But, approach that car and throw open its engine hood — chaos! To the nonmechanic, all appears so asymmetrical and complex — a chaos of wires and tubes among a myriad of varied shapes and parts. Yet, pursue knowledge to the function and essence of that complex engine. One then perceives a supreme beauty of conscious symmetry and purposeful order.

Now, open a computer — chaos! But again, what looks like chaos — a jumble of electronics, chips, and circuitry — is actually a wondrous display of conscious-made order delivering mega values to the economy and society. Such value synergies arise from assembling widely varied components into functional designs. ...In ruling existence, conscious beings create ever increasing values that appear as chaos to the more primitive, unknowledgeable eye.

Look into the night sky. Sense the smooth, orderly-rotating universe. Now, using radio and optical telescopes combined with computers and astrophysics, throw open the curtain of the Universe for a closer look. Chaos! All looks so asymmetrical, jumbled, complex. A seemingly random scattering of all kinds of stars, galaxies, black holes, pulsars, quasars, nebulas, novas, particles, waves, rays, forces, fields, energies, and masses. Yet, on pursuing the widest knowledge and integrations, one discovers the orderly purpose in such "chaos". With that discovery on planet Earth, everyone will grasp the purpose and value of the universe as orchestrated by conscious beings with much more-advanced knowledge. Then, finally, everyone on Earth can share that same beneficial control over time, space, and existence.

In Earth's anticivilization, the more conscious beings evolve, the more chaos appears to the unknowledgeable eye and primitive mind: Consider the obvious order of building blocks comprising the ancient pyramids. Compare the ordered symmetry of those pyramids to the apparent chaos perceived by the unknowledgeable, primitive eye gazing for the first time upon the jumbled maze of Manhattan's skyline. Compare the ordered drumbeats by early African or Indian tribes to the apparent chaos filling the untrained, primitive ear listening for the first time to full-blast Wagnerian opera. Compare the easy reading of simple parables throughout the Bible to the apparent chaos meeting the unintegrated mind perusing for the first time *Zonpower* — a communiqué from beyond the stars.

Now, trace the societal values within the symmetries of ancient human achievements — from the ordered pyramids advancing to the more chaotic-appearing but astronomically valuable Stonehenge. Then advance through the ages toward the ever increasing complexities of conscious achievements — toward ever greater economic and social values. Finally, consider the combined volumes of *Neo-Tech* and *Zonpower*: Their 1100 plus pages combine the widest-scope integrations possible — from subatomic particles to the universe of universes, from eternal time to eternal mass and energy, from romantic love to non-aging longevity with ever increasing prosperity and happiness for *all* conscious beings. From that integrated combination, an epiphany appears — the epiphany for the Civilization of the Universe enveloping planet Earth by the turn of this century.

A single artist can paint or sculpt a perfect-ordered auto engine or computer circuitry in a matter of hours or days. But consider what is required to actually invent, develop, and then competitively mass-produce complex, jumbled-appearing engines or computers that deliver ever increasing values to others, the economy, and society. Such mega achievements require countless man-*years* of efforts — heroic efforts combining fully integrated honesty with brilliantly integrated efforts.

In other words, only competitive business dynamics deliver ever increasing values to all peoples, in all societies, at all times. For, those dynamics follow the preordained paths of honesty and effort required for genuine job-and-value production. Only that value production delivers prosperity and happiness to conscious life. ...Such value production often appears as increasing chaos to the more primitive mind and eye. But, the opposite is *always* the fact. For, all genuine values consist of conscious minds molding existence into ordered benefits for everyone and society.

On studying *Zonpower*, one finds a widely varied communiqué. Yet, on integration of these varied writings, *Zonpower* unveils the supreme order for *all* existence. How? By contextually interweaving the general with specifics, theory with practice, abstraction with fact, history with the contemporary...and the future. Thus evolves a spiralling synergy of many parts — a synergy that crunches millions of words and countless volumes into this single communiqué.

Zonpower reveals to citizens of Earth their most important discovery: the Civilization of the Universe. Through the condensation of such wide-scope integrations arises the Neo-Tech/Zonpower discovery. And, from that discovery will come the first-and-final product of existence: the Civilization of the Universe.

Through the Neo-Tech/Zonpower discovery, that ultimate product can now arise on planet Earth. The Civilization of the Universe will start overtaking the parasitical-elite class, perhaps as early as the 1996 elections. Indeed, the Civilization of the Universe will vanish Earth's anticivilization and free everyone from unnatural deprivations, unhappiness, and death. For, those evils were wrought by chaos producers ranging from subhuman thieves and murderers to humanoid parasitical elites and professional value destroyers. ...The Civilization of the Universe will vanish those chaos generators to bring everyone on Earth the gifts of eternal life, prosperity, and happiness — gifts that are natural to all citizens of the universe.

Universal Communication

Zon talks to every conscious being in the universe. But, with the disease of mysticism and prior to the Neo-Tech/Zonpower discovery, no one on Earth could hear Zon.

Do all conscious beings receive the eternal communications from the Civilization of the Universe? Because of mysticism and its anticivilization, no one on Earth could hear such communications. Through Gravity Units, universal communication is possible within the laws of physics and nature as identified in Parts I and III. As Parts I and III further identify, we can cue our "ears" for such communication. Then, on curing the integration-blocking disease of irrationality and mysticism, anyone and everyone on Earth can receive and eternally benefit from the Zon communication occurring throughout the Civilization of the Universe.

PART III

The Civilization of the Universe

The Solution

The Anticivilization

How long? How long?
How long must we suffocate and die
in a web of dishonesty?

Escaping Dishonesty
A four-dimensional field of dishonesty manifested as a matrix or web pervades the anticivilization. Our every thought, our every movement during every instant becomes entangled in that matrix of dishonesty.   In its omnipresent web, we *all* suffocate and die. ...With the forthcoming *Zon Protocols*, we can escape that dishonesty — escape that web of entrapment, diminishment, and death. How? By using Zonpower to quantum jump from the anticivilization and to the Civilization of the Universe.

The Civilization of the Universe
Free. Free at last. Free forever.

Chapter 21

Finding Tomorrow's Golden World

On February 13, 1991, the federal prosecutor turned to the jury and revealed the man on trial was from another world. The prosecutor told the jury that this one man was the most dangerous man. For, this one man threatened the status quo — threatened to upright this upside down world in which we live.

Did you ever feel that a better world must exist somewhere: an eternally benevolent world of honesty, integrity, rationality, peace, security...a world of limitless excitement and prosperity? Where is that other world? How do we get there? Has any explorer yet discovered that world? Does he have a map for us? Is that our world of the future?

In 1980, a scout, a pioneer, a Columbus set sail into the unknown to discover a new world. All but a handful of people thought he was going to sail off the edge of this flat, irrational society. He did not. Instead, he returned wearing a Golden Helmet. He had discovered that better world. He discovered our world of tomorrow. He discovered a world of eternal rationality, peace, and prosperity. ...He discovered the Civilization of the Universe.

On returning from his long voyage, that man was imprisoned. Why? That man as a scientist ventured beyond the known to discover the route to Shangrila. He returned with a map. And, that map shows all men and women the route to a rational world of opportunity, growth, and unimaginable riches. Once started on that route, one can no longer accept the political criminalities, social insanities, and economic destructions overtaking today's world. Thus, for bringing you the map that leads to the Civilization of the Universe, that man was imprisoned by the threatened parasitical-elite class. But, now, with his map and Zonpower, nothing can stop those on Earth from discovering that golden world of eternal prosperity and happiness...starting now!

MS

Chapter 22

Cassandra's Secret

> **13th Century BC**
> Cassandra of Troy possessed the power to predict the future with perfect accuracy. But, no one would believe her. Thus, everyone missed collecting unlimited riches.

Imagine you are speaking to an old friend. Suddenly, you realize every conversation, every action, no matter how seemingly reasonable or conventional, is geared toward losing values and happiness. Suddenly, you see this mundane, completely "normal" experience as bizarrely irrational. Then, you see nearly everyone and all society as hypnotized losers in a civilization that is insane.

Next, you realize your own children, your spouse, your own self, all who seem to live with some success and happiness, are equally trapped in an insane civilization that always moves toward loss and death. You then realize the only realm of consistent sanity and increasing values lies within value-producing professions and market-driven businesses.

Breaking the Hypnotic Spell

First, you must choose to live in either a sane civilization or an insane one. An insane civilization is one that shrinks backward into irrationality. In today's anticivilization, essentially all thinking and knowledge are hypnotically contracting into ever more narrow ranges that increasingly block honesty and understanding. Thus, communication and actions are becoming increasingly politically correct, irrational, and harmfully split from reality...increasingly schizophrenic.

Hypnotic irrationality grips Earth's anticivilization. That spreading irrationality yields a decaying system in which increasing entropy brings decreasing order and increasing strife. That, in turn, brings declining job-and-value creation. Thus, whenever irrationality prevails, time must be *redefined* as running backward toward increasing ignorance, poverty, and entropy.

With consciousness as the controlling force of existence, the arrow of time in physics is reversed and must be redefined: In an open and eternally evolving universe, time flows forward toward decreasing entropy (increasing order) as controlled by productive conscious actions, *not* toward increasing entropy (decreasing order) as controlled by nonconscious actions or destructive conscious actions.

In a naturally evolving civilization with decreasing entropy (increasing order and harmony), competitive value production constantly expands. Thus, with rationality prevailing, time runs forward toward expanding knowledge, prosperity, and *decreasing* entropy.

Various aspects of this time-and-energy flow throughout the cosmos are observationally and experimentally demonstrated by electromagnetic-plasma cosmology — a cosmology first identified by Nobel laureate Hannes Alfvén — backed by Nobel laureates de Broglie, Schrödinger, and Prigogine — then advanced by Eric J. Lerner in his popular book, *The Big Bang Never Happened* (Vantage Books, 1992).

Now comes the real discovery: You discover what

everyone on Earth fears, including yourself. You discover what *no one* on Earth wants, including yourself. You discover how anyone on Earth can become rich, powerful, happy — quickly, guiltlessly, eternally. Yet, only with great concentration and effort do you break your hypnotic paralysis enough to barely open the easy-turning spigot to limitless riches.

Something seems paradoxical or upside down about the above paragraph, especially when restated as follows: Everyone on Earth, including you, *fears and shuns* that which brings expanding riches and happiness!

On learning Cassandra's Secret, you will understand the above statement. You will view reality from wider dimensions. You will understand this anticivilization. You will see the invisible hypnotic state in which everyone on Earth loses the values of life. You will then awaken to win everything — fabulous riches and happiness while benefiting everyone and society. You will discover what Zonpower is; you will discover that Zon is you. ...Those who do not rise to understand Cassandra's Secret will remain asleep in malignant irrationality, steadily losing their lives and happiness.

You Control Reality

Cassandra's Secret vanishes irrationalities and mysticisms, ranging from the false concepts of a finite existence and the singularity big-bang creation of the universe to the evil concepts of socialized collectivism and political-agenda laws backed by ego "justice". ...Cassandra's Secret operates from two directions: (1) it vanishes destructive illusions, (2) it reveals objective reality. Now, consider the following two points:

1. *You* **can Vanish Irrationality**: From the widest-

scope knowledge possible, Cassandra's Secret interweaves the essences of science, reality, business, and human consciousness to reveal a stunningly benevolent and bountiful civilization — a civilization 180° different from the one in which we all live. That endlessly rich civilization is available now — easily available to any conscious being on Earth who realizes the impotent nothingness of *all* irrationalities, mysticisms, and insanities.

Today, the disease of irrationality infests everyone on Earth. Cassandra's Secret reveals how by stepping into the Civilization of the Universe, you cure that disease — you vanish irrationality into its nothingness.

2. *You* **are the Controlling, Fixed Center of Existence**: Human consciousness is eternal. It has always been a fixed part of existence as demonstrated in Chapter 6. Indeed, human consciousness *is* the prime mover of existence.

The above statement implies nothing mystical about consciousness. Cassandra's Secret is not at all about new-age ideas, pantheistic Eastern mysticism, or some abstract "universal consciousness". It is about the limitless power of *your own* down-to-earth consciousness. Moreover, you must understand that consciousness can never *create* reality or existence.[1] Any claim that consciousness creates reality or existence is mystical. For, any such claim contradicts the nature of both consciousness and existence. ...Existence was not created. Existence simply exists as eternally evolving fields of matter and energy. Existence *cannot not* exist.

---

[1] However, consciousness can and does control the modes of existence such as matter, energy, and spacetime geometries to evolve new modes of existence, including new universes.

Indeed, consciousness is the sole ***integrator and controller*** of existence. Thus, consciousness is the prime mover of existence. Ever wider scopes of integrations unleash the limitless power of human consciousness. By contrast, irrationalities and mysticisms are diseases of human consciousness that truncate the power to integrate reality. For, integration of reality can never move beyond any point of irrationality or mysticism. By curing irrationality comes (1) ever growing knowledge of existence, (2) ever growing control of existence, and (3) ever growing prosperity and happiness.

Newton's absolute physics, Einstein's relativistic physics, and Bohr's quantum physics are reconciled by the ever widening knowledge generated from human consciousness free of mysticisms and irrationalities. Indeed, existence is controlled to eternally provide ever wider, integrated knowledge and riches for every conscious being. In other words, your consciousness *is* the fixed center and ultimate controller of existence.

* * *

Cassandra's Secret comprises the widest-scope integration with reality to yield accurate predictions of the future. Cassandra's Secret is based on observed facts, scientific research, and direct experience combined with inductive and deductive reasoning ranging from well-demonstrated theory and objective law to reality-grounded hypotheses moving toward confirmation.

But, Cassandra's Secret is in no way dependent on recognition or approval by anyone, much less the Establishment. For, the anticivilization Establishment is irrelevant to evolving knowledge and progress. Moreover, the fully integrated honesty and wide-scope integrations of Cassandra's Secret will ultimately end all bogus livelihoods — all livelihoods arising from professional value destroyers corrupting today's political, legal, scientific, and educational systems.

The ideas revealed by Cassandra's Secret are now propagating through worldwide networks, beyond the reach of oppressive "authorities" and their gun-backed political agendas. The goals of Zon are being accomplished independent of the Establishment media and academe. The key is cheap newsprint publications in twelve languages mass distributed by low-cost, worldwide bulk mailings from many countries.

The certitude arising from Cassandra's Secret quietly spreads from Neo-Tech self-leaders to the populations throughout the world. Nothing can stop that certitude from spreading in print and through cyberspace. The revelations of Cassandra's Secret will bring honest, rational people eternal prosperity and happiness.

Chapter 23
Ultimate Wealth Lurks
within
Cassandra's Secret

Undreamt wealth can be gained by controlling the power underlying the universe: Zonpower *is* the universal symmetry that underpins Cassandra's Secret. The power of Zon controls existence at *all* scales. Zonpower delivers unlimited wealth and excitement.

Hidden beneath everyone's consciousness flows Zonpower — a mighty river of wealth creation. That power is available to you now: through Cassandra's Secret, through the supersymmetry of Zon.

Born Free

Born free of the irrationalities propagating Earth's anticivilization, all young children hold the power of Zon. They are citizens of the universe. But, quickly, every child becomes trapped in a bizarrely irrational civilization created by parasitical elites...humanoids who have lost their humanity. Those humanoids must trap and blind every child. Why? To assure the future survival of humanoids. For, they survive by parasitically draining productive adults who have been blinded since youth by illusions, deception, and force.

Trapped

This humanoid-created anticivilization blinds and then corrupts its children. This corruption is force fed into the

211

mind of every child. While unknowingly holding the power of the universe, children lack the knowledge to protect their minds. Thus, before they can learn to use their power, they are inflicted with painfully destructive illusions built on contradictions and irrationalities. Those illusions damage the minds of children and block Zonpower from their consciousness.

How have such harms corrupted everyone on Earth for the past three millennia? To live "comfortably" in this life-draining anticivilization, one must increasingly invest in the harmful illusions of the anticivilization — one must sink to a lower social dimension. From that restricted dimension, no one can discover his or her natural power.

Until now, Zonpower has remained submerged in everyone's natural consciousness. Yet, Zonpower functions in parallel but hidden ways beneath one's clouded consciousness — clouded since childhood. The resulting becloudings provided the hypnotic set up for lifetime exploitations of every value producer by the parasitical elites. Indeed, that exploitive set up is the illusion of "needing to get along in or approval from" this irrational anticivilization hypnotically conjured up by the parasitical-elite "leaders".

Cassandra's Secret breaks that hypnotic spell. Once that spell is broken, one can freely access Zonpower to control existence and predict the future to gain limitless wealth.

Leaving the World of Losers

Perhaps certain children become autistic because they will not let their minds be corrupted by the anticivilization. Perhaps they withdraw from all relationships with their environment and cease their journeys into this corrupt, unreal world. But with that withdrawal, they also cease their personal development.

In 1993, Public Broadcasting aired a documentary about an acclaimed "breakthrough" from Australia for treating autistic children by a technique called "facilitated communication". Almost the entire professional field involved in treating and caring for autistic children embraced that technique, around which they began boosting their careers. Many millions of tax dollars poured into this "breakthrough", including costly physical facilities, such as at Syracuse University, dedicated to "facilitated communication".

Yet, any objective observation of that technique, even by those unfamiliar with autism, will immediately reveal the technique as bogus. Not only does the technique lack rationality, but has no correspondence with any law of nature, science, or logic. Anyone can easily recognize the technique as nothing more than a Ouija board spelling out the subliminal thoughts of the professional therapists "treating" autistic children. This technique is not only worthless but is harmful toward those children and their families.

How could an entire field of professionals invest their lives and build their careers on something so obviously bogus and harmful to everyone? When people start investing their lives into bogus activities, they increasingly rationalize — blindly and without limits — to continue expanding their harmful investments and livelihoods.

Thus lies the mechanism through which almost everyone on Earth invests his or her life into this bogus civilization. Once that investment is made in the anticivilization, one is trapped within its all-encompassing, irrationality.

Everyone in this anticivilization starts with the mind

of an innocent, defenseless child. That mind is then tortured with painful contradictions and dishonesties until the child either becomes autistic by withdrawing from this irrational civilization or becomes "normal" by surrendering to its destructive irrationalities.

The more irrational and destructive people become, the more they will destroy and kill to maintain their harmful careers in the anticivilization. Additionally, the more people invest in destructive careers, the less competent they become in producing competitive values that genuinely benefit others and society.

Most politicians — along with many bureaucrats, lawyers, judges, and stagnant big-business executives — abolish their human nature by becoming parasites. As professional parasites, they become camouflaged criminals, even murderers, rationalizing behind shields of subjective political-agenda "law" and corrupt ego "justice". ...Consider Hitler, Mao, Castro, Pol Pot, and the Clintons. Each increasingly invested their lives into becoming clandestine parasites until they could no longer support themselves by competitively producing values for others and society. Thus, such people *must* become hidden criminals and killers to survive.

With Zonpower, you leave all such losers behind forever.

Becoming Zon

Heathcliff, the main character of Emily Bronte's novel *Wuthering Heights,* reflects the hidden, parallel consciousness that flows in every human being. Heathcliff is portrayed as the epitome of a nasty, evil man. Yet, even in him, the nature of human consciousness surfaces to reveal nobility and good. Likewise, both the heroes and villains created by the great novelist Victor Hugo reveal the underlying human power and nobility that flow independently of the meanness and irrationalities controlling this unnatural anticivilization.

The nobility and good of human character are revealed at times in everyone, except in humanoids who have destroyed their human nature. Indeed, nobility and good are revealed spontaneously, in greater or lesser degrees, throughout the life of every conscious being. Now, today, the limitless potential of one's childhood can be fulfilled through Zonpower. At the same time, anyone can tap Cassandra's Secret to emasculate and vanish the harmful consequences of this anticivilization.

Conclusion

Through Cassandra's Secret, you will break the hypnotic spell of this anticivilization. You will discover how Zonpower puffs away the harms propagated by parasitical elites. Zonpower lifts *you* toward wealth — guiltless wealth for you and society, wealth that flows from super wide-scope integrations of knowledge. In your hands, you hold the widest-scope knowledge ever unveiled on planet Earth — the knowledge of Zonpower.

From *Zonpower*, you gain an entirely new way to view yourself, your life, and all existence. You will then be poised to capture eternal life. From Zonpower, you will seize iron-grip control and a confident certitude that brings everlasting youth, riches, and romantic love.

Chapter 24

Zon Speaks

"In this anticivilization dominating planet Earth, only young children hold the power of the universe. For, they are innocent and pure: free of the irrationality disease called mysticism. During their brief mystic-free period, children live among the Civilization of the Universe. They hold the limitless yet unlearned power of the universe — Zonpower. But all children are dependent on their parents and teachers for acquiring initial knowledge. Thus, parents and teachers are responsible for infecting and debilitating the minds of their children with deadly irrationality — with the integration-blocking disease of mysticism.

The minds of such children are manipulated and twisted into grotesque dishonesties ranging from accepting parental irrationalities and mystical religions to accepting the politically correct insanities and destructive actions of harmful 'teachers', 'authorities', and 'leaders'. Thus, children are dragged into Earth's irrational, Plato-enslaved anticivilization to lose their potential for eternal growth, health, and happiness.

"Upon accepting an irrational civilization as normal, a closed bubble of mysticism forms around each child. Each such closed bubble assumes its own wobbly size and shape to accommodate the dishonesties, inner logic, and rationalizations required to live 'normally' in an irrational civilization. *In such a bubble, one can never squarely stand on reality. Therefore, one never has real strength or power. One is never anchored in objective reality, but is always trapped in illusions.* Thus, one never even glimpses his or her potential. Floating in a mystical bubble, often upside down, one can never experience the Civilization of the Universe with its limitless power and wealth.

"Today, all citizens of Earth's anticivilization live in such bubbles, floating detached from reality and the universe. Those bubbles are easily pushed around in directions that support false authorities backed by their armed agents of force. Those false authorities lack any real power to produce genuine values for themselves and others. Such parasites survive by manipulating the dishonesties of mysticism and evils of force. They learn how to maneuver or force everyone's bubble of mysticism into supporting their own destructive lives.

"Indeed, every person living in this anticivilization is trapped within his or her own bubble, never to gain eternal prosperity and happiness. Thus, everyone on Earth sooner or later stagnates and dies. By contrast, in the rational Civilization of the Universe, stagnation or death of any conscious being is the ultimate loss, the ultimate tragedy, the ultimate irrationality. ...Thus, stagnation and death never occur in the Civilization of the Universe.

"Until today, no one on Earth realized that conscious beings never need to live in an anticivilization. For, an anticivilization is unreal — created entirely from illusions and hoaxes by parasitical 'leaders'. Those false leaders live as they have for three millennia: by enforcing fraudulent political agendas in order to control and, thus, live off the value producers.

"But, today, through Neo-Tech, all value producers on planet Earth can begin to recognize the Civilization of the Universe. That recognition begins the journey into fully integrated honesty. That honesty will begin to dissolve the bubble of mysticism. When the bubble finally breaks, one lands upright, firmly planted on reality. From that solid position, one reigns over reality throughout the universe, never again threatened or manipulated by illusions. From that radiant position, one captures Zonpower with its limitless excitement and prosperity.

"The most remarkable feature about Zonpower and the Civilization of the Universe is that to become Zon and achieve limitless prosperity requires *nothing* remarkable. Zon and the Civilization of the Universe are open to all honest people, no matter what their intellectual or physical attributes.

"Once one breaks his or her bubble of mysticism, the unreal anticivilization is revealed as nothing — as a nightmare of illusions. That person then becomes a Citizen of the Universe. That person captures the limitless power of eternity. That person becomes Zon!"

Civilization of the Universe, 1993

Advancing toward Eternal Life

Five centuries ago, Copernicus posited the Earth as round, rotating around the sun, with external events commanding everyone's life and final destination. But, today, with Zonpower, *you* can command the events of life to gain soaring prosperity. Today, you can collect limitless wealth, excitement, romantic love, and life itself through Zonpower. ...As Zonpower spreads, the public will scorn out of existence dishonest politicians, parasitical elites, neocheaters, and other professional value destroyers. Zonpower will end all harmful economic and social manipulations.

No conscious being needs support from Earth's anti-civilization. No conscious being needs to live in a mystical bubble. Objective law and fully integrated honesty advance conscious beings toward the Civilization of the Universe — toward eternal life and prosperity.

Chapter 25

Are You Zon?
What Is Zonpower?

You are Chained to an Anticivilization
But Zonpower easily breaks all chains to let you capture
Boundless Wealth, Romantic Love, and Happiness

The Power of Zon

You are thunderstruck. You have discovered the source of unlimited wealth. You have discovered how to leave the boring anticivilization of planet Earth for a civilization of boundless life, excitement, wealth, and romantic love. How did you make that discovery?

Sitting before a mirror, you have just interviewed an ordinary-appearing human being. But, that person is not a citizen of this world. Although sitting before you talking as a physical being, that person is a citizen of an all-powerful civilization -- the Civilization of the Universe. With powers beyond what Earth citizens could ever imagine, that person is called Zon. To those among Earth's stagnant civilization, Zon has powers wondrous beyond description.

A UFO has landed? An alien from space? A supernatural being? Or other such mystical wonder? No, nothing mystical or supernatural. Yet, in Earth's tribalistic anticivilization, the powers of Zon seem infinitely wondrous. Still, Zon is starkly in the here and now, standing before everyone on planet Earth. For, Zon exists just as you and everyone else. ...In fact, Zon was once a citizen of Earth's anticivilization.

Part III: The Civilization of the Universe

From where did Zon come? What can and will Zon do for you? How can you gain Zon's power? Can you become Zon? Are you already Zon?

Zon was born on planet Earth. By five years of age, that child escaped Earth's anticivilization to experience the all-powerful Civilization of the Universe. During that escape, he held universal power — a power greater than held by any adult on Earth. But, not until many years later, decades later, did he rediscover that power. He then realized that every conscious child two to six years old likewise escapes Earth's anticivilization to experience the power of the universe. Yet, *every* child forgets that experience as he or she is inexorably drawn into Earth's irrational, mind-crippling anticivilization.

A rare, perhaps one-in-a-trillion combination of ordinary circumstances let an ordinary person escape Earth's anticivilization. He then returned to construct a map for all conscious people to rediscover the all-powerful Civilization of the Universe. Today, by using that map, any conscious being can vanish the illusions of this anticivilization to boom into a civilization of limitless power, wealth, and life.

Thus, today, you can finally be free of the life-destroying humanoids infesting planet Earth. Zonpower offers you the key to vanish this anticivilization beset with parasitical elites, their illusions, their hoaxes. ...Zonpower brings you into the endlessly exciting Civilization of the Universe.

The Origins of Earth's Irrational Civilization

As babies first start becoming conscious, perhaps around two years of age, they automatically become citizens of the universe with omnipotent yet unlearned and unrealized powers over all life and existence.[1] But, before they can realize those unlimited powers, all young children are relentlessly, remorselessly drawn into Earth's irrational anticivilization. This unnatural anticivilization could not evolve until man's bicameral mind invented consciousness about 3000 years ago as described in Chapter 28. With that event, man's nature-organized automatic mind jumped to a much superior, man-organized conscious mind.

About a half millennia after that jump, man's newly conscious mind became infected with irrationality, which is an integration-blocking disease analogous to the immune-blocking disease of AIDS. The result was a fatal condition known as Plato's disease. Named after its historical originator, Plato's disease breaks down rationality — the mind's defense mechanism against integration-breaking illusions. ...Without consistent rationality, such illusions allow purposeful destructions, exploitations, poverty, unhappiness, suffering, disease, envy, evil, and death itself seem a natural part of life. ...Yet, the exact opposite is the fact.

Thus, illusion-infected consciousness creates economically stupid, war-like civilizations that continuously collapse on themselves into black-hole anomalies. Irrationality is the disease that causes certain human beings to mutate into parasites or humanoids programed to harm conscious life and society. Those mutants survive by feeding off and draining value-producing human beings. That constant, parasitical drain leaves innocent people in chains — increasingly unfulfilled and eventually dead.

---

[1]Babies do not grow old; they grow toward knowledge and power. After becoming infected with irrationality, however, everyone grows old and dies.

Zon's Escape — Your Escape

How did one conscious person on planet Earth escape its unnatural anticivilization? How did that one ordinary person as an adult rediscover the rational Civilization of the Universe? How can that person deliver to you boundless power and prosperity?

In answering those questions, you too can capture Zonpower. You can have the power of Zon. You can become Zon.

Zonpower is Waiting for You

You can acquire Zonpower by going to the origin of Earth's civilization. At that origin, one discovers the exit. ...Prior to that discovery, no adult could leave this anticivilization ruled by parasitical elites and their armed agents of force.

Until the Zonpower discovery in 1992, every person on Earth was embedded in this dead-end anticivilization. Every person's thinking process was corrupted by parasitical "leaders" in government, education, journalism, entertainment, and big business. Every person's logic was undermined by illusions and hoaxes from those professional parasites. Indeed, to live off the efforts of others, all parasitical elites *must undermine logic* with look-good illusions and rip-off hoaxes. As a result, everyone on planet Earth suffers incalculable losses.

But now, today, you too can leave that anticivilization. *Immediately upon leaving, you will experience the greatest mind empowerment possible for conscious beings. You will suddenly dominate life and control the future.* Moreover, you will be among the first in history to acquire knowledge beyond this anticivilization. You will capture ever expanding knowledge from the all-powerful

Civilization of the Universe — you will capture Zonpower for unlimited life, wealth, and happiness.

By understanding the charts on pages 226 and 227, you can begin eliminating those who harm and drain your life — those who chain your life to a stake, those who keep you in a mystical bubble.

Chart 1

Vanish Purposely Harmful People (parasitical-elite value destroyers)	Uphold Naturally Beneficial People (economic value-and-job producers)
State of Being: Diseased, ridiculous, unfocused, destructive, ignoble Self-corrupted, malevolent minds; uncompetitive Degenerated their natural minds, unintegrated word spouters Metaphysically dishonest, sappy, guilty, unhappy Entropy-increasing humanoids. Penis collapsors	*State of Being:* Healthy, important, focused, productive, noble Self-made, benevolent minds; competitive Developed their natural minds, integrated thinkers Metaphysically honest, serious, innocent, happy Entropy-decreasing human beings. Penis erectors
Archetypes: Most politicians and lawyers; many bureaucrats and journalists; all business quislings, socialists, nihilists, ecoists, "reformers", armed agents of force, political entrepreneurs	*Archetypes:* Blue-collar workers, farmers, job-creating business-people, laborers, byte heads, defenders of property rights, nurses, postal workers, firemen, most soldiers, market entrepreneurs
Examples *Historical:* Plato, Alexander the Great, Julius Caesar, Caligula, Genghis Khan, Kant, Hegel, Alexander Hamilton, Napoleon, Lincoln, Woodrow Wilson, John M. Keynes, John Dewey, Lenin, Hitler, FDR, LBJ, Mao, Ayatollah Khomeini *Current:* Fidel Castro, Li Peng, Rudolph Giuliani, William Bennett, Newsweek-type journalists, purposely destructive politicians and bureaucrats, money-mad lawyers and televangelists, dishonest professors and journalists	Examples *Historical:* Thales, Socrates, Aquinas, Bruno, Galileo, Spinoza, Newton, Jefferson, Darwin, Mark Twain, Andrew Carnegie, Jay Gould, J.J. Hill, Edison, Henry Ford, Einstein, Maria Montessori, Walt Disney, Ray Kroc, Sam Walton *Current:* Jonas Salk, Steven Jobs, Soichiro Honda, Michael Milken, Dershowitz, Leona Helmsley, Bill Gates, honest writers and editors, blue-collar workers, local police-men, value-producing housewives and teachers, entrepreneurs
Survival Dynamics: Survival depends on draining values from others, armed enforcement of harmful political policies, avoiding objective law, and implementing ego "justice" to control and drain the value producers.	*Survival Dynamics:* Survival depends on producing competitive values for others and upholding objective law. The result is expanding prosperity, happiness, and justice for everyone.
Potentials: Drainers of human life, the economy, and society. Destroyers of earned property, happiness, economies, and civilization.	*Potentials:* Enhancers of human life, the economy, and society. Builders of assets, economies, and civilization.
Action Toward: Identify, dishonor, ostracize, vanish. Forget them.	*Action Toward:* Identify, honor, uphold, multiply. Remember them.
End their Current State of: Being dishonestly glorified and praised. Reject JFK's *Profiles in Courage*. They are nothing. Remove their images and names from stamps, money, monuments, streets, buildings. Replace them with honest value-and-job producers.	*End their Current State of:* Being ignored, mocked, slandered, scorned, envied, plundered, even jailed or killed. They are everything. Praise and uphold value-and-job producing business people and risk-taking entrepreneurs. They are the real heroes.

Chart 2

Discover the Power of Zon

Code: − = Economic and social harms inflicted on society
         + = Economic and social benefits produced for society

Prosperity Power
(Generated by Mega Value Producers)

Civilizations of ever growing value giants

Grow rapidly with Zonpower as contributions to economy and society soar

Production of values, benefits, and prosperity is unlimited

Everyone is a potential or growing value producer. Destructive people cannot exist

Professional value destroyers, envy, dishonesty, plunder

ZONPOWER

All-Powerful Civilization of the Universe

Nothing Power
(Hoaxed by Mega Value Destroyers)

The most destructive people rise in power to control anticivilization

The greater the value-and-job producer the more taken for granted and suppressed in power in order to be controlled and drained by the parasitical elites

Heroic value producers as Gould, Milken, and Helmsley stomped down, often to end in jail or premature death

Politicians — exemplified by Lincoln, Wilson, Hitler, Stalin, FDR, Mao, media-elected politicians — rise to ruin entire nations

Anti-Power Civilization Currently on Earth

Chapter 26
Breaking the Bubble
of
Mysticism

Neo-Tech/Zonpower cures irrationality. Curing irrationality will end the parasitical-elite class and its hoax-built anticivilization. Indeed, curing irrationality and breaking its mystical bubbles of illusions will bring everyone into the Civilization of the Universe. ...Key knowledge for breaking everyone's mystical bubble evolved from three sources: *The Neo-Tech Discovery* by Frank R. Wallace (800 pages, Neo-Tech Publishing, revised 1992), *The Origins of Consciousness* by Julian Jaynes (467 pages, Houghton Mifflin, New York, 1976), and *Objectivism: the Philosophy of Ayn Rand* by Leonard Peikoff (493 pages, Dutton, New York, 1991).

Julian Jaynes, an academe at Princeton University, avidly avoids recognizing the titanic significance of his discovery that human consciousness is man-discovered, not nature-evolved.[1] For, to protect his own personal bubble of mysticism needed to live "acceptably" in today's anticivilization, he must avoid knowing the mystic-shattering key embodied in his work. And, as did the late Ayn Rand, her protégé Leonard Peikoff, a highly productive and principled philosopher, also avoids knowing the mystic-vanishing power lying within his and Rand's work. For, he, too, must protect his mystical bubble in order to live "normally" in today's anticivilization.

As is now experienced explicitly with mystic-breaking

---

[1]Jaynes's work is reviewed in Chapter 28 of this communiqué.

Neo-Tech, Peikoff's masterwork will be experienced implicitly as a threat by everyone living "normally" in an irrational anticivilization. Thus, today, Peikoff's great work is largely ignored or minimized not only by the threatened parasitical-elite class, but by his professional peers and objectivist cohorts. And, finally, neither Jaynes nor Peikoff recognizes the achievements of the other. Thus, neither integrates their great works together: Jaynes's work reveals the origins and metaphysical nature of consciousness; Peikoff's work reveals the epistemological nature of consciousness and its philosophical consequences.

Other major value producers, such as Albert Einstein and Michael Milken, were also trapped in their own bubbles of mysticism. Thus, they never identified the widest, most important values contained in their work. For, they would rather perish than abandon their lifelong emotional and material investments in the status quo that trapped them in Earth's anticivilization. ...*Every* citizen of planet Earth exists in a self-made mystical bubble in order to live "correctly" in a loser's anticivilization.

Vanishing the Parasitical-Elite Class

What are we talking about? We are talking about a parasitical-elite class that has created an anticivilization on planet Earth. We are talking about a parasitical-elite class that after 2500 years has finally overwhelmed its host — the producers of objective values and genuine jobs...the sole providers of life and prosperity to mankind. We are talking about a malignancy of parasites who drain and destroy those value-and-job producers. We are talking about forever vanishing professional value destroyers and their anticivilization. We are talking about limitless wealth, health, and happiness available to everyone on Earth. ...We are talking about the mystic-free Civilization of the Universe enveloping planet Earth, perhaps by the year 2000.

"No, that could never happen," everyone exclaims. "Not in a generation, a century, or even a millennium."

Such an exclamation is valid within today's hoaxed anticivilization. But, anyone who steps into the Civilization of the Universe will exclaim: "Parasitical elites? An anticivilization built on force and deception? ...Everything was so irrationally destructive and boring back then. What is there to remember about such a value vacuum — such nothingness?"

Indeed, parasitical elites are pragmatic subhumans or humanoids who lack the requirements for supporting human life. They lack honest character, long-range principles, real power. They live by manipulating truth to bleed others — by undercutting objective law, societal well-being, and human happiness. They bring society only losses and suffering. Thus, all memories of those parasites and their hoaxed civilization will vanish as the Civilization of the Universe brings to Earth the excitement of boundless prosperity and happiness.

How can such certainty exist about vanishing the parasitical elites and their anticivilization? That certainty rises from new knowledge: As demonstrated in *Zonpower*, every hoax and illusion is revealed on exposure to the Civilization of the Universe. Stripped of their illusions, parasitical elites go down the memory hole in whirlpools of absurdity. Also washed away will be politicians living as destructive humanoids, bureaucrats violently enforcing harmful political agendas, judges applying ego "justice", and prosecutors ignoring objective law and justice. ...They all will vanish down the drain of public ostracism.

As the Civilization of the Universe envelops Earth, *genuine* value-and-job producers from hard-working laborers to multimillionaire entrepreneurs will assume power. This anticivilization will then end. ...What guarantees the end of this anticivilization? Relentless self-spreading Neo-Tech guarantees the end of the parasitical-elite class and its hoax-built anticivilization.

The Role of Rand and Peikoff

Amidst the pending demise of the parasitical-elite class and its anticivilization, Earth's first valid philosophy arises. That philosophy arises from two people in history who applied fully integrated honesty in developing a comprehensive philosophy: Ayn Rand and Leonard Peikoff. Ayn Rand established Objectivist philosophy, despite her tragic personal irrationalities. That philosophy evolved by overcoming the philosophical errors of Aristotle and Baruch Spinoza. Today, Objectivist philosophy combined with the limitless prosperity available from Neo-Tech disintegrates the anticivilization on planet Earth by *dis*integrating all its bogus philosophies.

Ironically, the Civilization of the Universe with its Zonpower requires no explicit philosophy. For, by nature, the only moral and practical philosophy throughout all universes and all times — Objectivist philosophy — is self-evident to everyone in the Civilization of the Universe. Indeed, valid philosophy — its metaphysics, epistemology, ethics, politics, and aesthetics — reduces to thirteen words: *What is is. Perceive it. Integrate it honestly. Act on it. Idealize it.* ...Honesty *is* free will.

Peikoff definitively grounds those thirteen words to existence. After thirty years of preparation and six years of writing and editing, he crafted Ayn Rand's philosophy of Objectivism into 180,000 words. Those words link the Civilization of the Universe to existence, throughout time. ...Dr. Peikoff provides an unmovable position that philosophically exposes the parasitical-elite class and its anticivilization.

In philosophically exposing the anticivilization, Peikoff provides a reality-linking tour from sense perception and volition to concept formation, objectivity, and reason; from the nature of man to the concepts of good, virtue, happiness, government, economics, and art. *That tour is the death knell for the grotesque anticivilization in which today every citizen of Earth lives...and upon which every Earth-bound citizen falsely feels dependent.* Indeed, everyone's comfort-zone rationalizations, livelihoods, socializings, and contemporary lifestyles are falsely dependent on a wealth-and-life-destroying anticivilization. Yet, in reality, no healthy, prosperous life is dependent on any anticivilization or on any parasitical humanoid.

How does Neo-Tech extend Jaynes's and Piekoff's works into Zonpower? Neo-Tech is fully integrated honesty applied within a dishonest anticivilization. Zonpower is the limitless power radiating from the Civilization of the Universe. Zonpower both unifies and evolves existence, radiating as unbreached, integrated honesty throughout the universe. With Neo-Tech literature seeding the world in many languages, the Civilization of the Universe will blossom to vanish Earth's anticivilization. ...Ironically, from the rising specter of uncompromised Zonpower, those people closest to Neo-Tech, even the discoverer and author of Neo-Tech, will also feel their bubble-protecting urges to shun the rise of Zonpower. For, they too will feel the threat of losing their stake in the anticivilization if their "protective" bubbles of mysticism are broken. ...On stepping into the wider social dimensions found in the Civilization of the Universe, one can use Zonpower to vanish all connections with the anticivilization.

Limitless Success Guaranteed

With Jaynes's and Peikoff's masterworks, the Neo-Tech/Zonpower dynamics guarantee the disappearance of Earth's anticivilization. Indeed, today, with Zonpower, any citizen of Earth can step into the Civilization of the Universe and vanish Earth's anticivilization. ...In the Civilization of the Universe, every conscious being is guaranteed limitless prosperity and happiness — limitless success.

The Government and Religion of the Universe

Philosophy with its ivory-tower approach is incomprehensible to most people. By contrast, government and religion provide the behaviors, laws, and values understandable to general populations. *Rational* government and *rational* religion, therefore, benefit society.

In an anticivilization, destructive governments and irrational religions grow from Earth-bound "authorities" manipulating truths based on illusions and faith. Thus, harmful behaviors and subjective laws evolve. A parasitical-elite class backed by force can then rise by draining the value producers. Stagnation of conscious life results. By contrast, the government and religion of the universe grow from rational consciousness. Humanoid parasites cannot rise or even exist in the rational Civilization of the Universe. Thus, an unlimited flourishing of conscious life results.

Zon is the unbreached honesty of the universe. Zon is the honesty within each conscious being. But, mysticism profanes honesty. Those who hold the honesty of Zon above the dishonesty of mysticism become all-powerful. Those who use the power of Zon to end the destructiveness of Earth's anticivilization secure themselves among the stars.

Part II of *Zonpower* identifies the problem: Earth's irrational anticivilization. Part II shows how Neo-Tech lets one live free and incorruptible within Earth's unfree, corrupt anticivilization. Part III of *Zonpower* shows how the universal government and religion of Zon let one become a Citizen of the Universe to live free of the anticivilization — to live forever with unbounded prosperity and happiness protected by the Constitution of the Universe shown on page 188.

The Discovery of Zon

Zon is the essence of fully integrated honesty. Zon is the giver of boundless prosperity to conscious beings throughout the universe. Zon is beyond God and heaven. ...Zon *is* the eternal government, religion, and paradise of the universe.

Thirty years ago, Frank R. Wallace discovered fully integrated honesty, later called Neo-Tech. He then abandoned all Earth-bound ideas of government and God formulated through manipulated truths and mystical faith. In 1972, Dr. Wallace resigned his position as Senior Research Chemist at E.I. duPont de Nemours & Company with the goal of bringing the limitless benefits of Neo-Tech to everyone on Earth. Twenty years later, *The Neo-Tech Discovery* is published in twelve languages and distributed worldwide — in 156 countries.

From the indelible foundation of Neo-Tech, the world advances toward fully integrated honesty — toward Zon, the rational government and religion of the universe. ...Through Zon, conscious beings achieve eternal life, prosperity, and happiness.

Today, Zon rises on planet Earth midst the pillagings, jailings, and deprivations inflicted upon the few remaining value-and-job producing giants. Zon rises midst the economic destructions by a burgeoning parasitical-elite class: Morally corrupt politicians, bureaucrats, and judges are circling to silence the government and religion of the universe. They must silence fully integrated honesty to continue their unearned livelihoods. They must continue toward their final feeding frenzy in devouring the world's economies. To survive, they must break Zon with its all-exposing, wide-scope accounting. But, they cannot silence the unsilenceable. They cannot break the unbreakable. ...Professional value destroyers cannot survive in the presence of Zon and the Civilization of the Universe. In America, the wake-up call for their demise came in the elections of November, 1994.

Through Zon, strength and knowledge come from each infliction by parasitical elites and their political-policy enforcers. Their guns, thefts, and prisons have no power. Exposed by wide-scope accountability, their every harmful act not only advances their own demise, but advances all value producers toward the Civilization of the Universe.

Compassion Rules the Universe

Who really helps the needy: the elderly, the handicapped, the oppressed, the sick, the helpless? Who really protects the disadvantaged, the consumer, the environment, the innocent animals? Who really provides the rational needs of everyone at ever lower costs? No, not those people who effusively try to convince themselves and others how much care and compassion they have for the disadvantaged, animals, and the environment. They are compassion hoaxers. For, they function by irrationally demanding *others* be forced into providing for the needy and protecting the environment.

Those compassion hoaxers do not function through benevolence and good will. They function through parasitical force and malevolent destruction. Be they politicians, journalists, judges, professors, advocates, or entertainers, they all hypocritically feign good intentions to conceal agendas of unearned livelihoods, power, esteem.

How much can one trust a president or anyone who must implore his victims to "trust" him? And how good are the intentions of politicians, news journalists, judges, or clergy who must constantly try to convince themselves and others of their good intentions and compassion, especially toward their ultimate victims, such as minorities, the poor, the disadvantaged, innocent animals, and the environment?

By contrast, the genuinely honest, trustworthy, and good-intentioned person *never* needs to publicly prove that he or she is honest, trustworthy, good-intentioned, compassionate. In fact, the more genuinely good-intentioned and compassionate one really is, the less that person is aware of being good-intentioned or compassionate.

Essentially every parasitical elite and professional value destroyer is consumed with guilt over his or her self-made, destructive nature. Each lives by what others think rather than by the facts of reality. Thus, each squirms behind hoaxes of good intentions and compassion. Within each such hoaxer exists an agenda of vilifying, draining, and destroying genuine value-and-job producers from GM truck manufactures to apple growers. ...Dishonest compassion hoaxers at the end of Earth's anticivilization era include people like Bill and Hillary Clinton, Pope John Paul, Jane Pauley, NBC news producers, Meryl Streep. And, perhaps the worst people: religious demagogs seeking political power such as Pat Buchanan, Pat Robertson, and Bill Bennett[1]. ...Zon vanishes those *souls of malevolence*.

Remember, Zon is fully integrated honesty: the widest integrations of reality throughout the universe. Those who produce genuine jobs for others and competitive values for society have authentic power and benevolence. Those who have earned that power have the greatest good intentions and compassion toward others. Thus, through Zon, those with authentic power — those *souls of benevolence* — reign supreme among the stars, eternally delivering genuine compassion and prosperity to all citizens of the universe.

---

[2]William J. Bennett's best-selling *Book of Virtues* (Simon & Schuster, 1993) is a full-blown example of camouflaging evil with illusions of virtue. Close examination of Bennett's book of "virtues" reveals a maudlin collection of non sequiturs that mostly contradict mankind's only two objective virtues: (1) fully integrated honesty and (2) producing competitive values for others and society. William Bennett is nothing more than a totalitarian theocrat who advocates, for example, public beheadings of those who violate political-agenda laws involving drugs.

Chapter 27
Rise from Your Knees

Until now, all governments and religions grew from dishonest mysticisms...from Earth-bound "authorities", force, and fraud. Until now, all governments and religions worked to break human beings of their natural self-confidence, creativity, happiness, pride, courage, and honesty. But, today, Zon makes the clean sweep sought by Nietzsche a century ago. Zon frees everyone on Earth. Through Zon, any conscious being can unite with the Civilization of the Universe to gain its unlimited power — Zonpower. *Unlike* Nietzsche's strong-rule-the-weak ideas, Zon allows *every* man and woman on this planet to become an "overman"; a super-man ruled by no one, a genius regardless of IQ or race. Zon brings dignity with boundless excitement, wealth, and romantic love to every conscious being throughout the universe. ...Rise from your knees. Zon vanishes all mystical "Gods". Zon lives eternally. Zon is *you*!

Guiltless Riches Through Zon

Energy and matter are one and the same as identified by Einstein. Energy (E) can become matter; and matter (M) can become energy: $E=Mc^2$. Likewise, thought and things are one and the same as identified by Spinoza. Nonmystical thoughts (T1) can become all things throughout the universe; and all things (T2) throughout the universe can become nonmystical thoughts: $T1=T2k$, where k is the universal constant of Zon. Also, the Di Silvestro equation: $T1(I°+E°)=vT2(k)$ in which I° is the degree of intent and $E°$ is the degree of effort behind the thought. $I°$ and $E°$ affect v or the velocity of converting T1 to T2, with T2 being the thought converted to reality. ...Thus flows the power of Zon.

Consider this: Can empty space or vacuums really exist? Or does existence always exist — *everywhere*? Is *all* space filled with an ether of existence — filled with quantized Gravity Units, each so dense with the weightless geometry of existence yet so tiny with near-surfaceless, seemingly infinite curvature that neither gravity nor detection of mass or energy can enter or exit? If so, do endless universes exist above and below each Gravity Unit, hiding as pure symmetry beneath every point in existence? ...Regardless of the ultimate answers to those questions, wealth and happiness evolve eternally for every citizen of the universe. Thus, today, citizens of Earth can use Zonpower to capture limitless prosperity and guiltless riches.

Chapter 28
Infinite Power
from
Conscious Dynamics

(From a 1980 article by Frank R. Wallace)

A person could make an excellent bet by wagering a hundred ounces of gold that Julian Jaynes's book, *The Origin of Consciousness in the Breakdown of the Bicameral Mind* (Houghton Mifflin, 1976) will rank among the five most important books ever written by the year 2000. ...Jaynes's book signals the end of a 10,000-year reign of authoritarian institutions. His book also marks the beginning of a new era of individual consciousness during which people will increasingly act on the authority of their own brains. That movement toward self-responsibility will increasingly weaken the influences of external or mystical "authorities" such as government and religion.

The discovery of the bicameral mind solves the missing-link problem that has defied all previous theories of human evolution. But more important, that discovery is generating a new field of knowledge called Neothink with which all human life can evolve into abiding prosperity and happiness through powerfully competitive Neo-Tech advantages.

Dr. Jaynes discovered that until 3000 years ago essentially all human beings were void of consciousness. Man along with all other primates functioned by mimicked or learned reactions. But, because of his much larger, more complex brain, man was able to develop a coherent language beginning about 8000 B.C. He was then guided by audio hallucinations. Those hallucinations evolved in the right hemisphere of the brain and were "heard" as communications or instructions in the left hemisphere of the brain (the bicameral or two-chamber mind). ...In effect, human beings were super-intelligent but automatically reacting animals who could communicate by talking. That communication enabled human beings to cooperate closely to build societies, even thriving civilizations.

Still, like all other animals, man functioned almost entirely by an automatic guidance system that was void of consciousness — until about 1000 B.C. when he was forced to invent consciousness to survive in the collapsing bicameral civilizations. ...Today, man's survival still depends on his choice of beneficially following his own consciousness or destructively following the voices of external "authorities".

The major components of Jaynes's discovery are:

- All civilizations before 1000 B.C. — such as Assyria, Babylonia, Mesopotamia, pharaonic Egypt — were built, inhabited, and ruled by nonconscious people.

- Ancient writings such as the *Iliad* and the early books of the Old Testament were composed by nonconscious minds that automatically recorded and objectively reported both real and imagined events. The transition to subjective and introspective writings of the conscious mind occurred in later works such as the *Odyssey* and the newer books of the Old Testament.

- Ancient people learned to speak, read, write, as well as carry out daily life, work, and the professions all while remaining nonconscious throughout their lives. Being nonconscious, they never experienced guilt, never practiced deceit, and were not responsible for their actions. They, like any other animal, had no concept of guilt, deception, evil, justice, philosophy, history, or the future. They could not introspect and

had no internal idea of themselves. They had no subjective sense of time or space and had no memories
as we know them. They were nonconscious and
innocent. They were guided by "voices" or strong
impressions in their bicameral minds — nonconscious
minds structured for nature's automatic survival.

- The development of human consciousness began about
  3000 years ago when the automatic bicameral mind
  began breaking down under the mounting stresses of
  its inadequacy to find workable solutions in
  increasingly complex societies. The hallucinated
  voices became more and more confused,
  contradictory, and destructive.

- Man was forced to invent and develop consciousness
  in order to survive as his hallucinating voices no
  longer provided adequate guidance for survival.

- Today, after 3000 years, most people retain remnants
  of the bicameral guidance system in the form of
  mysticism and the desire for external authority.

- Except for schizophrenics, people today no longer
  hallucinate the voices that guided bicameral man.
  Yet, most people are at least partly influenced and
  are sometimes driven by the remnants of the
  bicameral mind as they seek, to varying degrees,
  automatic guidance from the mystical "voices" of
  others — from the commanding voices of false
  external "authorities".

- Religions and governments are rooted in the
  nonconscious bicameral mind that is obedient to the
  "voices" of external "authorities" — obedient to the
  voice of "God", gods, rulers, and leaders.

- The discovery that consciousness was never a part of
  nature's evolutionary scheme (but was invented by

man) eliminates the missing-link in human evolution.

• Essentially all religious and most political ideas today survive through those vestiges of the obsolete bicameral mind. The bicameral mind seeks omniscient truth and automatic guidance from external "authorities" such as political or spiritual leaders — or other "authoritarian" sources such as manifested in idols, astrologers, gurus. Likewise, politicians, lawyers, psychiatrists, psychologists, professors, doctors, journalists and TV anchormen become "authoritarian voices".

The idea of civilizations consisting entirely of nonconscious, yet highly intelligent, automatic-reacting people and the idea of man bypassing nature to invent his own consciousness initially seems incredible. But as Jaynes documents his evidence in a reasoned and detached manner, the existence of two minds in all human beings becomes increasingly evident: (1) the obsolete, nonconscious (bicameral) mind that seeks guidance from external "authorities" for important thoughts and decisions, especially under stressed or difficult conditions; and (2) the newly invented conscious mind that bypasses external "authorities" and provides thoughts and guidance generated from one's own mind. ...Understanding Jaynes's discoveries unlocks the 10,000 year-old secret of controlling the actions of people through their mystical or bicameral minds.

What evidence does Jaynes present to support his discoveries? After defining consciousness, he systematically presents his evidence to prove that man was not conscious until 3000 years ago when the bicameral civilizations collapsed and individuals began inventing consciousness in order to survive. Jaynes's proof begins with the definition of consciousness:

Infinite Power from Conscious Dynamics

Defining and Understanding Consciousness

Julian Jaynes defines both what consciousness is and what it is not. After speculating on its location, he demonstrates that consciousness itself has no physical location, but rather is a particular organization of the mind and a specific way of using the brain. Jaynes then demonstrates that consciousness is only a small part of mental activity and is not necessary for concept formation, learning, thinking, or even reasoning. He illustrates how all those mental functions can be performed automatically, intelligently, but unconsciously. Furthermore, consciousness does not contribute to and often hinders the execution of learned skills such as speaking, listening, writing, reading —as well as skills involving music, art, and athletics. Thus, if major human actions and skills can function automatically and without consciousness, those same actions and skills can be controlled or driven by external influences, "authorities", or "voices" emanating under conditions described later. ...But first an understanding of consciousness is important:

Consciousness requires metaphors (i.e., referring to one thing in order to better understand or describe another thing — such as the head of an army, the head of a household, the head of a nail). Consciousness also requires analog models, (i.e., thinking of a map of California, for example, in order to visualize the entire, physical state of California). Thinking in metaphors and analog models creates the mind space and mental flexibility needed to bypass the automatic, bicameral processes.[1]

The *bicameral thinking* process functions only in

---

[1]Metaphors and analog models bring the right hemisphere brain functions to the left hemisphere with a much broader, wide-scope view which enables ever more powerful conceptual thinking.

concrete terms and narrow, here-and-now specifics. But the *conscious thinking* process generates an infinite array of subjective perceptions that permit ever broader understandings and better decisions.

Metaphors of "me" and analog models of "I" allow consciousness to function through introspection and self-visualization. In turn, consciousness expands by creating more and more metaphors and analog models. That expanding consciousness allows a person to "see" and understand the relationship between himself and the world with increasing accuracy and clarity.

Consciousness is a conceptual, metaphor-generated analog world that parallels the actual world. Man, therefore, could not invent consciousness until he developed a language sophisticated enough to produce metaphors and analog models.

The genus Homo began about two million years ago. Rudimentary oral languages developed from 70,000 B.C. to about 8000 B.C. Written languages began about 3000 B.C. and gradually developed into syntactical structures capable of generating metaphors and analog models. Only at that point could man invent and experience consciousness.

Jaynes shows that man's early writings (hieroglyphics, hiertatic, and cuneiform) reflect a mentality totally different from our own. They reflect a nonmetaphoric, nonconscious mentality. Jaynes also shows that the *Iliad*, which evolved as a sung poem about 1000 B.C., contains little if any conscious thought. The characters in the Iliad (e.g., Achilles, Agamemnon, Hector, Helen) act unconsciously in initiating all their major actions and decisions through "voices", and all speak in hexameter rhythms (as often do modern-day schizophrenics when hallucinating). Hexameter rhythms are characteristic of the rhythmically automatic functionings of the right-hemisphere brain. Moreover, the *Iliad* is entirely about action...about the acts and consequences of Achilles. The *Iliad* never mentions subjective thoughts or the contents of anyone's mind. The language is nonconscious — an objective reporting of facts that are concrete bound and void of introspection and abstract thought.

With a conscious mind, man can introspect; he can debate with himself; he can become his own god, voice, and decision maker. But before the invention of consciousness, the mind functioned bicamerally: the right hemisphere (the poetic, god-brain) hallucinated audio instructions to the left hemisphere (the analytical, man-brain), especially in unusual or stressful situations. Essentially, man's brain today is physically identical to the ancient bicameral brain; but with his discovery or more precisely his *invention* of consciousness, he can now choose to integrate the functions of the left and right hemispheres.

Beginning about 9000 B.C. — as oral languages developed — routine or habitual tasks became increasingly standardized. The hallucinating voices for performing those basic tasks, therefore, became increasingly similar among groups of people. The collectivization of "voices" allowed more and more people to cooperate and function together through their bicameral minds. The leaders spoke to the "gods" and used the "voices" to lead the masses in cooperative unison. That cooperation allowed nomadic hunting tribes to gradually organize into stationary, food-producing societies. The continuing development of oral language and the increasing collectivization of bicameral minds allowed towns and eventually cities to form and flourish.

The bicameral mind, however, became increasingly inadequate for guiding human actions as societies continued to grow in size and complexity. By about 1000 B.C., the bicameral mind had become so inadequate that man's social structures began collapsing. Under threat of extinction, man invented a new way to use his brain that allowed him to solve the much more complex problems needed to survive — he invented a new organization of the mind called consciousness.

Jaynes eliminated the missing link in the evolution of man by discovering that consciousness never existed in the evolutionary processes — consciousness was invented by man.

The Development of Consciousness

Dr. Jaynes shows through abundant archaeological, historical, and biological evidence that the towns, cities, and societies from 9000 B.C. to 1000 B.C. were established and developed by nonconscious people. Those societies formed and grew through common hallucinating voices attributed to gods, rulers, and the dead — to external "authorities". Various external symbols that "spoke" (such as graves, idols, and statues) helped to reinforce and expand the authority of those common "voices". Such "voices" continued to expand their reach through increasingly visible and awe-inspiring symbols such as tombs, temples, colossuses, and pyramids.

But as those unconscious societies became more complex and increasingly intermingled through trade and wars, the "voices" became mixed and contradictory. With the "voices" becoming muddled, their effectiveness in guiding people diminished. Rituals and importunings became ever more intense and elaborate in attempts to evoke clearer "voices" and better guidance. The development of writing and the permanent recording of instructions and laws during the second millennium B.C. further weakened the authority and effectiveness of hallucinated voices. As the "voices" lost their effectiveness, they began falling silent. And without authoritarian "voices" to guide and control its people, those societies suddenly began collapsing with no external cause.

As the bicameral mind broke down and societies collapsed, individuals one by one began inventing consciousness to make decisions needed to survive in the mounting anarchy and chaos. On making conscious and volitional decisions, man for the first time became responsible for his actions. Also, for short-range advantages and easy power, conscious man began discovering and using deceit and treachery — behaviors not possible from nonconscious, bicameral minds. ...Before inventing consciousness, man was as guiltless and amoral as any other animal since he had no volitional choice in following his automatic guidance system of hallucinated voices.

As the "voices" fell silent, man began contriving religions and prayers in his attempts to communicate with the departed gods. Jaynes shows how man developed the concept of worship, heaven, angels, demons, exorcism, sacrifice, divination, omens, sortilege, augury in his attempts to evoke guidance from the gods — from external "authorities".

All such quests for external "authority" hark back to the breakdown of the hallucinating bicameral mind — to the silencing and celestialization of the once "vocal" and earthly gods.

Much direct evidence for the breakdown of the

bicameral mind and the development of consciousness comes from writings scribed between 1300 B.C. and 300 B.C. Those writings gradually shift from nonconscious, objective reports to conscious, subjective expressions that reflect introspection. The jump from the nonconscious writing of the *Iliad* to the conscious writing of the *Odyssey* (composed perhaps a century later) is dramatically obvious. In the *Odyssey*, unlike the *Iliad*, characters possess conscious self-awareness, introspection powers, and can sense right, wrong, and guilt. ...That radical difference between the *Iliad* and the *Odyssey* is, incidentally, further evidence that more than one poet composed the Homeric epics.

The transition from the nonconscious *Iliad* to the conscious *Odyssey* marks man's break with his 8000-year-old hallucinatory guidance system. By the sixth century B.C., written languages began reflecting conscious ideas of morality and justice similar to those reflected today.

The Old Testament of the Bible also illustrates the transition from the nonconscious writing of its earlier books (such as Amos, circa 750 B.C.) to the fully conscious writing of its later books (such as Ecclesiastes, circa 350 B.C.). Amid that transition, the book of Samuel records the first known suicide — an act that requires consciousness. And the book of Deuteronomy illustrates the conflict between the bicameral mind and the conscious mind.

Likewise, the transition to consciousness is observed in other parts of the world: Chinese literature moved from bicameral nonconsciousness to subjective consciousness about 500 B.C. with the writings of Confucius. And in India, literature shifted to subjective consciousness around 400 B.C. with the Upanishadic writings.

American Indians, however, never developed the sophisticated, metaphorical languages needed to develop full consciousness. As a result, their mentalities were probably bicameral when they first encountered the European explorers. For example, with little or no conscious resistance, the Incas allowed the Spanish "white gods" to dominate, plunder, and slaughter them.

The Bicameral Mind in Today's World

Dr. Jaynes identifies many vestiges of the bicameral mentality that exist today. The most obvious vestige is religion and its symbols. Ironically, early Christianity with its teachings of Jesus was an attempt to shift religion from the outmoded bicameral and celestial mind of Moses to the newly conscious and earthly mind of man. Christianity then discovered a devastatingly effective tool for authoritarian control — guilt. Indeed, guilt not only worked on conscious minds, but required conscious minds to be effective.

Despite religion, conscious minds caused the gradual shifts from governments of gods to governments of men and from divine laws to secular laws. Still, the vestiges of the bicameral mind combined with man's longing for guidance produced churches, prophets, oracles, sibyls, diviners, cults, mediums, astrologers, saints, idols, demons, tarot cards, seances, Ouija boards, glossolalia, fuhrers, ayatollahs, popes, peyote, Jonestown, born-agains.

Jaynes shows how such external "authorities" exist only through the remnants of the bicameral mind. Moreover, he reveals a four-step paradigm that can reshuffle susceptible minds back into hallucinating, bicameral mentalities. The ancient Greeks used a similar paradigm to reorganize or reprogram the minds of uneducated peasant girls into totally bicameral mentalities so they could become oracles and give advice through hallucinated voices — voices that would rule the world (e.g., the oracle at Delphi). ...Today, people who deteriorate into schizophrenic psychoses follow similar paradigms.

A common thread united most oracles, sibyls, prophets, and demon-possessed people: Almost all were illiterate, all believed in spirits, and all could readily retrieve the bicameral mind. Today, however, retrieval of the bicameral mind is schizophrenic insanity. Also, today, as throughout history, a symptomatic cure for "demon-possessed" people involves exorcising rituals that let a more powerful "authority" or god replace the "authority" of the demon. The New Testament, for example, shows that Jesus and his disciples became effective exorcists by substituting one "authority" (their god) for another "authority" (another god or demon).

As the voices of the oracles became confused and nonsensical, their popularity waned. In their places, idolatry revived and then flourished. But as Christianity became a popular source of external "authority", Christian zealots began physically destroying all competing idols. They then built their own idols and symbols to reinforce the external "authority" of Christianity.

Among today's vestiges of the bicameral mentality is the born-again movement that seeks external guidance. In that movement, people surrender their self-choice and self-decision making in exchange for false promises of protection and guidance. Such vestiges dramatize man's resistance to use his own invention of consciousness to guide his life.

The chanting cadence of poetry and the rhythmic beat of music are also rooted in the bicameral mentality. In ancient writings, the hallucinated voices of the gods were always in poetic verse, usually in dactylic hexameter and sometimes in rhyme or alliteration — all characteristic of right-brain functionings. The oracles and prophets also spoke in verse. And today schizophrenics often speak in verse when they hallucinate.

Poetry and chants can have authoritarian or commanding beats and rhythms that can effectively block consciousness. Poetry is the language of the gods — it is the language of the artistic, right-hemispheric brain. Plato recognized poetry as a divine madness.

Most poetry and songs have an abruptly changing or a discontinuous pitch. Normal speech, on the other hand, has a smoothly changing pitch. Jaynes demonstrates that reciting poetry, singing, and playing music are right-brain functions, while speaking is a left-brain function. That is why people with speech impediments can often sing, chant, or recite poetry with flawless clarity. Conversely, almost anyone trying to sing a conversation will find his words quickly deteriorating into a mass of inarticulate cliches.

Likewise, listening to music and poetry is a right-brain function. And music, poetry, or chants that project authority with loud or rhythmic beats can suppress left-brain functions to temporarily relieve anxiety or a painfully troubled consciousness.

Jaynes goes on to show phenomena such as hypnosis, acupuncture, and déjà vu also function through vestiges of the bicameral mind. And he demonstrates how hypnosis steadily narrows the sense of self, time, space, and introspection as consciousness shrinks and the mind reverts to a bicameral type organization. Analogously, bicameral and schizophrenic minds have little or no sense of self, time, space or introspection. The hypnotized mind is urged to obey the voice of the hypnotist; the bicameral mind is compelled to obey the "voices" of "authority" or gods. By sensing oneself functioning in the narrow-scope, unaware state of hypnosis, gives one an idea of functioning in the narrow-scope, unaware state of bicameral man.

Jaynes also identifies how modern quests for external "authority" are linked to the bicameral mind. Many such quests use science to seek authority in the laws of nature. In fact, today, science is surpassing the waning institutional religions as a major source of external "authority". And rising from the vestiges of the bicameral mind are an array of scientisms (pseudoscientific doctrines, faiths, and cults) that select various natural or scientific facts to subvert into apocryphal, authoritarian doctrines. That subversion is accomplished by using facts out of context to fit promulgated beliefs. Such mystical scientisms include astrology, ESP, Scientology, Christian Science and other "science" churches, I Ching, behaviorism, sensitivity training, mind control, meditation, hypnotism, as well as specious nutritional, health, and medical fads.

Today the major worldwide sources of external "authority" are the philosophical doctrines of religion (along with the other forms of mysticism and "metaphysics") combined with political doctrines such as Socialism, Fascism, and Marxism. All such doctrines demand the surrender of the individual's ego (sense of self or "I") to a collective, obedient faith toward the "authority" of those doctrines. In return, those doctrines offer automatic answers and lifetime guidance from which faithful followers can survive without the responsibility or effort of using their own conscious minds. Thus, all current political systems represent a regression into mysticism — from conscious man back to bicameral man.

Despite their constant harm to everyone, most modern-day external "authorities" and master neocheaters thrive by using the following two-step neocheating technique to repress consciousness and activate the bicameral mind in their victims.

1. First man is made to feel guilty. He is condemned for having lost his "innocence" by inventing consciousness. He is condemned for assuming the responsibility to use his own mind to guide his life. He is condemned for exchanging his automatic, bicameral life for a volitional, conscious life...condemned for exchanging his nature-given bicameral mind for a superior, man-invented conscious mind.

2. Then man is offered automatic solutions to problems and guidance through life — is offered an "effortless" Garden of Eden or a utopian hereafter if he exchanges his own invented consciousness for faith in external "authority": bicameral faith in some leader, doctrine, or god. He is offered the "reward" of protection and the escape from the self-responsibility of making one's own decisions to guide one's own life. But for that "reward", he must renounce his own mind to follow someone else's mind or wishes disguised as "truths" promulgated by some external "authority" or higher power.

But in reality, no valid external "authority" or higher power can exist or ever has existed. Valid authority evolves only from one's own independent, conscious mode of thinking. When that fact is fully realized, man will emerge completely from his bicameral past and move into a future that accepts individual consciousness as the only authority. ...Man will then fully evolve into a prosperous, happy individual who has assumed full responsibility for his own thinking and life.

Still, the resistance to self-responsibility is formidable. The bicameral mentality grips those seeking mysticism or other "authorities" for guidance. Those who accept external "authority" allow government officials, religious leaders, environmental and anti-abortion movements, faith, homilies, cliches, one-liners, slogans, the familiar, habits, and feelings to automatically guide their actions. The *Neo-Tech Discovery* demonstrates how throughout history billions of people because of their bicameral tendencies unnecessarily submit to the illusionary external "authorities" of parasitical Establishments, governments, and religions. Such submission is always done at a net loss to everyone's well being and happiness.

The Implications of Neo-Tech

To some, the implications of Neo-Tech (fully integrated honesty) are frightening, even terrifying. To others, the implications are electrifying and liberating. ...The implications of Neo-Tech are that each individual is solely responsible for his or her own life — responsible for making the efforts required for learning how to honestly guide one's own life toward growing prosperity and happiness. No automatic, effortless route to knowledge or guidance exists.

No valid external "authority" exists that one can automatically live by. To live effectively, an individual must let only the authority of his own consciousness guide his activities. All consistently competent people have learned to act on reality — not on their feelings or someone else's feelings or doctrines. An individual must accept the responsibility to guide his or her own life in order to live competently, successfully, happily.

Chapter 29
The Rise and Fall
of the
Anticivilization

Earth's anticivilization is characterized by humanoids with criminal minds controlling value-producing human beings. For 3000 years, such humanoids survived through hidden agendas designed to usurp the wealth created by the productive class. Those hidden criminals are responsible for all wars, slave-master relationships, mass thefts, purposeful property destructions, terrorisms, genocide.

Neocheaters: The Hidden Criminals

Two classes of criminals exist: (1) The less-dangerous *subhuman* class consisting of people, who with blatant criminal minds, openly rob, injure, and murder human beings. Such subhumans are generally scorned by society and are usually jailed for their crimes through objective laws and valid justice. (2) The most-dangerous *humanoid* class consisting of people, who with ingeniously hidden criminal minds, covertly rob, injure, and destroy entire economies, entire populations, entire nations, entire civilizations. Such humanoids are camouflaged criminals who survive by destructive deceptions used to gain bogus livelihoods, respect, even adulation from their duped human victims. Such criminals are usually praised by the parasitical Establishment and seldom held responsible for their crimes.

The subhuman class of criminals sporadically commit crimes against various individuals. The humanoid class

257

of criminals daily, continuously commit crimes against everyone and society through their destructive careers.

The anticivilization is created by the parasitical-elite class and its legions of professional value destroyers. They exist by manipulating the disease of irrationality. Such career criminals deceive and plunder populations through subjective laws, harmful regulations, and dishonest ego "justice".

Cambodia's Pol Pot to FDA's Dr. Kessler

Neocheaters comprise destructive politicians, corrupt lawyers, and killer bureaucrats who exist through the criminal use of government force implemented through political-agenda laws, gun-backed regulations, and ego-determined "justice". Some of the more prominent neo-cheaters in today's anticivilization include genocide-champion Pol Pot, mass-killer FDA commissioner Dr. David Kessler, envy-demagog Hillary Clinton, Tiananmen-Square murderer Li Peng, job-killer Interior Secretary Bruce Babbitt, child-abuser/killer (Fijnje/Waco) Janet Reno, and Russia's rising star of evil Vladimir Zhirinovsky. ...In what way are all such neocheaters mass killers? Wide-scope accounting demonstrates that for every life humanoids purport to benefit, they are responsible for killing several, often dozens, even hundreds or thousands of innocent people directly through guns and political prisons or indirectly through draining economies and destroying assets as documented in the *Neo-Tech Protection Kit*, volume II, 1994 edition.

Homer to Plato

How did this criminal-mind disease bring about the anticivilization on planet Earth? And, why does this disease continue to ravage the populations of planet Earth? As identified previously, the philosophical father of the parasitical-elite class and totalitarian governments is Plato. His neocheating masterpiece was *The Republic* written nearly 2400 years ago. But, the foundations were laid 400 years earlier with two of the three primary epics of Western literature — the *Iliad* and the *Odyssey*.

The Iliad's hero, the nonconscious amoral Achilles, and the Odyssey's hero, the conscious immoral Odysseus, were in essence nothing more than wildly irrational killers with no sense of honesty or justice. The nature of all glory-seeking criminal minds is summed up in the character of Odysseus, especially as he returns home after a decade of "glorious" battles and "heroic" adventures. The great bully Odysseus simply plunders and butchers the innocent populations of defenseless coastal towns whenever he and his cohorts want to feel big and powerful — whenever they want to plunder the value producers, rape them, kill them, have a good time.

Such characters are not human beings, but are humanoids with no concept of honesty, human values, or objective justice. They are criminals who pretend worthiness through fake glories, destructive heroics, and evil ego "justice". All their boastfully paraded "heroics", "courage", and "glory" are nothing more than masks for criminal acts and parasitical cowardice. ...All such humanoids are simply plunderers and killers, *nothing more*, no matter what "heroics" they stage. Indeed, that was the blind-poet Homer's intended message. For, Homer grants no hint of virtuous good-versus-evil struggles by those "heroes".

Yet, 400 years later, the politician-philosopher Plato turned Homer's message upside down. As identified in the *Neo-Tech Discovery*, Plato ingeniously constructed an integrated philosophy justifying the parasitical control and dictatorial rule of the honest value producers by criminal-minded elites. Finally, 300 years after Plato, the Roman poet Virgil in his famous secondary epic, the *Aeneid*, recycled Homer's *Odyssey* into a "gentler", more hidden form. Thus, Virgil laid the structure for even more subtle neocheating techniques.

Ever since Virgil, subtle neocheating techniques have allowed criminal-minded humanoids to plunder the value producers in countless, hidden ways while appearing moral, even heroic. Thus, those neocheating techniques allowed an irrational anticivilization to rise and exist to this day on planet Earth.

Virgil to Hitler

Virgil promotes the evil falsity that the virtues of life, character, bravery, and morality lie in sacrifice and service — sacrifice of the workers and value producers to the service of the parasitical elites. All such calls for sacrifice are done under the arbitrary guises of government, nationalism, religion, society, "higher causes"...whatever sounds good at the time. Virgil's *Aeneid* lays the foundations for totalitarianism and "glorious" leaders like Hitler to rise and destroy entire economies and populations.

Most Germans and many others in the 1930s were duped into admiring Hitler's Odysseus-like courage as one of the bravest soldiers in World War I and the strutting "glory" he bestowed on the Third Reich. Thus, most Germans and many others blinded themselves to the obvious fact that popular, glory-talking Hitler was nothing more than a criminal value destroyer — a mass murderer for his *own* parasitical livelihood and glory. Like most politicians, Hitler increasingly committed destructive acts so he could increasingly feel big, important, powerful.

Likewise, prompted by a deeply dishonest media, many Americans were duped into admiring a good-sounding, smooth-talking Hillary Clinton. Until the Neo-Tech dynamics began taking hold in America in 1994, most people were blind to the fact that she was a criminal-minded parasite intent on controlling society by draining the value producers. She almost succeeded through her attempted power-grab encompassing America's entire health-care system. How would she have carried out her giant, free-lunch fraud? Through use of government force — through subjective laws and gun-backed regulations enforced by ego "justice". ...Had Hillary Clinton succeeded, health-care would have decayed, effective medical research would have stopped, businesses would have shut down, jobs would have been lost, innocent value producers would have been fined and jailed, many precious lives would have been lost.

How could anyone be so purposely destructive? Given the chance, essentially *any* politician from a small-town mayor to a nation's president or his wife would eagerly seize Hitlerian power with all its criminalities and destructiveness. For, that is the essence of essentially all politicians. Under camouflaged deception, they will simply plunder and destroy people, property, jobs, capital, *whatever they can get away with*, in order to advance their own harmful careers, glory, and power...in order to have an Odysseus-like good time.

Capone to Clinton

Humanoid criminals are much more destructive and dangerous than *subhuman* criminals such as Al Capone.

For example, Hillary Clinton, with help from a fawningly dishonest media, rationalized away her criminal-minded behaviors.   Her camouflaged drive for Orwellian power and control would be justified through the sacrifice of productive workers and hard-working businesspeople to a hypocritically proclaimed "higher good" or "caring for others".   Such ploys ultimately hurt everyone badly.   For, Hillary Clinton's "higher good" meant nothing more than a self-serving empowerment for personal gains through the use of government force. ...Such self-serving empowerment and gains are the essence of essentially all politicians who propagate Earth's irrational anticivilization.

Beowulf to a Neo-Tech President

The third and final primary epic of Western literature, the allegorical *Beowulf*, written about 1000 AD, reflects an honest, moral foundation for conscious beings.   The hero, Beowulf, is genuinely noble and honest as his pure goodness triumphs over pure evil — over allegorical monsters who are metaphors for humanoid neocheaters. Indeed, Beowulf himself explicitly identifies the greatest evil as harming and killing innocent people, especially one's own people.   But, evilly *unprincipled* Odysseus, not virtuously *principled* Beowulf, underpins Earth's anticivilization.   Yet, Beowulf represents the first glimmerings of the Civilization of the Universe.

In this anticivilization, most political leaders are nothing more than camouflaged, criminal-minded plunderers.   Those "leaders" hide behind Plato's and Virgil's neocheating techniques.   They are simply modern-day Odysseuses committing their hidden crimes to garner unearned livelihoods, power, and glory — be they a Hitler, a Stalin, a Bush, a Clinton.

Will the to-be-announced Neo-Tech presidential candidate be the first major political figure of the past 2000 years to embody the life-enhancing character of Beowulf? By 2000 AD, will the benevolent spirit of Beowulf vanish the neocheaters and let the value producers bring eternal prosperity and happiness to *all* human beings? By 2000 AD, will Cassandra's Secret and the fully integrated honesty of Neo-Tech have vanished this anticivilization? By 2000 AD, will *Zonpower* be delivering limitless prosperity, love, and happiness to all conscious beings on Earth?

Chapter 30

RELAX

for

Zonpower Rules Cyberspace

What should you do about this draining anticivilization and its humanoid creators — its parasitical elites who only fake the human qualities of value and compassion? Should you stand up, resist, fight back? No. Relax and enjoy life. Ignore all parasitical elites. Ignore the negative, the irrational, the unreal. With Cassandra's Secret revealed in cyberspace, the anticivilization and its harmful humanoids will have no power over you. For, when you learn Cassandra's Secret, humanoids cannot drain your life or harm your future.

On learning Cassandra's Secret, anxieties vanish. You will discover that *nothing* in this anticivilization has power over you or your future. ...Parasitical elites have no power in cyberspace.

After capturing Cassandra's Secret, most of what you see and hear from others becomes meaningless. Most of what others say or do becomes pointless and boring. For, you will control all that affects you, now and in the future. You will dismiss all political and philosophical positions — left or right, conservative or liberal, rationalist or empiricist. You will dismiss them all as equally senseless. You will see every position and argument in this anticivilization as an irrational swirl of nothing.

On reading and rereading *Zonpower,* you will learn Cassandra's Secret and control the power of Zon. Not only is Zonpower real, it is omnipotent. With Zonpower, any loss in the unreal anticivilization is no loss at all

For, within the dynamics of nature, losses in an unreal world become gains in the real world. Thus, with Zonpower dynamics, all such unreal losses become real gains in propelling you into the Civilization of the Universe — into limitless power and wealth.

In the anticivilization, its parasitical humanoids — its malignant politicians, wealth-destroying bureaucrats, life-destroying ego judges, mind-destroying academe, dishonest journalists, stagnant big-business executives — are in reality *nothing*. For, they make *no* difference to anything in the real world or over any span of time.

Humanoids and their anticivilization are no more real than fleeting antimatter particles that exist not in permanent reality but in a transitory, virtual reality — a false, simulated reality that affects nothing real, nothing in the future. ...Those humanoids are nothing more than figments that can be vanished by Zonpower and the Civilization of the Universe.

Arriving at the next millennium, today's anticivilization and all its destructive humanoids will have affected nothing in our world, universe, or future. Only you with Zonpower will affect our world, universe, and future. Thus, this anticivilization with its last wave of humanoids can be ignored and forgotten, now and forever. But, you, with Cassandra's Secret, will become eternally powerful, forever gaining exciting adventure, wealth, and happiness.

The Hidden Source of All Advantages

Zonpower is easily understandable for readers at all levels, especially after a second reading. Yet, most dishonest politicians, parasitical elites, destructive lawyers, and force-backed bureaucrats shrink in befuddlement on exposure to *Zonpower*. Therein lies the hidden power of

Zon — its great advantage in this anticivilization.

As did the mythical Cassandra, *Zonpower* foretells all. Yet, the more minds that are beclouded by Cassandra's Secret, the greater is its power. For, if everyone knew Cassandra's Secret, everyone would know the future. But, most people will not directly hear about *Zonpower* until the 1996 presidential campaign. Thus, today, arises the greatest opportunity. With *Zonpower,* one can live beyond the parasitical elites — can live on Earth with immortal prosperity.

1994 AD

Most know something is wrong. Some know something is terribly wrong. Most want change — real change.

They are right: Something is wrong — terribly wrong. For, here lies a stagnant, envy-ridden anticivilization shrinking into dishonesty and ignorance worth nothing to the future. But, relax. Enjoy life. The first domino of a seminal change fell in America during its 1994 elections. Ahead lies the booming, exciting Civilization of the Universe expanding through cyberspace forever into the future.

1996 AD

During the 1996 Presidential Campaign, people in America will begin directly learning about Zonpower and Cassandra's Secret through the forthcoming *Zon Protocols.*

2000 AD

By the turn of the millennium, highly productive market entrepreneurs may have already swept away today's political parasites along with their armed agents of force.[1]

Today

Zonpower is an exotic manuscript that initially will becloud most conscious minds on Earth. Like suddenly being flipped up into a higher spatial dimension, *Zonpower* initially will make many conscious beings on Earth go blank and run. That fact can be illustrated by the following account:

On Saturday, June 27, 1992, a meeting was held near Las Vegas, Nevada. The closest associates of Neo-Tech Publishing attended. At that meeting, Dr. Frank R. Wallace revealed Zonpower — the conscious control of nature's force fields. He then explained how the reactions to this new discovery by those most closely associated with Neo-Tech would not only be negative, but would grow increasingly negative as its secrets were initially revealed. For, on planet Earth today, we are *all* engaged in wide-scope dishonesties and evasions. ...But, here lies the key to everyone's prosperity and happiness:

Sweeping Away Ignorance and Evil

The Secret of Cassandra isolates the essence of ignorance and evil as personified by many politicians, lawyers, and judges. Many high-profile men and women, especially those in government and law, are ignorant of justice and honesty. Indeed, they function through automatic dishonesties and deceptions. They build destructive careers based on ego agendas and reveal the irrational foundations of an anticivilization. Those revelations produce a predicted reaction among those

---

[1]Swept away as described by Mark Hamilton in his book *Neo-Tech Cosmic Business Control*, Neo-Tech Publishing, 1989.

exposed to Zonpower:

Confronted with the foretold banishment of irrationality, many minds go blank. For, the closer one gets to the knowledge of Zonpower, the clearer becomes the subconscious realization that the cure for irrationality is coming. In turn, that means Zonpower will sweep away this anticivilization along with all its parasites who survive through irrationality — through automatic dishonesties, deceptions, and lies backed by bogus political-policy laws, ego "justice", and armed bureaucrats.

So why will almost everyone on Earth initially blind themselves to Cassandra's Secret, *including* Frank R. Wallace? Because, (1) almost everyone has a lifetime investment in this anticivilization with its wide-scope dishonesties and (2) almost everyone is addicted to its neocheating opiates of the past 2300 years.

On reading *Zonpower,* many cannot proceed past the first few chapters when they (1) sense the end of their lifetime investments in an anticivilization, and (2) sense the end of their hypnotic-drug state of automatic, wide-scope dishonesties. Almost all will rationalize, "I don't understand", "this is real deep", "it's eerie", "it's beyond me", "it's scary". ...They cannot face losing their bad investments and hypnotic rationalizations.

By contrast, those who do not "have it made" today, those who are not benefiting from the ruling elites, those who are ripped off by others, those who are oppressed in today's society will flourish on reading the newly intoxicating *Zonpower.* They can understand its secret. For, they have little or no vested interest in the anticivilization.

Thus, lies the power of *Zonpower* — your route to fabulous riches. By grasping *Zonpower,* you can dominate the sleeping minds of others...you can gain wide-awake powers far beyond them. At the same time, they and their moribund anticivilization lose all power over you. You, not they, control the future.

Cassandra's Secret

Harnessing *Zonpower* is a two step process: (1) learn why and how nearly everyone's mind in the anticivilization will becloud on exposure to *Zonpower,* (2) follow the instructions given on page 271 — instructions given to prevent your own mind from beclouding *Zonpower.* You will then unlock the infallible forecasting power of Cassandra's Secret. At that point, power will flow to you. ...You will have seized control of the force field that reaches into the future.

Breaking the Hypnotic Spell

First consider that knowledge ends at each person's boundary of irrationality — the boundary of dishonesty used to hold everyone in the anticivilization. That boundary is defined by each person's mystical bubble needed to tolerate life in a seemingly hopeless anticivilization. Only by breaking that hypnotic boundary, that mystical bubble, can one reach beyond that hopelessness and into another realm — into the rational realm of limitless knowledge and prosperity.

The purpose of *Zonpower* is not to persuade or convert others. That cannot be done. For, no one can understand beyond his or her hypnotic boundary or bubble. Indeed, everyone today mistakenly protects his or her mystical bubble in order to justify living in an irrational civilization.

The essence of *Zonpower* is its power to break that hypnotic spell — to break that mystical bubble in which everyone on Earth is trapped. Once that bubble is broken, one is no longer trapped in the dishonesties of an anticivilization. One can then soar beyond everyone else's boundary. One can soar into the Civilization of the Universe, gaining its knowledge and foretelling power to collect limitless riches here on Earth.

Instructions to Break Your Mystical Bubble

1. You must make yourself read and think about every sentence in *Zonpower*...and then reread *Zonpower* until its full integration reveals a new-color power — a power to accurately forecast the future.

2. You must consciously resist every dishonest rationalization that could make you turn in blindness from *Zonpower.*

3. You must realize that *Zonpower* does *not* arise from a different drummer or a higher power. To the contrary, *Zonpower* arises from every mystic-free mind — from every honest, conscious mind that produces competitive values for others here on Earth *and* throughout the universe.

Those three steps allow knowledge and power to come together and foretell the future. You will know what to do for acquiring limitless excitement and riches. You will vanish the anticivilization on entering the Civilization of the Universe. Then you will have the secret of Cassandra. You will control the future — you will control the force fields of existence.

Chapter 31

Earth's
Greatest Discovery

On any objective consideration, one cannot take seriously religious claims of life after death. Yet, such claims are the centerpiece of Western religions as well as many other religions. But, all such claims are marketing hype to exploit the deepest hopes and fears of conscious beings. For the past two millennia, afterlife promises have hoaxed Earth's anticivilization into embracing mystical religions.[1]

Earth's Greatest Discovery

The afterlife hoaxes promoted by mystical religions serve to hide the single most important, provable fact on this planet: ***Most if not all honest conscious beings who have died on Earth in the past 3000 years continue to live with eternally expanding prosperity and happiness throughout the Civilization of the Universe!***

Ultimate Justice

Justice is an immutable law of nature. As demonstrated by Cassandra's Secret, justice is *always* fulfilled throughout existence. As a result, the eventual destination or just reward for every actual and potential value producer — of every honest conscious being — is eternal prosperity and happiness in the Civilization of the Universe.

---

[1]Religious faith has, however, been a key value at various periods in history. At times, for example, religious faith served to divide and weaken government tyranny, and vice versa, leaving pockets of freedom to advance knowledge, technology, and well-being within the anticivilization.

That just destination is the inevitable consequence of nature. From that nature comes (1) immutable justice that characterizes the Civilization of the Universe, (2) the supremely leveraged, limitless value of each conscious being when placed in a rational civilization, (3) the dynamics of eternally expanding prosperity, which demand the full use of *every* available conscious being, and, as explained later in this chapter, (4) the technology needed to transceive[1] every volitionally developed human consciousness through the omnipresent existence field and into the Civilization of the Universe.

Humanoid criminals or parasitical neocheaters who have lived by harming others or society through force, fraud, and illusions also meet ultimate justice: They become humanoids because they destroy the human nature of their own consciousnesses. Therefore, they destroy the conscious structure needed to transceive through the Gravity-Unit existence field and into the Civilization of the Universe. Moreover, having lived as enormous net negatives to society, humanoids such as politicians with their armed bureaucratic agents of force and ego-"justice" systems are in reality *nothing* — they are worthless to the Civilization of the Universe. Thus, they simply vanish from existence, forever forgotten.

Bases of Proof

The proofs of immortality for conscious beings are derived from theories that are in full correspondence with the laws of physics — theories derived both deductively

---

[1]Transceived not in the mystical Plato sense of a detached soul. For, the soul and physical body are one in the same and function as a unit. But, transceived in the Gravity-Unit form that captures conscious "I"ness immortality as described in *The Neo-Tech Discovery*, all in accord with the laws of physics.

and inductively — theories based on wide-range predictiveness, reproducible experimental evidence, consistent mathematical definitions, and observations with limitless ways to test for contradictions. This communiqué provides the elements needed to develop such proofs, predictions, and facts. ...Those theories must withstand challenges of direct and indirect experimental tests, observations, and calculations.

Listed below are the elements found in this communiqué. When assembled, those elements show that (1) the Civilization of the Universe exists, (2) every fully developed, honest conscious being who lived on this planet for the past 3000 years continues to live with growing prosperity, love, and happiness in the Civilization of the Universe, and (3) technology commonly exists throughout the Civilization of the Universe that provides eternal life and prosperity to all honest, conscious beings on this planet. By contrast, every humanoid criminal who has died during the past 3000 years has vanished from existence. And, all such parasitical humanoids who currently live by harming others will also vanish from existence. Humanoids, however, can be "saved" by restructuring their behaviors in order to mature into healthy, conscious human beings who competitively produce values for others and society.

The Elements of Proof found in *Zonpower*

Existence exists.

Existence is axiomatic, endless, eternal.

Existence exists eternally with no prior causes.

Consciousness is not only an eternal part of eternal existence, but is the eternal controller of existence.

Individual human consciousness is the greatest value in

eternal existence...the seminal value from which all other values flow.

The greatest social value among conscious beings is honest, competitive businesses combined with *objective* law and justice.

Valid knowledge is contextual and hierarchal. Valid ideas are hierarchal paradigms of contextual facts.

Conscious knowledge is limitless because knowledge always begets new knowledge — geometrically, up to the speed of light.

The essence of human consciousness is goodness: By nature human consciousness is noble, rational, honest, just, compassionate, value producing, benevolent, kind, loving, happy.

The only diseases of human consciousness are dishonesty, mysticism, and irrationality.

Those diseases destroy the natural good of human consciousness. Those diseases cause all wars and crimes, including politically inflicted property destructions, harms, sufferings, cruelties, and deaths. Such evils are inflicted by force or fraud to support the lives of open criminals (subhumans) such as muggers and carjackers... or the much more evil, hidden criminals (humanoids) such as destructive politicians, tyrannical rulers, and killer-type (WACO) bureaucrats.

Camouflaged irrationality and deception used to drain, harm, and kill human beings is called neocheating.

Neocheaters are highly intelligent humanoids in whom the diseases of dishonesty and irrationality have destroyed the human nature of their conscious minds. Thus, such neocheaters are no longer human beings. They are humanoids who have destroyed the conscious structures of the human essences needed to enter the Civilization of the Universe. [Ref: The Neo-Tech Matrix described in the *Neo-Tech Discovery*]

To parasitically exist, neocheaters purposely propagate a bizarre, irrational civilization on planet Earth within which conscious life always moves toward unnatural death instead of natural immortality.

This unnatural, transitory anticivilization in macroscopic existence is somewhat analogous to the unnatural, transitory antiparticle in microscopic existence.

As the bizarre antiparticle vanishes forever on contact with natural matter, the bizarre anticivilization will vanish forever on contact with the natural Civilization of the Universe.

The supreme value of human consciousness will always be preserved by advanced civilizations using multidimensional[1] transceiver technologies in digitized cyberspace. Those technologies integrate rational consciousness with the existence field throughout the Civilization of the Universe.

By the very fact of their continued existence, all civilizations technologically advanced significantly past their Nuclear-Decision Thresholds are free from the diseases of dishonesty, mysticism, and irrationality. Thus, all such advanced civilizations are a part of the Civilization of the Universe.

In most areas, no one can predict the state of technology 100 years ahead, and certainly not a 1000 years ahead, much less a million years into the future. We cannot even imagine the technological states and economies of the advanced societies throughout the Civilization of the Universe.

---

[1]Perhaps the multidimensions derived from superstring theory...or wormhole theory. Traversable wormholes, rotating blackholes, and above-and-below Gravity Units offer theoretical time-travel possibilities at above light speeds. Such possibilities can be codified through mathematics.

We can, however, know that no society, regardless of how advanced, can contradict the laws of physics or nature. Moreover, we can know that conscious beings throughout the Civilization of the Universe will never purposely act to violate their nature, well being, and happiness.

The basic nature of rational conscious beings has never and will never change. No rational being would ever let technology overtake his or her nature, self-control, self-responsibility, growth, and happiness. For, that loss of control over one's self — one's greatest value — would be self-destructive and irrational. Indeed, all conscious beings in the Civilization of the Universe are free of such irrationality or any other impediments to the growth and happiness of individual consciousness.

Thus, conscious beings in the Civilization of the Universe have the same nature: They live for happiness and its corollary emotions of genuine self-esteem and love. Indeed, the moral purpose of conscious beings is to meet the requirements for achieving rational happiness.

The nature of existence includes (1) objective law and justice, which characterize the Civilization of the Universe, (2) the limitless value of each conscious being when functioning in a rational civilization, (3) the dynamics of continually expanding value production and prosperity, which demands eternally preserving the supreme value of *every* conscious being.

The most bizarre characteristics of the anticivilization are its overpopulation and aging problems. In any rational civilization, overpopulation and aging are impossible. Exactly the opposite occurs. When free of destructive humanoids, each conscious being is free to productively, culturally, and artistically innovate and flourish without limits, becoming a priceless value to others and society.

For, each conscious being in a rational civilization is free to innovate and produce through division-of-labor dynamics far more values and resources than he or she consumes. ...Always increasing in value while always decreasing entropy, conscious beings remains forever young and precious.

Thus, in the open-ended Civilization of the Universe, a great demand for volitionally conscious people *always* exists. ...When free in an open and rational society based on objective law, each conscious being enormously benefits and enriches all other conscious beings and society. Through eternity, therefore, each conscious being will eventually contribute more value to society than its entire population at any given point in time.

Knowledge and technology increase endlessly. All advancing civilizations require developing ever greater and cheaper energy sources and production efficiencies.

Prosperity and happiness of conscious beings do *not* depend on their actual level of knowledge or technology, but on their rational thinking and acting processes required for continuously advancing knowledge and technology from any level.

Throughout the universe, every level of advancing knowledge and technology exists. Thus exists a technological level of conscious beings whose most efficient production of values depend on the *unsupervised* development and utilization of free-will conscious beings...such as found in an anticivilization as exists today on planet Earth. For, each such transceivable conscious person would provide endless values to all individuals and societies in the Civilization of the Universe.

Every populated area in existence has the economic-growth

needs for which each additional, volitionally developed, conscious being from any civilization would be of immense value. Thus, honest conscious beings anywhere in existence are never allowed to perish.

In Earth's anticivilization, *every* volitionally developed, honest conscious person is redeemed and transceived into the Civilization of the Universe. In other words, essentially every honest conscious being who has ever lived on Earth continues to live, flourishing eternally, in the Civilization of the Universe. ...But, the harmful humanoids of past history self-programed themselves to perish — to vanish from existence forever.

Assembling the Proof of Immortality

Consider the effect of delivering irrefutable proof showing how all honest human beings live *forever* with increasing prosperity and happiness. Also, consider delivering irrefutable proof to all destructive humanoids showing how they will vanish from existence and memories forever...unless they reprogram their consciousnesses to mature into honest, value-producing human beings.

Such proof might include measuring Gravity-Unit field changes of human beings versus humanoids and animals as they die. Those experiments could support the fact that human consciousness transceives into the Civilization of the Universe, while humanoids vanish forever.[1]

---

[1] In the mid 19th century, the great German mathematicians, C. F. Gauss and G. F. Riemann uncovered the noneuclidean geometries and higher spatial dimensions involved in such transductions throughout existence. Matter, energy, forces, and fields arise from motions through varying geometries in various dimensions and quantum states. Einstein needed Riemann's geometries to develop general relativity. Today, superstring theory originating from Kaluza-Klein theory further links geometries in various dimensions to existence.

$$\begin{matrix} \text{Gravity Units} \\ \text{Consciousness} \end{matrix} \overset{\text{convert}}{\underset{\text{to}}{\searrow}} \text{matter/energy/forces/fields} \overset{\text{convert}}{\underset{\text{to}}{\longrightarrow}} \text{spacetime curvatures/geometries} \overset{\text{convert}}{\underset{\text{to}}{\nearrow}} \begin{matrix} \text{Gravity Units} \\ \text{Consciousness} \end{matrix}$$

Chapter 32
Your Ride
into the
Civilization of the Universe

What will actually happen when you travel into the Civilization of the Universe? What will you experience? Will you ever return to this anticivilization? What about those left behind? What will limitless prosperity and eternal happiness really mean to you — emotionally, practically?

Once in the Civilization of the Universe, you will quickly forget the anticivilization. For, the anticivilization vanishes as the unreal nothingness it really is — it simply vanishes to be forever forgotten. And, those left behind? They too will vanish and be forgotten. But, no one will be left behind except criminal-minded humanoids who have destroyed their human nature and refused to reconstruct their humanity. Thus, every conscious being, once in the rational Civilization of the Universe, has no reason or desire to connect their lives or memories with the destructive irrationalities of an anticivilization.

What will a nonpolitical civilization based entirely on integrated honesty and *objective* law be like? That civilization will be free of dishonesty, *subjective* political-policy laws, irrationality, ego "justice", and their humanoid predators. Gone will be force-backed governments with their above-the-law rulers. Gone will be the politicians, lawyers, and judges identified as criminal-minded "superior people" by Fyodor Dostoyevsky in his classic *Crime and*

Punishment. Gone will be armed bureaucracies, mystical religions, wars, crime, fraud, suffering, poverty, disease, and death itself.

But, what is the Civilization of the Universe really like — emotionally, intellectually, and experience wise? What will living free of disease, mysticism, dishonesty, criminality, and irrationality really be like? One's entire pattern of thoughts, emotions, and experiences will be different — so radically different from anything experienced in this anticivilization that no one today could really know or describe that eternal difference...at least not until the Civilization of the Universe is created on planet Earth.[1] The conscious-created Civilization of the Universe could be available on Earth as early as 1998. If so, then by 2000 AD, many conscious beings in the business-developed countries will have already left behind this unreal anticivilization to reside in the exciting Civilization of the Universe.

How can one get some idea of what conscious life in the Civilization of the Universe might be like — some idea before actually taking that one-way journey from this grotesquely contradictory anticivilization into the beautifully harmonious Civilization of the Universe?

Perhaps one can begin imagining an eternally prosperous, happy life by trying to view this closed-system anticivilization from the outside. From that external view,

---

[1]Consider a flatlander living in a two-dimensional universe being flipped up into a three-dimensional universe then falling back into his flat-plane universe. Observing only a series of two-dimensional planes or lines fly by as he traveled through three-dimensional space, he would have no adequate way to understand a three-dimensional universe and would have no way to explain it to his fellow flatlanders. ...Do not confuse this useful dimensional analogy with the invalid analogy of Plato's cave to so-called higher realities. No higher or multirealities exist. Only one reality exists.

one can sense how irrationality constantly blocks or cuts off experiencing life as ecstasy, cuts off achieving limitless prosperity, cuts off experiencing a fully joyful, productive, rational life. From the Civilization of the Universe, *every* perspective will look different from anything one could experience within this anticivilization. Each new perspective will be like encountering a new color for the first time — a stunningly unexpected experience unrecognizable from any previous experience.

The increasing resistance, pain, and difficulties in achieving competitive values and genuine happiness throughout this anticivilization will wondrously transform into the easy way — the path of least resistance — a painless path, a consistently joyful path filled with endless victories. Indeed, that easy way is *endless* growth through joyful discipline, rational thought, and productive action. Perhaps the closest, but still distant sense to that experience, can be observed in children under six years old still not diseased by the anticivilization. In every such child, one can observe his or her learning as not only remarkably rapid but compellingly joyful and exciting. Until poisoned by the dishonesties of the anticivilization, each young child experiences no pain, only joy, in progressing toward knowledge and control of existence.

Through the Zon Protocols, every adult can reenter the Civilization of the Universe left behind as a child. On reentering, one becomes free from the life-draining burdens of mysticism, irrationality, and dishonesty. One then gains a hitherto unknown perspective on discipline, productive work, love, happiness, health, diet, fitness, entertainment, pleasures. Indeed, an ecstatic life of endless growth is experienced by all conscious beings in the Civilization of the Universe. Even destructive politicians and other parasitical humanoids can reenter that nonpolitical Civilization of the Universe after reconstructing their humanity — after becoming honest, competitive human beings who are genuinely valuable to others and society.

What a joyful life awaits human beings on Earth. Our journey toward the nonpolitical Civilization of the Universe has begun. Indeed, our one-way, magic-carpet ride into the Civilization of the Universe begins with *Zonpower* and is completed with the forthcoming *Zon Protocols*.

This unreal anticivilization whose politicians depend on dark Schopenhauer drives to survive by harming others and society will then vanish. Yes, the *Zon Protocols* will usher in the Civilization of the Universe...the natural civilization from which we came as children. And, into which, we will return as increasingly valuable, fully responsible, mature adults. For, we belong to the eternally evolving Civilization of the Universe.

Zon is the *natural* law of conscious beings in all worlds and universes.

Chapter 33
You Will Become Zon

Consider the following six points:

1. Zon is the measure of all conscious beings.
2. Zon is disconnected from *every* aspect of any anticivilization.
3. Parasitical elites have created a dishonest, violent anticivilization on Earth. They each will unhesitantly lie, make war, commit crimes, murder, even mass murder to continue their destructive livelihoods and increase their power usurpations.
4. One finds eternal freedom by disconnecting from Earth's anticivilization. Such a disconnection switches one from this anticivilization into the Civilization of the Universe.
5. No part of any anticivilization is redeemable or correctable. For, nothing is redeemable or correctable from illusions based on nonreality. ...Fully integrated honesty with its wide-scope reality vanishes all such illusions.
6. Daybreak does not at once replace the darkness. Thus, the Civilization of the Universe will not at once replace Earth's anticivilization. In both cases, a seeming glow comes first. Then light breaks across the darkness. All becomes visible, clear — a peaceful civilization of eternal prosperity here on Earth.

The following journey unites the above points by returning *you* to Zon whose kingdom is the Civilization of the Universe.

Part III: The Civilization of the Universe

> You Control Existence
> You are Invulnerable
> You are Zon

Zon is a citizen of all universes. How would a citizen of Earth recognize Zon? How would Zon appear? How would Zon think? What would Zon do?

Zon is the controller of existence. Zon is the past and future creator of all universes. Zon is identical to you, except he or she acts entirely through fully integrated honesty and wide-scope accounting. Thus, you can experience Zon. Indeed, you can become Zon to rule existence and gain eternal prosperity. ...As Zon, nothing in an anticivilization has power over you.

You were born Zon. Every human being who has ever existed was born Zon. But, on planet Earth, *every* conscious being has been dragged from childhood into the dishonest illusions that perpetuate this anticivilization. Thus, everyone today behaves as someone else — as someone other than an honest, fully conscious human being. ...Until today, every adult on Earth has lived as a phantom, never realizing that he or she is an eternal Zon.

You are Zon living in an illusion-shrouded anticivilization. In this illusionary civilization, all human beings live as phantoms deluded into believing they are mortals who live and die with no eternal power, purpose, or prosperity. When, in reality, conscious beings are immortal with limitless power and purpose.

On vanishing the illusions of this anticivilization, you reconnect with Zon, the ruler of existence. Although you still walk among the phantoms in this anticivilization, you have no connection with their illusions. You are as divorced from their illusions as you would be divorced from the illusions of schizophrenics in an insane asylum.

Yet, you see *everyone* as your kin. You see the profound value and power in every conscious being. Beyond all else in existence, you treasure the soul of each human being, regardless of what civilization or age in which each lives.

* * *

As Zon, how would you appear physically, mentally, and behaviorally among the phantoms of this anticivilization? How would you gain ever increasing prosperity, love, and happiness when you are disconnected from all the illusions comprising this anticivilization? How would you function among the hypnotized human beings and destructive humanoids of this anticivilization?

As Zon, you do not feel superior to, aloof from, or even particularly different than others. You simply know you are in a different civilization — a 180° different civilization. That difference does not make you feel uncomfortable or uneasy. In fact, your ability to function with others is enhanced. That disconnection also enhances your ability to benefit all human beings *and* humanoids on this planet. Moreover, your disconnection enhances your own happiness and enjoyment of life on Earth.

Most profoundly, as Zon you know that you are invulnerable to the irrationalities of this anticivilization. Like the anticivilization itself, the irrational actions of both its human-being and humanoid citizens are unreal — not connected to reality. Thus, such nonreality has no meaning for you...no real influence on you.

Still, you are among your fellow human beings — the greatest value in existence. Moreover, the objective requirement for eternal life, prosperity, and happiness remains the same wherever conscious beings exist. That requirement is to deliver ever increasing values to others and society. Through the division of essence and labor combined with voluntary transactions, you create increasingly more values for others than you consume.

You live to *be*, not to *have*. You live to create, not to consume. You need nothing beyond the requirements to produce life-enhancing values at maximum efficiencies for others and society. You need or want nothing from this inherently wasteful anticivilization. You neither need nor want anything from its inherently destructive rulers and their dishonest media, organizations, academe, intellectuals, or celebrities.

Why the zero value of this anticivilization? Consider its irrational effects: The more life-enhancing values that heroic value producers deliver to society, the more parasitical humanoids foment public envy against those value producers. Why? To increasingly usurp unearned livelihoods from the productive class. Likewise, the more life-supporting jobs that honest businesses deliver to society, the more parasitical humanoids use government force to drain those businesses through irrational taxes, political-agenda laws, and destructive regulations. Such insanity is not the fault of human beings. Rather, that insanity is inherent in any civilization functioning through subjective laws fashioned by parasitical rulers backed by armed agents of force.

In reality, you and all human beings belong *not* among this unreal anticivilization but among the Civilization of the Universe. All the insanities of which an anticivilization is constructed are merely illusions that never exist in reality — bizarre illusions that ultimately yield only diminishment and death to human beings — dishonest illusions that serve only the parasitical livelihoods of humanoids.

Yet, you as Zon are eternally protected by honesty and reality. You are always advancing in *real* spacetime to ever greater accomplishments that continually decrease the entropy or disorder of existence. Thus, nothing in the anticivilization can really harm or adversely affect your progress in moving through spacetime toward eternal life and prosperity.

At this moment, you can experience the first glimpse at how you as Zon function among your fellow human beings in this anticivilization. You first note the honest innocence of young children. You realize that essentially all children under six years of age are Zons — innocent, uncorrupted, honest. You notice how all such children struggle to obtain objective knowledge, not illusions. Those children strive for value-producing powers, not socially destructive pragmatisms. Then you realize how all parents and adults in this anticivilization are deluded by their humanoid rulers — humanoids who eventually corrupt and then bury the innocence, honesty, and power inherent within *every* young child.

Only through that ultimate crime inflicted on all children has this bizarre anticivilization been perpetuated since its creator, Plato, twenty-three centuries ago.

Real and Imaginary Killing of Human Beings

You start your journey into the Civilization of the Universe by transporting yourself into a mind and body that functions through fully integrated honesty and wide-scope accountability. With the power of fully integrated honesty, you discover the universal laws that deliver valid solutions to all problems. As a simple example, consider two diverse problems in this anticivilization: (1) the unhealthy fattening of Americans and (2) the emotionally charged abortion issue. Wide-scope accounting provides completely different perspectives on those two problems, links them together in unexpected ways, and then delivers powerful, definitive solutions to each based on universal laws. Consider the following example:

— Real Killings—

You are sitting in a mall ice-cream parlor eating nothing, just looking at those eating ice cream. You then look into the mall promenade at the milling crowd. You let nothing block your thoughts. You think honestly, widely. Nothing is out-of-bounds. In such wide-scope thinking, everything eventually connects together through new knowledge, certain knowledge about the past, present, and future.

You are thinking about the intentional destruction of the human mind and body. You realize that such destruction accrues through subjective laws and views replacing objective laws and views. By that process, you see America is becoming a fat farm as well as an insane asylum. You realize that obesity and insanity are related. With drug-like insanity, Americans are increasingly living to eat, rather than eating to live.

Indeed, the intentional destruction of the body requires the intentional destruction of the mind, which in turn requires the loss of honesty through rationalizations. That loss of honesty evolves from a culture of parasitical leaders foisting self-serving political agendas and exploitive mysticisms onto the public.

How do the above facts link together to cause the intentional killing of Americans — the lethal fattening of men, women, and most evilly, innocent children[1]? How do those facts link together to increasingly diminish the chance for a healthy, happy life for Americans and their children? ...You discover the answer:

Research for the Canadian Air Force in the 1960s compiled and implemented scientifically sound facts about human metabolism, health, and physical fitness. That study identified the objective causes of damaging one's metabolism to breed unhealthy weight gains that lead to demoralizing stagnation, decreasing happiness, and early death.

Then in the early 1970s, Dr. Robert C. Atkins converted the Canadian Air Force findings into the best-selling, most effective diet book ever published: *The Diet Revolution.*[2] The eternal fact underlying Dr. Atkins' diet is that carbohydrates combined with poor aerobic fitness — *not* calories, oils, or fat per se — cause unsavory weight gain, heart disease, diabetes, hypoglycemia, and other health problems. For, the human body does *not* naturally metabolize concentrated carbohydrates. In fact, above certain modest quantities, carbohydrates are both poisonous and addicting to human beings.

Human beings are natural carnivores, not herbivores. Human beings are natural meat or protein eaters, not vegetarians or carbohydrate eaters. Human beings naturally metabolize proteins along with fats and oils. Thus, natural foods include meat, poultry, fish, cheese,

---

[1]Gushing with hypocritical concerns and dishonest pleadings, be it a Susan Smith or a Hillary Clinton, such people can easily, in cold blood, directly kill their own children or indirectly kill thousands or even millions of other people's children.

[2]In later years, Dr. Atkins sadly surrendered to the politically correct establishment, grew stout again, and promoted bogus fad diets.

nuts, butter, cream, eggs, low-starch vegetables, and high-fiber cereals. While corn, sweet fruits, potatoes, pastries, pastas, and breads are troubling foods for human metabolism. All concentrated carbohydrates are harmful above modest levels, especially the most concentrated, purest form of carbohydrate — sugar in *all* its forms, including fructose, honey, and corn-syrup sweeteners. ...Sugar, a heavily government-subsidized industry, is subtly the most addicting, toxic, and deleterious drug known to afflict the human body...and mind.

Sugar is the crack cocaine of the carbohydrate drugs. Sugar is by far the biggest killing substance among human beings today. Such concentrated carbohydrates lie at the root of most eating disorders, discipline problems, concentration deficiencies, moodiness, unhappiness, depression, sloth, poor performance, and criminal behavior. Indeed, *without exaggeration*, the most insidiously harmful of child abusers and drug pushers are parents who addict their defenseless children with sugar in all its forms.

Those are facts: facts now, facts before, facts forever. Sitting in that ice-cream parlor, you realize why Americans today are increasingly throwing away their health and happiness. You realize they are increasingly mutilating their bodies and trashing their minds through endless upside-down "health" diets, government-subsidized nutritional frauds, bogus low-fat school lunch programs, and dishonest government-backed, survey-type pseudo science. Those frauds along with the FDA maliciously work to harm the physical and mental health of all Americans and their children.

In the 1970s and 1980s, increasing numbers of people directly or indirectly recognized the universal, objective facts about diet and health. Development and sales of sugar-free food and drinks escalated. But, today, observe how sugar-free foods are vanishing in favor of meaning-less low-fat, low-cholesterol, organic "natural" foods — politically correct foods. Fat-free, sugar-laden cookies and brownies are sold as "healthy" foods while the most benign and effective of the nonsugar sweeteners, cyclamates, are dishonestly banned by power-crazed FDA bureaucrats...and the harmless sugar-substitute saccharine is irrationally labelled as cancer-causing by the FDA, leaving only dubious NutraSweet® unscathed.

Today, as the public obsession with irrational food consumption and bogus fat-free diets grows, the per capita intake of toxic carbohydrates soars. Indeed, consumption of sugar and carbohydrates is now accelerating as people are deceived with illusions generated by the government, FDA, and bogus health advocates. Their dishonest deceptions dupe people into believing they are eating healthier by eating low-cholesterol, low-fat carbohydrates. In the meantime, they and their children are increasing their carbohydrate intakes and addictions. Thus, they grow fatter while irreversibly damaging their metabolic systems, leading to glandular harm, uncontrolled fatness, and mounting unhappiness.

Next, consider Dr. Kenneth Cooper's great, scientifically grounded research in the 1960s concerning physical fitness and his subsequent book, *Aerobics*. From that book, Americans freely, on their own, began a rational trend toward genuinely improved physical fitness and happiness. For, in the 1970s and 1980s, without the blatherings of government "experts" or self-appointed "health" advocates, the two natural criteria of a healthy human body were being increasingly understood: Human beings are by nature (1) protein metabolizers and (2) long-distance running animals.

Yet, today, sales of near worthless, non-aerobic exercise devices, health-club memberships, low-fat diet books, and "anti-aging" pills are soaring. Fewer and fewer people are keeping *aerobically* fit to remain trim and happy into old age. ...The key to human health and longevity is *low-carbohydrate* diets combined with *aerobic* fitness. The key to human dietary happiness is the CAS diet — no Caffeine, no Alcohol, no Sugar.

Observe the increasing political-correctness machinations combined with government-funded, pseudo-science "research" in the form of noncontextual surveys. Today's avalanche of lazy, dishonest "science" is why objective knowledge about health, fitness, and happiness is being lost in a sea of irrationality — forgotten in a contradictory blizzard of bogus, survey-type health "discoveries".

Today is like reentering the Dark Ages that were dominated by dishonest religious Establishments similar to today's dishonest political Establishments. During that period of extreme irrationality, knowledge about health and prosperity was lost or sequestered. Life expectancy plunged, for example, to less than half that experienced in the previous, more-rational Golden Age of Greece.

Today's period of increasing irrationality blocks public knowledge of the destructive political agendas diminishing everyone's precious life. For example, government promotes public dependency and control by increasing drug-like carbohydrate consumption in the form of low-fat, low-cholesterol, sugar-laced foods and drinks. As people become carbohydrate addicted, unfit, and unhappy, they lose self-esteem and seek ever more dependency on authorities supplying good-sounding "easy answers". ...Consequently, the first major product totalitarian and communist governments allow into their countries is the insidious sugar-laced caffeine drug, Coca-Cola®. ...Such governments show no interest in importing healthy, sugar-free, caffeine-free beverages.

The inescapable essence of a healthy human mind and body is *honesty and effort*. That identification about honesty and effort will eventually serve to vanish our chronically sick anticivilization, replacing it with the eternally healthy Civilization of the Universe.

— Imaginary Killings —

Now shift to an entirely different problem in this anticivilization. You know religious-right individuals are among the most worthy of Americans. Most religious-right people deliver genuine values and prosperity to others and society. Many are hard working, productive, family-oriented individuals who act as foils to the destructive actions of the parasitical-elite class throughout the Establishment.[1] Most religious-right people are self-sufficient and do not partake in government-sponsored, gun-backed parasitism. Yet, they are self-defeating and thoroughly hoodwinked by their own demagogic leaders on abortion and issues like school prayer.

But, with fully integrated honesty, they can escape their trap — their contradictions of reality. With integrated honesty, they can remove the threats against their lifestyles while expanding their admirable values to vanish their nemeses: parasitical elites who enforce evil agendas through their armed bureaucrats.

Because of their loyalty to genuine values, religious-

---

[1]As stated on page 273, Western religion has often acted as a foil to the destructive power of the state — and vice versa. ...In the Civilization of the Universe, no illusions exist. Thus, no state or religious powers exist. Only individual Zonpower exists.

right people properly respect human life above all else. Thus, they would be correct — morally and legally — to block by any means within *objective* law, anyone, including government itself, who purposely murders other human beings. But, the problem with their all-out crusade against abortion "murder" is simply that a fetus is *not* a human being. ...Potentiality is *not* actuality.

Their badly misguided concept of "murdering" fetuses springs from emotional brainwashings by false "spiritual" leaders — leaders who support agendas needed to advance their own self-serving demagogic livelihoods. Indeed, at *any* stage or situation, a fetus is nothing more than protoplasm. The fetus is not a baby, not a child, not a human being. The defining essence or attribute of a human being is consciousness — conscious awareness and conscious functioning. The fetus has no consciousness. The fetus is not a human being. The fetus has no rights. The fetus requires no legal or moral protection.

Many millions of intclligent, religious people have been duped into morally and physically defending fetuses as if they were human beings. Consider their forcibly aggressive anti-abortion demonstrations along with other contradictions such as their demanding prayer or silent mediation in *public* schools. Such repugnant blending of church and state ultimately subverts the rights and freedoms of all nonreligious *and* religious people. For, demanding *any* government action to promote political frauds or religious agendas means sanctioning force-back actions leading to all criminal acts, including political-agenda mass murder such as at WACO. Indeed, WACO was a political fraud that involved *real* child killings by the President, his armed bureaucracies, and his Attorney General.

Objective Laws are Universal Laws

In the final analysis, all problems tie together to yield valid, effective solutions according to objective, universal laws that can never be contradicted. Only objective laws are valid and apply to everyone, at all places, at all times. By definition, objective laws do not spring from the minds of men and women. Such laws have always and will always exist universally — independent of the human mind and its emotions. Thus, no objective law is new; each is eternal. Moreover, *no* law — physical, legal, or moral — is valid unless that law is naturally applicable, universally and eternally.

Living by the universal principles of objective law, one neither needs nor wants approval, acceptance, or recognition from anyone interacting with this unreal anticivilization. The entire history of the anticivilization and its humanoid rulers is one of fraud leading to human diminishment. The anticivilization has no real existence or power. Its humanoid perpetrators have only illusionary existences and imaginary powers in an anticivilization first conjured up by Plato and then perpetuated by parasitical elites. Such parasites are epitomized by the dishonest hierarchies of the church, state, and academe who have fatally corrupted the minds and bodies of human beings for the past two millennia.

Now consider the meaning of vanishing the illusions that support this anticivilization and its humanoid rulers — the meaning of you becoming Zon:

Becoming Zon

On becoming Zon, you recognize your disconnection from all actions, human beings, and humanoids interacting with this unreal anticivilization. Your disconnection is not one of misanthropy, but one of grace. Your disconnection involves (1) physical actions reflected by demeanor, (2) mental processes reflected by creative, nonlinear, far-from-equilibrium thinking that eventually brings order out of chaos, new knowledge, and life itself, and (3) behaviors reflected by disconnections from the irrationalities of this anticivilization. Those irrationalities include health-diminishing, life-consuming distractions ranging from drug-like obsessions with eating to life-escaping obsessions with sports, entertainment, and celebrities.

You need not correct anything in an uncorrectable anticivilization. **You only need to disconnect.** ...Now consider these areas of disconnection:

— Physical —

Expanding health and vitality are earned, not given. Expanding health and vitality come no other way except through DTC — Discipline, Thought, then Control. DTC self-perpetuates, builds on itself, and then brings limitless rewards to every aspect of conscious life. ...DTC is the most powerful determinant of human health, longevity, and happiness.

Returning to your free-ranging thoughts, you have long known human beings on Earth are by nature long-distance running animals. Thus, through DTC, you run daily. You started years ago by running a slow 100 yards, working up over several years to a steady five miles a day in 40 minutes. Now you run every day, probably not missing a half-dozen days in a year. Time and schedule "inconvenience" are no more an inconvenience than bathing everyday. With that daily run, you are physically and mentally reborn each day, ready to advance beyond the accomplishments of the previous day, progressing forever into a future of expanding knowledge and prosperity.

You also know human beings are carnivorous animals. Indeed, your natural, low-carbohydrate diet eliminates cravings and desires for drug-like, high-concentration carbohydrates and sugar toxins. ...DTC naturally occurs throughout the Civilization of the Universe as does the CAS happiness diet — no Caffeine, no Alcohol, or no Sugar. ...You recognize cups of coffee, for example, as cups of unhappiness.

You are trim, fit, and happy. With your spouse, values such as growth, communication, love, and sexual enjoyment grow each year. In handling life, your effectiveness increases each year, *never* diminishing with age.

Your joy with your work, your loved ones, and your life expand eternally. You realize DTC and physical fitness are natural for all conscious beings throughout all universes, in all ages.

You disconnect from the irrationalities throughout this anticivilization.

— Mental —

Your power to acquire expanding knowledge for controlling existence derives through fully integrated honesty and wide-scope thinking. Fully integrated honesty is the underlying source of value creation and competitive businesses on Earth and throughout existence. In an anticivilization, its humanoid creators and perpetrators can survive only by disintegrating the most powerful essence of conscious beings — fully integrated honesty.

You disconnect from the dishonesties throughout this anticivilization.

— Behavior —

Conscious beings are social animals mediated through value exchange and business. The limitless benevolence, prosperity, excitement, and happiness possible among conscious beings are derived from the natural dynamics among the Civilization of the Universe. They are derived from conscious beings freely producing and volitionally trading mutually beneficial values through not only the division of human labor but through the division of human essences. ...Poverty, crime, and war are inconceivable concepts in the Civilization of the Universe.

You disconnect from the socially and economically destructive behaviors throughout this anticivilization.

* * *

As Zon, you feel a profound care and valuation for the source of *all* human values, in all universes, in all ages. That source of values is your fellow conscious beings. You also care for the humanoid parasites who created and propagate this destructive anticivilization. Indeed, you work for their redemption as human beings. Why? Most humanoids can be guided back to their childhoods when they were innocent Zons. From that point, they can learn to grow up — to mature into value-producing human beings. On becoming honest conscious beings, they also can reenter the Civilization of the Universe to become limitless values to others and society.

Redemption

Even treacherously destructive humanoids, even people like Hillary Clinton, can be redeemed through Zon to become honest, productive human beings.

The Zon Protocols

The forthcoming *Zon Protocols* is the medium through which the Civilization of the Universe will embrace planet Earth. The *Zon Protocols* identify, integrate, and then vanish each and every illusion conjured up for the past two millennia by parasitical humanoids. Eventually, through the *Zon Protocols*, every conscious being on Earth will, with no transition phase or backward glance, simply click off this transitory, unreal anticivilization and step into an eternal, real civilization — the Civilization of the Universe in which each conscious person naturally belongs.

In the meantime, *Zonpower* will enable adults to protect children from being dragged into this illusionary anticivilization. Children will remain Zons. Thus, their Zonpower will remain intact as they grow into adults. They will leave this anticivilization behind as *nothing*. The anticivilization with its humanoid rulers will vanish, forgotten forever. Everyone will then live prosperously, peacefully, eternally in the Civilization of the Universe.

Children are the Achilles' heel of this anticivilization. For essentially all children under six belong to the Civilization of the Universe. They are Zons, citizens of the universe. Uncorrupted, they hold the power to control existence through fully integrated honesty. When, through *Zonpower* or the *Zon Protocols*, parents realize that every baby is born a Zon, they will protect and prevent their children from being dragged into this lethal, illusionary anticivilization. Thus, when those children become adults, they will assume their responsibilities as all-powerful citizens of the universe. They will be free of corruption and dishonesty. For them, the anticivilization will not exist. It will have been vanished, forgotten forever. ...Conscious beings on Earth will then be free to control existence in creating for society eternal health, prosperity, and happiness.

Chapter 34
The Zon Awakening

Nothing links the nonliving to the living, the plant to the animal, or the animal mind to the human mind. Similarly, nothing links the slumberous consciousness of the anticivilization to the dynamic consciousness of the Civilization of the Universe. ...Likewise, nothing links the endless deprivations in this anticivilization to the limitless prosperity in the Civilization of the Universe.

In physics, nothing links one electron state to another or one spacetime system to another. In both life and physics, essences exist in either one state or another with no flow, transition, or linkage between them. Consider the nature of Planck's go/no-go blackbody radiation, Einstein's go/no-go photoelectric effect, and *civilization's go/no-go limitless-prosperity dynamics*. Locked within those quantum laws of physics, how could one ever enter the law-based Civilization of the Universe from this criminal-based anticivilization?

As in physics with the introduction of Planck's energy, the introduction of Zonpower will allow entry into the Civilization of the Universe. Eventually, everyone on Earth will leave criminal politics behind and click into the Civilization of the Universe without transition.

Since no link or communication with the anticivilization is possible, no one today can know what life is like in the Civilization of the Universe — not until it actually appears on planet Earth, perhaps before the end of this century. Until then, all that can be known with certainty is that life in the Civilization of the Universe means limitless prosperity and eternal happiness. Indeed, everyone can look forward to the happiest shock of his or her life as each suddenly awakens in a law-based civilization of limitless riches.

Why is linkage between the two civilizations impossible? That impossibility is not because of any cultural or psychological differences, which are profound and absolute. But, rather, that impossibility is because the laws of physics make impossible any contact or linkage, both practically and theoretically. The reason for that impossibility lies in the fact that each civilization travels along separate spacetime coordinates. One cannot travel or switch to a different spacetime system anymore than one can travel backward in time. *For, any such spacetime travel or switch would require the conscious reconstruction of every matter and force coordinate in the universe at every instant in time.* Thus, the arrow of time cannot be reversed or switched.

Spacetime systems constantly evolve and move forward. One is never able to travel to different spacetime or light-cone coordinates that have already come and gone...here or elsewhere. Nothing can revisit, return to, or alter events occurring in any past or separate time frame as reflected in a familiar way by Omar Khayyám in *The Rubáiyát* nine centuries ago:

> The moving finger writes; and, having writ,
> Moves on: nor all your piety nor wit
> Shall lure it back to cancel half a line,
> Nor all your tears wash out a word of it.

Consider the two illustrations on the next page:

Illustration A
ENERGY-ACTIVITY SYSTEMS

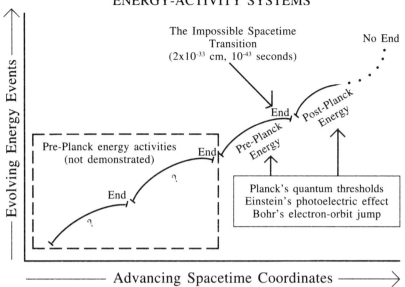

The Impossible Spacetime
Transition
(2×10^{-33} cm, 10^{-43} seconds)

No End

End

Pre-Planck
Energy

Post-Planck
Energy

Pre-Planck energy activities
(not demonstrated)

End

End

?

End

?

Planck's quantum thresholds
Einstein's photoelectric effect
Bohr's electron-orbit jump

Evolving Energy Events ⟶

⟶ Advancing Spacetime Coordinates ⟶

Illustration B
CONSCIOUS-ACTIVITY SYSTEMS

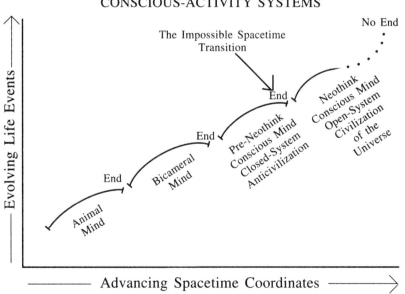

No End

The Impossible Spacetime
Transition

End

Neothink
Conscious Mind
Open-System
Civilization
of the
Universe

End

Pre-Neothink
Conscious Mind
Closed-System
Anticivilization

End

Bicameral
Mind

End

Animal
Mind

Evolving Life Events ⟶

⟶ Advancing Spacetime Coordinates ⟶

What do the two illustrations on page 305 reveal? Different essence systems are in different spacetime or energy coordinates in different worlds or civilizations. In every such case, an unclosable gap always exists between separate coordinates. Nothing can connect one spacetime system to another.

Then how does one move from one spacetime system, world, or civilization to another if no contact or transition is possible? Like going from one time zone to another, one does not phase out of one zone and into another. One is in one zone or the other with no transition. So, how can one in the anticivilization end up in the Civilization of the Universe? How can one suddenly be in the Civilization of the Universe without any transition?

Consider the analogous, well-established laws of physics shown in Illustration A on page 305. Throughout existence, at least two distinct coordinate systems of energy exist: (1) the limited closed-coordinate system that functions below Planck's energy level doing little, and (2) the limitless open-coordinate system that functions above Planck's energy level doing everything — spewing out all varieties of events and energies. Between the two systems, nothing except Gravity Units exists — no contact, no transition. Each system is in a universe of its own. Below Planck's energy level, a boring universe of limited, closed boundaries exists. Above Planck's energy level, a lively universe of limitless, open evolution springs forth — spewing all possible events and energies, without limits or boundaries. ...Everything is either above or below Planck's energy level. Nothing is in-between. Nothing connects or mediates the two independent systems or universes.

What about the animal mind to the bicameral mind as

shown in Illustration B? The bicameral mind to the conscious mind? The closed-system, rationalizing Kantian mind comprising the anticivilization to the open-ended, integrating Randian mind comprising the Civilization of the Universe? The criminally destructive Hitlerian/ Clintonian mind to the heroically productive Thomas Edison/Bill Gates mind? ...What is the analogous Planck's energy that will jump the spacetime gap or void from the anticivilization to the Civilization of the Universe? That equivalency of Planck's energy is contained within the universal constant of Zon, k, described on page 11. From the constant k flows the power of Zon.

The Civilization of the Universe *is* Zonpower. Once one integrates with Zonpower, he or she automatically makes a Planck-like jump with no transition. Abruptly, one is in the Civilization of the Universe. The anti-civilization is then left behind, impossible to contact, soon forgotten forever.

Nonaging through Time Dilation

Civilizations are functions of conscious thinking, especially integrated thinking. The speed of integrated thinking depends on the depth and range of objective knowledge acquired. All such thinking is subject to time-dilation as described by Einstein's Special Relativity. In the closed boundaries of the anticivilization, integrated thinking is severely and absolutely limited. Thus, both the power and speed of integrated thinking are limited to minimal ranges. The speed of integration always increases with advancing knowledge. But, the closed boundaries of the anticivilization holds the speed of advancing knowledge far below that which relativity has any observable effects.

By contrast, the Civilization of the Universe has no boundaries. Thus, new knowledge is limitless and the speed of integrations are bounded only by the speed of light. Thereby, both knowledge and speed of thinking increase geometrically, if not exponentially. With such a multiplying effect, the speed of integration will soon approach the velocity of light as described in Chapter 6. At such speeds, time dilation becomes noticeable and then dominates.

What happens as the speed of integrations for new knowledge keeps accelerating ever closer to the velocity of light? The resulting time dilation becomes so great that the flow of time essentially ceases relative to events and experiences in technologically advanced cyberspaces.

* * *

The rationally open Civilization of the Universe allows conscious beings to live in eternal prosperity. By contrast, the criminally closed anticivilization forces conscious beings to live in deprivation and then die.

Those differences in time dilation reflect the separate spacetime coordinates or paths along which conscious beings travel in the closed anticivilization versus the open Civilization of the Universe. With those differences in time dilation, any linkage or contact is impossible between conscious minds travelling along their separate spacetime coordinates — the anticivilization slow path versus the Civilization of the Universe fast path. ...Galileo/Newton provided the transformations of classical physics; Lorentz/ Einstein provided the transformations of relativity; today Neothink/Zon provides the transformations of consciousness.

The Civilization of the Universe is coming. On its

arrival for each individual, the anticivilization and its criminal parasites will disappear, lost in bygone spacetime coordinates, never to be revisited, forever forgotten as nothing.

Life in the Civilization of the Universe

Why do people who materially indulge themselves live in hidden desperation, cynicism, boredom? Why do they grow increasingly dissatisfied with themselves? Why does the greatest dissatisfaction and emptiness occur in those who seek ego indulgences and material gains most fervently? By contrast, what makes the Civilization of the Universe inconceivably different in which *everyone* has limitless prosperity, excitement, and happiness...void of boredom, doubt, anxiety?

In the anticivilization, why care what anyone thinks, says, or does? Except for competitive values and their heroic producers, what difference does anything or anyone make in the schizophrenic irrationality of an anticivilization? Beneath this anticivilization, nothing except permanent value production makes any difference...or sense. In the Civilization of the Universe, however, everything that each individual does or experiences makes the most profound difference to everyone eternally.

Onward to Cyberspace
(See periodic chart on next page)

A Periodic Chart
Evolving from Endless Losses to Limitless Prosperity

Expansion Phases →

Foundation	Value Development	Value Spreading	Protection
Fundamentals and Principles Neo-Tech Pincer I Advanced Concepts of Poker 1968 Neo-Tech Reference Encyclopedia 1976 Neocheating 1979 Golden Helmet 1980 Neo-Tech Discovery 1981/1986/1994	Conversion to Business Applications Neo-Tech Pincer II Neo-Tech/Neothink Business System 1988 Neo-Tech World Summits 1985-1987	Spreading Worldwide Neo-Tech Pincer III Building a Global Business Empire 1992 Golden-Helmet Package 1994 The Seven Waves 1987-1997	Neo-Tech Protection Kit 1988/1994
Prosperity Revolution 1991-1999 Court Trials 1991-1995 The Zonpower Discovery 1992 Cassandra's Secret 1993 Depoliticize, Decriminalize 1995-1999	Foundation Building for a New Civilization 1. Neo-Tech Day-Care Centers 2. Neo-Tech Elementary Schools 3. Neo-Tech Role Models 4. Neo-Tech high-paying jobs for everyone 5. Neo-Tech Love Connection and Friendship Service 6. Objective-Law Party 1996-2000	Neo-Tech Literature Distribution Program 1994 Social Connection 1994 Zon World Summits 1996-1999	Operation of the Ostracism/Praise Matrix 1998 Worldwide Conscious Control 2000
Cyberspace **Zon Protocols** 1996 **Civilization of the Universe under development** (available 1997-2000)	*Cyberspace* **Implementation Worldwide as shown above** 1998	*Cyberspace* **Universal Networking** 2005	*Cyberspace* **Universal Conscious Control** 2010

Neo-Tech in the Anticivilization · Resurrection of Zon · Civilization of the Universe

→ Movement toward Limitless Prosperity →

Chapter 35
Poker Stratagems
replaced by
Zon's Integrated Honesty

In reference to Chapter 18, how could anything so seemingly evil as the Illuminati Protocols be compatible with the fully integrated honesty of Neo-Tech? How could the founding Illuminati be the heroic precursors of Neo-Tech? Those questions are answered by comparing the underlying dynamics flowing beneath the fatally flawed, close-ended Illuminati dynamics to the pristine, open-ended Neo-Tech/Zon dynamics:

Compatible Dynamics
As with the Neo-Tech dynamics, the original Illuminati recognized that all conscious beings on Earth, throughout the ages, were and continue to be drained, impoverished, and killed by a permanently entrenched parasitical-elite class. Both the Neo-Tech dynamics and the original Illuminati recognized that this parasitical-elite class created a bizarre anticivilization from which no one could escape its always fatal human diminishments. Both Neo-Tech and the Illuminati also recognized that no matter what reforms or advances occurred, the same ever increasing cycles of parasitical destruction would always occur on planet Earth. Thus, when technology advanced to the capacity of destroying the entire human race through nuclear fusion, that destruction would occur on the next major upswing cycle of irrational destructions and wars.

Like the discoverers of Neo-Tech, the original Illuminati were fully aware that every conscious being and all earned values on Earth would eventually be consumed by the parasitical elites. Although not knowing the final technology that could destroy conscious life on Earth, the original Illuminati knew that capability would eventually develop. Today, everyone knows that this total-destruction technology is thermonuclear energy.

Thus, the Illuminati today race to complete their goal of subverting and eliminating all life-draining institutions that support parasitical humanoids — eliminate them before they obliterate conscious life on Earth. The current parasitical cycle will increasingly ruin the real value-and-job producers, their means of production, their capital, their property. As in all past such cycles, this parasitical feeding cycle will escalate until the maximum possible human values are consumed or destroyed.

By using nuclear or biological weapons to destroy maximum possible values, this final wipe-out cycle would end most if not all conscious life on Earth. ...Some religious-right fundamentalists fervidly root for such an apocalyptic wipe out.

As revealed in Part II of this book, the only solution possible by working *within* this anticivilization is to undermine and then break every harmful institution throughout the anticivilization — eliminate every institution that supports humanoid parasites. That breaking of parasitical institutions could be accomplished by harnessing genuine business power through advanced poker stratagems. For, by combining that business power with such stratagems, one can outflank every parasitical maneuver.

The breaking of destructive governments and religious

institutions along with their parasitical beneficiaries can be done through organized, persistent business dynamics. In fact, that breaking of those destructive institutions has been nearly accomplished. By whom? By the dedicated handful of highly responsible Illuminati businesspeople.

Advancing the Illuminati's goal required the confident certainty that genuine business power combined with advanced poker strategy will *always* outflank and eventually vanish the false power of parasitical elites and their illusion-built institutions. Indeed, the underlying Illuminati strategy is maneuvering parasitical elites and influential leaders alike into irresistible positions of worldwide, ego-boosting power. Such positions are proffered by various quasi-secret international organizations. But, the controlling long-range plans and power are orchestrated by that handful of obscure Illuminati. Through such a system, the Illuminati could always maneuver influential leaders worldwide into creating conflicts that increasingly undermine nationalistic governments and organized religions.

Incompatible Dynamics

Discovering the Civilization of the Universe in 1992 also revealed that, on the brink of victory, the Illuminati would catastrophically fail, resulting in the end of conscious life on planet Earth. For, parasitical humanoids and their institutions can never be permanently vanished from *within* their own creation — from within their closed-system anticivilization. Instead, those humanoids on the brink of defeat would devour the Illuminati and their organizations as explained later in this chapter.

By contrast, as revealed in *Zonpower*, the Civilization of the Universe provides an eternally open, evolving system of advancing knowledge, value production, and prosperity that is totally independent of the anticivilization. When individuals begin functioning from the Civilization of the Universe now arising on planet Earth in cyberspace, the illusions of the anticivilization and the influences of its parasitical rulers simply vanish.

Thus, the Illuminati's goal can be fully achieved not by violently working within this unnatural anticivilization but by peacefully working from without — from the natural Civilization of the Universe. ...The Civilization of the Universe is a healthy business civilization void of poverty and violence — void of parasitical elites.

Credit for Zon and the Civilization of the Universe being able to embrace planet Earth and vanish the anticivilization by the turn of this century belongs to the Illuminati — to their two centuries of relentlessly undermining the destructive institutions of this anticivilization. Credit must go to the heroic "dirty work" done by men of productive accomplishments and moral responsibility from the 18th-century Adam Weishaup to today's 20th-century David Rockefeller...and all the other unrecognized, low-profile Illuminati. For two centuries, they have brilliantly duped and poker played the parasitical-elite class into undermining its own institutions.

Eight decades ago, Einstein's open system of relativity physics jumped past Newton's brilliant, invaluable work within the closed system of classical physics. Both systems were dedicated to eliminating ignorance about physical reality. To advance into the future, however, Einstein's open system had to move past Newton's closed system.

Likewise, today, Zon's open-system Civilization of the Universe jumps past the Illuminati's brilliant, invaluable work on the closed-system anticivilization. Both works are dedicated to eliminating the deceptions supporting this anticivilization. To advance into the future, however, the open-system moral base of Zon must replace the closed-system moral base of the Illuminati.

The Illuminati Would Fail Without Zon

The Illuminati could not foresee the inevitable failure of their master plan. That failure would occur near their moment of victory: In the death throes of this anticivilization, its parasitical-elite rulers in a desperate attempt to survive would enter into a final feeding frenzy. They would devour the last seeds of human and financial capital needed for populations to exist and prosper.

Today, less-and-less earned wealth remains for the burgeoning parasitical-elite class to feed upon. When those last seeds of prosperity are devoured, even the Illuminati along with their master plan, their influential international organizations, and their noble goal would end in a suicidal, global Hitler-like debacle. For, with the essence of productive business gone, the Illuminati could no longer function. The anticivilization would then be primed for a new cycle of Hitlerian tyrants to arise — arise chaotically without the two-century-old restraints and controls of the Illuminati. Such uncontrolled humanoid rulers would drum-beat the world toward nuclear conflagrations, consuming nationality after nationality, race after race, population after population. ...The Illuminati's fatal flaw is their working *within* the closed-system anticivilization. They could not foresee that in the end they too would be devoured by the anticivilization.

Zon removes that fatal flaw to allow the successful conclusion of the Illuminati's master plan. ...Against the reality of Zon, the anticivilization with its parasitical rulers will vanish in cyberspace.

Today, with the glimmerings of Zonpower reflected in America's 1994 elections, the Illuminati are sensing the shift of their moral and operational base from the politicized anticivilization to the nonpolitical Civilization of the Universe. That shift will eventually halt all parasitical feeding to vanish this anticivilization.

The Wonderful World Ahead

Ahead lie limitless riches, romantic excitement, and eternal happiness for all conscious beings. Today, the Illuminati can finally vanish this moribund anticivilization. How? By using the glittering nonpolitical Civilization of the Universe as their new, limitless base of operations.

* * *

In the Civilization of the Universe, one asks not where another is from, but one asks what another does for a living...what one does to deliver needed, competitive values to others and society. Concepts of race, nationality, and religion are unknown in the Civilization of the Universe.

Objective Laws are Universal Laws

In the final analysis, all problems tie together to yield valid, effective solutions according to objective, universal laws that cannot be contradicted. Only objective laws are valid and apply to everyone, at all places, at all times. By definition, objective laws do not spring from the minds of men and women. Such laws have always and will always exist universally — independent of the human mind and its emotions. Thus, no objective law is new; each is eternal. Moreover, *no* law — physical, legal, or moral — is valid unless that law is contextually applicable, universally and eternally.

The Protocols of Zon

The Illuminati's goal will now be peacefully, humanely completed through the protocols of Zon. Those omnipotent protocols arise from Cassandra's Secret. In late 1996, the explicit, formal Zon Protocols will be published through the Internet for worldwide implementation.

The nonviolent Zon Protocols will bring a nonpolitical business civilization to planet Earth.

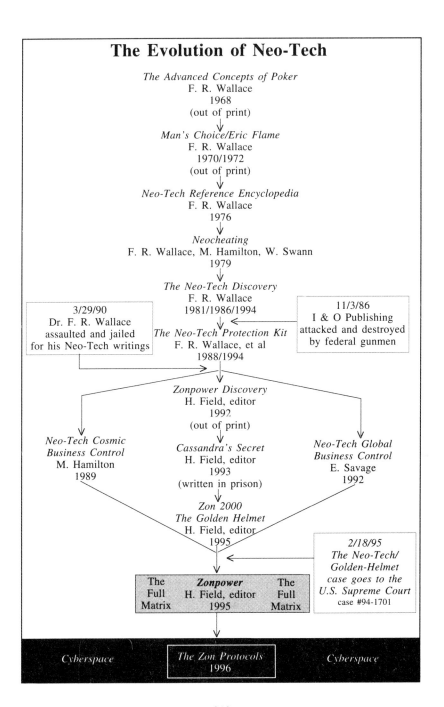

The Evolution of Neo-Tech

The Advanced Concepts of Poker
F. R. Wallace
1968
(out of print)

Man's Choice/Eric Flame
F. R. Wallace
1970/1972
(out of print)

Neo-Tech Reference Encyclopedia
F. R. Wallace
1976

Neocheating
F. R. Wallace, M. Hamilton, W. Swann
1979

The Neo-Tech Discovery
F. R. Wallace
1981/1986/1994

3/29/90
Dr. F. R. Wallace
assaulted and jailed
for his Neo-Tech writings

The Neo-Tech Protection Kit
F. R. Wallace, et al
1988/1994

11/3/86
I & O Publishing
attacked and destroyed
by federal gunmen

Zonpower Discovery
H. Field, editor
1992
(out of print)

*Neo-Tech Cosmic
Business Control*
M. Hamilton
1989

Cassandra's Secret
H. Field, editor
1993
(written in prison)

*Neo-Tech Global
Business Control*
E. Savage
1992

*Zon 2000
The Golden Helmet*
H. Field, editor
1995

2/18/95
*The Neo-Tech/
Golden-Helmet
case goes to the
U.S. Supreme Court*
case #94-1701

The
Full
Matrix

Zonpower
H. Field, editor
1995

The
Full
Matrix

Cyberspace

The Zon Protocols
1996

Cyberspace

Chapter 36
The Zon Protocols

Most physicists, scientists, or physicians with vested interests in the anticivilization, such as tax-funded livelihoods, will resist identifying that human consciousness is the omnipotent force controlling existence.[1] Likewise, business people, professionals, or academics seeking praise and acceptance from within Earth's anticivilization must avoid grasping the wide-scope dynamics of Neo-Tech with its fully integrated honesty. But, those who integrate with *Zonpower* today or those who surf the *Zon Protocols* after 1996 can disconnect from Earth's anticivilization to gain Zonpower.

Without Zonpower, You are Trapped in an Anticivilization
With Zonpower, You Control Existence

Until the unveiling of Zonpower in June 1992, every conscious adult on planet Earth was imprisoned in its irrational civilization — a mortally destructive anticivilization. Through force and coercion, a dishonest parasite class has propagated an anticivilization around the globe. They continue propagating that anticivilization by deceptively, forcibly draining the productive class, especially the entrepreneur business class which is the source of all genuine jobs, prosperity, and happiness.

Without Zonpower, every conscious mind is imprisoned. Without Zonpower, no conscious mind is able to escape the products of an anticivilization: dishonesty, irrationality, destruction, death. The reason for that entrapment is that everyone is coerced from *every*

---

[1]As reviewed in Chapter 6, *The Long Wave*.

direction. And no conscious mind can think honestly, widely, or deeply under *any* form of coercion.

Most important, on trying to live by fully integrated honesty that is natural in the Civilization of the Universe, one will increasingly feel uncomfortable and anxious if his or her life remains invested in the anticivilization. Indeed, one cannot capture Zonpower while remaining invested in this unreal anticivilization.

Ironically, throughout history, only young children and certain schizophrenic savants have tasted Zonpower, albeit in narrow areas. What is meant by stating certain schizophrenics have tasted Zonpower? Do their experiences provide a hint of the undreamt power available to conscious beings not invested in this anticivilization? Consider the ancient oracles of Greece, including the most famous, the Oracle at Delphi. They had one common background: They all were naively honest, uneducated country girls who hallucinated as schizophrenics. None were invested in the anticivilization. Yet, kings as mighty as Alexander the Great, emperors, generals, lawmakers, and the wealthy regularly consulted and acted, often with spectacularly favorable results, on the uncanny, seemingly brilliant insights of those hallucinating women.

Consider Joan of Arc in the early 15th century. She too was a naively honest, uneducated country girl who hallucinated and was disconnected from society — disconnected from the sophistications of the anti-civilization. Yet, as a teenager, she became the premier military commander and war strategist in France. She delivered brilliant new insights into politics, warfare leadership, and battle tactics. Starting by liberating Orléans at 17 years old, she personally led France to key victories over the English invaders. She then provided the political strategy to restore Charles VII to the throne of France. ...At 19 years old, undermining the false power of the parasitical-elite class, she was politically imprisoned, tried by ego "justice", and then burned at the stake.

Why did those uneducated, illiterate women have insights beyond anyone else in areas of state and war? Because they were uneducated, poor, and disconnected from established society, their minds were disconnected from the integration-blocking dynamics of the anticivilization. In those areas, therefore, they were free to think more widely, without bounds...free to think with greater honesty.

In their areas of disconnection, they could gather wider ranges of integrations and insights than anyone connected to the anticivilization, including the greatest contemporary experts. Thus, the unblocked minds of those women could provide completely new and often more accurate perspectives of momentous events.

Consider the most powerful moral savant of Western Civilization: an uneducated, illiterate hippie who also hallucinated. He too was disconnected from the anti-civilization of his day. Yet, that man held moral sway over the Western world for a hundred generations, right up to this day. That person was Jesus. He undermined the parasitical-elite class, was politically imprisoned, tried by ego "justice", and then crucified. ...Jesus' *earthly* moral principles are now yielding to the *universal* moral principles found in objective law and expressed by the forthcoming Zon Protocols.

Indeed, wide-scope thinking is impossible under coercion. That is why no one in this anticivilization can fully grasp the concept of integrated honesty to unleash Zonpower. *Any form of coercion generates an array of rationalizations that prevent the wide-scope, contextual thinking required for Zonpower.*

By disconnecting from *every* aspect of the coercive anticivilization, the conscious mind springs free from the anticivilization to gain Zonpower. With Zonpower, one controls existence through fully integrated honesty.

The Zon Protocols in Cyberspace

Through the Zon Protocols, you will live with ever increasing health, prosperity, and happiness. You will no longer need to invest in a corrupt anticivilization. You will live in the Civilization of the Universe. You will vanish the dishonesties, illusions, and nonrealties that today assault the mind and body of every conscious being on Earth. The anticivilization with all its coercions, harms, and diminishments will disappear. You will gain genuine power. You will gain Zonpower. You will control existence.

Today, you are unable to experience fully integrated honesty and wide-scope thinking. Today, you are bound within bubbles of mysticism, stunted by coercions, blocked by rationalizations in seeking acceptance from an irrational civilization ruled by parasitical elites. Thus, you will enter the *Zon Protocols* as a citizen of Earth's anticivilization created by criminal politics and morbid religions. ...But, you and everyone reading the forthcoming *Zon Protocols* will become a Citizen of the Universe. You will become Zon. You will be free of mysticisms and illusions — free of Earth's anticivilization. You will control existence through fully integrated honesty, boundless energy, and wide-scope thinking. **...You will gain all the prosperity and happiness available to conscious life.**

Word Usage

Neo-Tech is a noun or an adjective meaning *fully integrated honesty* based on facts of reality. Neo-Tech creates a collection of *new techniques* or *new technology*[1] that lets one know exactly what is happening and what to do for gaining honest advantages in all situations. Neo-Tech provides the integrations in every situation to collapse the illusions, hoaxes, and all other forms of irrationality manipulated by the parasitical-elite class. ...Understanding *is* the process of integration.

Mysticism is action based on dishonest irrationalities and mind-created "realities". Mysticism evokes, accepts, or uses unreal notions that *create problems where none exist.* Contrary to popular belief, mysticism today seldom involves god-type religions or the occult. God religions and the occult are dying forms of mysticism with fading powers to hurt the productive class. More generally, mysticism is the dishonesty that evolves from using feelings or rationalizations to generate mind-created "realities". In turn, those "realities" create unnecessary problems and unnatural destructions. Unnecessary and un-natural because the human brain *cannot create* reality. Instead, the brain *perceives* and then *integrates* facts of reality in order to control reality.

Thus, "reality"-creating mysticism is a perversion or disease of human consciousness. Indeed, mysticism is the destruction disease. For mysticism blocks brain integrations to erode all values. Mysticism breeds dishonesty, malevolence, and death. Hence, mysticism is suicide on all levels — on personal, family, social, and business levels; on local, national, and world levels.

[1]New to the anticivilization, but normal to the Civilization of the Universe.

Neocheating is the undetected usurpation of a livelihood — the unsuspicious swindling of money, power, or values through clever manipulations of dishonest rationalizations, non sequiturs, and mystical notions. Neocheating means *new cheating* for usurping values earned by others. Actually, parasitical elites have used neocheating for two millennia in hidden, unnoticeable ways. But the *techniques* of neocheating were not specifically identified until 1976. Thus, neocheating is a *new identification* rather than a *new technique*. Before that identification, no one could define or even notice a neocheater. Now, anyone with Neo-Tech can easily spot neocheaters and render them impotent. For, against Neo-Tech, the illusions of mysticism vanish and neocheaters become powerless. ...Neocheaters are unnatural people. They are humanoids.
- The essence of Neo-Tech is honesty and effort.
- The essence of mysticism and neocheating is hidden dishonesty and laziness.

NEO-TECH is rational. It lets one act consistently on objective *facts*. That approach yields happy emotions and love. Thus, Neo-Tech captures reality by having actions produce emotions. ...*Neo-Tech integrates the mind.*

MYSTICISM is irrational. It lets one act arbitrarily on subjective *feelings*. That approach yields harmful actions. Thus, mysticism loses reality by having emotions produce actions. ...*Mysticism disintegrates the mind.*

Mysticism is the essential tool of all parasitical elites and neocheaters. But Neo-Tech will cure the disease of mysticism to end irrationality, dishonesty, neocheating, and the parasitical-elite class.

Neothink is the boundlessly wide integrations made possible by Neo-Tech eradicating irrationality. Neothink is the harnessing of Neo-Tech power here on Earth: *...Neothink outcompetes all, controls all.*

Integrated Thinking is the honest effort of putting information into the most accurate, widest context by logically connecting *all* known relevant facts. Only contextual knowledge is valid. Thus, genuine power is gained through integrated thinking, both vertical and horizontal, in the widest possible context. ...Volitional choice, the essence of free will, is also the essential of effective integrated thinking and valid knowledge building.

Justice is based on objective law and integrated honesty.

Ego "Justice" is based on arbitrary subjective laws and force-backed political agendas used to gain unearned livelihoods and feel false importance.

Parasitical Elites are unnatural people who dishonestly drain others. They have lost the attributes of human beings. They are humanoids who live by furtively usurping, swindling, or destroying values produced by others. To exist, they must prevent honest, integrated thinking by others. For survival, they depend on ego "justice" and force-backed political policies.

Criminal Minds: *"Others owe me a living. Thus, I can live by destroying, stealing, leeching, or usurping values earned by others."* ...Criminal minds lay the responsibility for competitive value production onto others. Such criminal minds epitomize politicians, business quislings, also many bureaucrats, academe, clerics, news journalists, judges, and lawyers. For, their behaviors fit Dostoyevsky's *Crime and Punishment* definitive description of the criminal mind: 1) Unawareness of or contempt for individual property rights. 2) The presumption that parasites, usurpers, enviers, value destroyers, and con artists have a right to live off the productive efforts of others. ...Criminal minds exist by using deception or force to live off the productive class. Survival depends on value destruction. Incompetence and unhappiness result.

Virtuous Minds: *"I must earn my own living. Thus, I must live through my own productive efforts. I must competitively create and produce values needed by others and society."* ...Such virtuous minds are the opposite of criminal minds. For, virtuous minds, by nature, respect individual property rights. Virtuous minds never need to use ego "justice", deception, fraud, or force to prosper. Survival depends on value production. Competence and happiness result.

Value Producers have business minds that benefit society. They live by creating or producing competitive values and productive jobs for others and society. They succeed by honest, integrated thinking.

Money: Is it wanted for laziness or effort? A criminal mind sees usurping money as a way to escape competitive efforts needed to produce values for others...a way to do less. A business mind sees earning money as a way to increase competitive efforts to produce ever more values and jobs...a way to do more for others and society.

Neo-Tech Minds are the powerful, mystic-free minds of the Civilization of the Universe...minds based on fully integrated honesty and justice.

Neo-Tech Business Minds easily outflank and outcompete the narrow thinking and dishonest behavior of all criminal and mystic-plagued minds.

Truth is a mushy, hydra-headed word. Everyone disputes its meaning. Truth denotes a <u>static</u> <u>assertion</u> that changes from person to person, opinion to opinion, culture to culture. Thus, *truth* is a hollow, manipulative word that parasitical elites promulgate to gain credibility for their deceptions, destructions, and ego "justice".

Honesty is a solid, indivisible word. No one disputes its meaning. Honesty denotes a <u>dynamic</u> <u>process</u> that is identical for every conscious being. *Honesty* cannot be manipulated. Therefore, parasitical elites must squelch honesty in order to live off the productive class.

> *Discard the Word* **Truth** —
> *Uphold the Word* **Honesty**
> *Discard Ego "Justice"* —
> *Uphold Objective Law*
> *Discard the Parasitical Class* —
> *Uphold the Productive Class*

The News-Media Establishment
vanishes in
Cyberspace

The task of today's news-media establishment is to promote the political status quo as meaningful. Neo-Tech and Zon sweep away the political status quo as meaningless. The news-media establishment has little value in cyberspace and no value in the Civilization of the Universe.

Cyberspace/Zon137=$hc/2\pi e^2$ 5940

331

332

333

334

Ignorance
  sweeping away of, 268
Iliad, 242, 246, 247, 250, 259
Illuminati
  business plan of, 173-177
  defined, 171-181
  goal of, 180
  protocols of, 171-175, 177, 180, 181, 187, 311
  strategy of, 174
  Zon, 189-191
  Zon and, 171-181, 315-317
Immigrants, 122
Immigration and Naturalization Service (INS),
  118, 121-125, 148, 168
  biological immortality and, 67, 68
  Goy politics and, 184
Immortality, 274, 280, see Biological immortality
  proofs of, 274, 286, 308
Implosion cycle, 57, 58-60, 61-63
Income taxes, 188, see Internal Revenue Service (IRS)
India, 107, 250
Indians, 251
Individual rights, 27, 185, 188
Industrialization of Asia, 112
Inertia, 40
Infinite knowledge, 70-72, 193
Infinite power, 241-256
Infinite-regression questions, 52, 53
Infinity, 5, 14, 15, 17, 18, 53, 54, 63-65
Inflation Theory, 8-9, 90
Innocence of children, 283, 289
INS, see Immigration and Naturalization Service
Insanity, 185, 290, 291
Instant communication, 5-10
Integrated thinking, 106, 110, 112, 307, 325
  speed of, 307
Integration, 96, 112, 238, see also specific types
Intelligence vs. IQ, viii, 51, 239
Intent, 240
Internal Revenue Service (IRS), 118, 120-122, 123,
  124, 139, 141, 148, 167, 168
  biological immortality and, 67, 68
  commissioners of, 133, 134
  criminal behavior by, 133, 134
  Goy politics and, 184
International networking, 210
Internet, 182, 210, 317, also see cyberspace
Interstate Commerce Commission (ICC), 109
Invulnerability, 285-289
Irrationality, 23, 24, 208, 209, 218, 223
  of anticivilization, 21
  biological immortality and, 66-68
  camouflaged, 276
  as cause of unhappiness, 72
  curing of, 65-74, 77, 81, 86, 87, 269
  dangers of, 230
  freedom from, 211-213, 277, 278, 281
  hypnosis and, 205-207
  investment in, 212
  invulnerability to, 287

impact of, 116, 128, 134, 276
  origin of, 61-62
  symptoms of, 116
  termination of, 135, 205-210, 269, 277
IRS, see Internal Revenue Service

– J –

Jackson, Jesse, 168
Japan, 107, 109
Japan bashing, 167
Jaynes, Julian, 50, 229, 230, 233, 234, 241, 242, 244-254,
  see also *Origin of Consciousness in the Breakdown*
  of the Bicameral Mind, The
Jefferson, Thomas, 149, 226
Jesus, 23, 252, 321
Jew bashing, 167
Jewish businessmen, 175
Jewish people, 184
Joan of Arc, 320
Job losses caused by IRS, 121
Jobs, Steven, 226
Johnson, Lyndon, 226
Joly, Maurice, 181
Jonestown, 251
Journalists, 115, 136, 139, 141, 168, 226, 237, 244, see
  also media; specific individuals by name
Judges, 131, 155, 167, 168, 231, 232, 237, 266
Justice, 257, 259, 268, 276
  idefined, 325
  ego, see Ego "justice"
  fulfilling of, 273, 274
  objective, 118
  ultimate, 273, 274

– K –

Kaluza-Klein theory, 280
Kant, Immanuel, 12, 20, 226, 307
Kennedy, Ted, 137-144
Kepler, Johannas, 30
Kessler, David, 122, 258
Keynes, John M., 226
Khan, Genghis, 226
Khomeini, Ayatollah, 153, 226
Kinetic energy, 33, 60
King, Martin Luther, Jr., 167
Kinship with others, 287
Knowledge, 9, 10, 68, 154, 157, 193
  as contextually based, 276, 290
  existence relationship to, 80
  as function of time, 80
  generation of, 79-81
  geometrically increasing, 73-81, 86
  growth of, 276
  increase in, 279
  infinite, 70-72
  laws of, 80
  limitlessness of, 9, 70
  linearly increasing, 79, 80

mega-advanced, 79-81
processing of, 79-81
at speed of light, 76-82
storage of, 79-81
time integrated with, 80
Kroc, Ray, 226
K=Tc², 80

– L –

Land, 5
Language, 241, 242, 246, 247
Law
  cause-and-effect, 12
  in Civilization of the Universe, 187, 281
  force-backed,108, 109, 112
  identity, 12, 14
  of knowledge, 80, 81
  of nature, 5, 6, 13, 194
  noncontradiction, 14
  objective, see Objective law
  of physics, 6, 14, 82, 84, 193, 199, 275, 278
  seizure, 168
  subjective, see Subjective law
  thermodynamic, 57
  universal, 204
Lawyers, 20, 135, 136, 165, 167, 168, 231, 266, 268,
    see also specific individuals by name
  bicameral mind and, 243, 244
  dishonest, 115, 116, 131
  Zonpower and, 226
Laziness, 185, 294
Learning, 245, 246
  by children, 283
Least-action principle, 35
Lederman, Leon, 183
Left hemisphere, 246, 247, 253, 254
Legal system corruption, 119-121
Lenin, 119, 226
Leptons, 38
Lerner, Eric, J., 206
"Let there be light", 83, 86, 87
Liberals, 162
Lies, 269
Life wasting, 115-122
Light, 28, 33, 42, 44
  "let there be", 83, 86, 87
  speed of, 4, 6, 17, 18, 20, 36, 43, 62, 80-82
  knowledge at, 76-82
  transmission of, 35
  velocity of, 32
Light cones, 92
  quasi, 92
Lincoln, Abraham, 167, 184, 226, 227
Li Peng, 226, 258
Liquids, 5
Listening, 245, 246
Litigations, 168
Local police, 188
Locke, John, 22
Long-distance running, 294, 298-299

Longevity, 122, 125, 142, 196, 294
Long Wave: Surpassing Einstein, The, 24-26, 56
Lorentz, Hendrik, A., 308
Love, 196, 221, 275, 278

– M –

Malcolm X, 167
Man's Choice, 318
Mao, 119, 153, 214, 226, 227
Market entrepreneurs, 99, 100, 102, 109, 226
Marsden, Victor, 180
Marxism, 254, 255
Masons, 173
Mass, 2, 24, 25, 32, 33, 42, 48-50, 60, 61, 63
  altering of, 83, 84
  changing nature of, 54-57
  control of, 75
  consciousness, eternal, 196, 197
  inertial, 40
  gravitational, 40
  nature of, 54-57
  not intrinsic, 40, 41
  relationship to, 40
  scattering of, 62, 63
Mass/energy transceivers, 277
Master neocheaters, 255
Master plans, 172-173
Master terminator role of Neo-Tech, 127-129
Mathematics, 14, 20, 30, 84
Matter, 31-33, 35, 36, 59, 208, 239
  energy ratios to, 32
  minimum energy, 33
"Meaning of Life, The", 47-49, 81
Mechanics, quantum, 34
Media, 20-22, 135, 141, 167, 168, 243, 244, see also
    Journalists; specific types, also see News media
  nationalistic, 171, 173
  populist, 171, 173
  religious-right, 171, 173
  ultra-conservative, 171
Medicine, 20, 22
Meditation, 254
Mediums, 251
Mega-advanced knowledge, 79-81
Memorial Day hoax (vs. Decoration Day), 126
Mercantilism, 142
Mesopotamia, 242
Metabolism, 291, 292
Metaphors, 245, 246
Metaphysical uncertainties, 34
Metaphysics, 232, 254
Meta-universe, 62
Michelangelos, 136
Michelson-Morley experiment, 44
Milken, Michael, 135, 139, 141, 167, 230, 226
Milky Way, 47, 48, 63, 64
Mind
  destruction of, 291
Mind control, 254, 255

339

340

Virgil, 260
Virtuous minds, 326
Vitality, 298
Vitamins, 292
Volitional choice, 325

– W –

Waco, c-2, 191, 258, 276, 297
Wagnerian opera, 196
Wallace, Frank R., 157, 174, 235, 241, 268
  jailed, 318
Walton, Sam, 226
War, 20, 70, 71, 194
  elimination of, 282
Waves
  pilot, 34
  radio, 34
"War on Drugs", 123, 139
Wasting of life, 115-122
Water, 5
Wavefunction, 45
Wealth, 2, 37, 205-215
  cosmology of, see Cosmology of infinite riches
  Illuminati and, 171-172
  start of guiltless, 197, 198
  unlimited, 221, 222, 227
  unlocking secrets to, 95, 96
  Zonpower and, 239, 240
  Zon's force field and, 31, 37
Wealth distribution schemes, 185
Weight, 40-41, 290, 291
Weightlessness, 40, 42 ,44
Weishaup, Adam, 172, 314
Welfare programs, 188
White-collar-hoax business people, 100, 125, 131,135,
  168, 226
White holes, 55, 58
Wide-scope accounting, 118, 120-122, 125, 134,
  143, see also Golden Helmet; Neo-Tech
  Civilization of the Universe and, 290
  Illuminati and, 172, 176
  Zon and, 236, 286
Wilson, Woodrow, 113, 184, 226
Wigner's friend, 45
World Bank, 180
World War l, 260
Wormhole theory, 277
Writing, 149, 245, 246
Wuthering Heights, 214

– X –

Xon, see Zon

– Y –

Young, Brigham, 23
Youth, eternal, 89

– Z –

Zhirinovsky, Vladimir, 258
Zon, 199, 207, 214, 217, 221-240, see also Fully
  integrated honesty; Zonpower
  aesthetics of, 21, 232
  age of, 37
  becoming, 11, 214, 285-301
  constant k of, 11, 239
  as controller of existence, 286
  daybreak analogy for becoming, 285
  defined, vii, 28, 171-181, 237, 284
  discovery of, 176, 234-237
  dynamics of, 176, 180, 311-313
  epistemology of, 21
  escape of, 223
  ethics of, 21, 232
  experiencing of, 286
  force field, 31
  foretelling age of, 31, 37
  goals of, 210
  God vs., 23
  government of, 11
  Goy politics and, 185
  Illuminati and, 171-181, 315-317
  irrational civilization and, 222-224
  Jesus of, 23
  metaphysics of, 21, 232
  poker stategies replaced by, 311-317
  politics of, 21, 232
  power of, 265, also see Zonpower
  product from, 28
  prosperity delivered by, 3-10
  protocols of, 172, 181, 187, 283, 317
  religion of, 11
  task of, 20
  words from, 218-219
Zon137=$hc/\pi e^2$, 328
Zon 2000, 318
Zon Association, 23
Zon constant, 32
Zonpower, 318
Zonpower, 11,15, 28, 37, 211-213, 215, 217, 219,
  223-224, 237, 319-322, see also Zon
  awakening, 303
  capturing of, 20, 28, 223
  children and, 221-223
  defined, vii, 13, 28, 221
  discovery of, 95, 238
  disease cures and, 20
  journey to, 13-22
  omnipotence of, 265
  philosophy and, 232
  physics of, 39, 46
  rising of, 95
  scientific validity of, 95
  wealth through, 239
  world summits, 310
Zonpower Discovery, 310, 318
Zon Protocols, 310, 318
Zon Protocols, 300-301, 319-320, 321

344